TRUE CRIME CASE HISTORIES

VOLUME 12

TRUE CRIME CASE HISTORIES
BOOK 12

JASON NEAL

IDIGITAL GROUP

Great effort and research have gone into the compilation of this material. It is the author's intention to represent the information within as accurately as possible. However, the author and publisher do not guarantee the accuracy of the text, graphics, and information presented. Any errors, omissions, or misinterpretations of this publication are not the responsibility of the author, copyright holder, or publisher. Although based on fact, some character names may have been changed, and/or scenes and dialogue may have been fictionalized. This publication is produced solely for informational and entertainment purposes and is not intended to hurt or defame anyone involved.

Cover images of:

Nancy Brophy: (top-left)

Joseph Edward Duncan III: (top-right)

Stephen Beadman: (bottom-left)

Estibaliz "Esti" Carranza: (bottom-right)

More books by Jason Neal

Looking for more?? I am constantly adding new volumes of True Crime Case Histories. The series **can be read in any order**, and all books are available in paperback, hardcover, and audiobook.

Check out the complete series at:

https://amazon.com/author/jason-neal

All Jason Neal books are also available in **AudioBook format at Audible.com.** Enjoy a **Free Audiobook** when you signup for a 30-Day trial using this link:

https://geni.us/AudibleTrueCrime

FREE BONUS EBOOK FOR MY READERS

As my way of saying "Thank you" for downloading, I'm giving away a FREE True Crime e-book I think you'll enjoy.

https://TrueCrimeCaseHistories.com

Just visit the link above to let me know where to send your free book!

INTRODUCTION

Those of you who have read my True Crime Case Histories series since the beginning know what to expect when reading a true crime book. If you're one of those readers, you also know that I start each volume with a quick warning for those unfamiliar with the genre.

True crime is not for everyone. Most people would rather avoid the unsettling truth that happens in our world, while others of us are drawn to it. Maybe we're searching for truth and justice or a better understanding of the criminal mind. Or perhaps the armchair detective in us wants to know how the crimes were solved.

Either way, I like to make sure my new readers are aware that these stories can be distressing. Many television crime shows gloss over the truly disturbing parts of true crime. In my books, however, I do my best to include the details, regardless of how gruesome they may be.

I spend hours researching these cases—reading court transcripts, first-hand accounts, autopsy reports, and police files.

In my books, I lay out all the facts, regardless of how horrific they are. My goal is not to shock but to give readers an unfiltered look into the mind of a killer.

We may never fully understand what drives someone to commit such evil acts. But by examining the cold, hard facts, we can at least begin to comprehend the twisted psychology behind them.

In this volume of True Crime Case Histories, you'll read about a young East German boy who walked to the cinema to meet friends, but disappeared somewhere along the snow-packed sidewalks. When his body was later found, the only clue investigators had was a crossword puzzle filled out with green ink.

There's also the story of a fourteen-year-old boy who claimed to be triggered to kill when his teacher uttered a single word.

In another story, a female ice cream shop owner, who had felt the urge to kill since she was a child, acted on her impulse and kept her victims' dismembered bodies hidden in the cellar of her ice cream shop.

Another woman, struggling to raise her three boys, felt that her youngest sons were foreign to her, and she believed she could be a much better parent to the eldest son if the other two were in heaven.

You are about to read several more stories in this volume that are shocking and disturbing, but they're also true. These things really do happen in the world. The stories paint a picture of human depravity that many would prefer to remain hidden. However, it is only by dragging evil into the light that we can begin to understand its terrible allure.

Several of the stories in this volume were suggested by my readers. I am constantly looking for new stories for future books, and I prefer stories that can't already be found online.

With each volume, many of my readers send me stories they remember happening in their hometowns. In many of these cases, the stories had gone largely unreported anywhere other than the original reports in local newspapers—these are precisely what I'm looking for. If you remember a story that happened years ago, has been forgotten, and you'd like to see it written about, please send me any details you can remember, and I will do my best to research them.

Before you continue, I encourage you to join my mailing list for discounts, updates, and a free e-book. You can sign up for that at

TrueCrimeCaseHistories.com

Additional photos, videos, and documents pertaining to the cases in this volume can be found on the accompanying web page at:

https://TrueCrimeCaseHistories.com/vol12/

Thank you for reading. I sincerely hope you gain some insight from this volume of True Crime Case Histories.

- Jason

CHAPTER 1
THE CROSSWORD MURDER

Built as East Germany's largest new city after World War II, Halle-Neustadt was envisioned as a modern, socialist paradise for workers at the local chemical plants. It was built as the city of the future, and planners had imagined up to 110,000 people living in the carefully designed urban space.

Impersonal concrete tower blocks dominated the urban landscape of Halle-Neustadt in the early 1980s. The streets had no names at the time, only generic numbers. Addresses were simply the block number—residents lived in Block 483 or Block 318, and so on.

Young Lars Bense and his family lived in one of these massive, concrete structures that were carbon copies scattered across the planned community. Their home was in Block 483, an austere building that housed hundreds of families behind its monotonous exterior. It exemplified the efficient-but-bleak living spaces propagandized as model Soviet-style apartments.

Within this maze of dreary, identical blocks, it was easy to feel lost and anonymous. The lack of street names and individualized addresses stripped away personal identity from the environment. People almost became extensions of the buildings, lost in the standardized concrete cityscape.

It was a snowy Thursday in January 1981 when seven-year-old Lars Bense finished his first-grade classes for the day and planned to meet with friends to see a movie.

Lars' mother had given him money for a movie ticket, sending him off to meet friends. They planned to see the animated film Thumbelina, based on the classic Hans Christian Andersen fairy tale, at the city center cinema.

Lars bundled up warmly against the swirling snow and headed out with his older sister, trudging along the icy sidewalks. They walked until the city center was in view a few hundred feet further, and Lars' sister felt he could manage the short distance alone. She turned back, trusting he would soon join his friends.

But the expected rendezvous never happened as the snow piled higher that afternoon. Lars' friends waited at the city center, toes numbing in the drifting snow, but Lars never arrived. Somewhere in that last stretch of frozen path, he had vanished.

When Lars didn't arrive home after the movie ended, his parents began to worry. He was always punctual. They quickly called his friends, but no one had seen him since school. With dread clutching their hearts, Lars' parents reported him missing to the Volkspolizei, the police of the former East Germany.

The police launched a search right away, scouring the snowy streets and apartment blocks late into the night, but little Lars was nowhere to be found. His disappearance gripped the community with fear. Had he gotten lost? Had there been an accident? Or had someone taken their beloved child?

The following days brought no answers, only agonizing silence—a week passed with no breaks in the case. Lars' anguished parents waited by the phone day and night, desperate for news. But their bright, shy boy seemed to have disappeared into the icy winter.

Two weeks had passed when Uwe Theuerkorn, a nineteen-year-old railway worker, was making his rounds on long stretches of railroad between Halle-Neustadt and Leipzig. He was looking for frozen switches or network damage when an abandoned suitcase covered with snow caught his eye.

It lay scratched and weathered with broken latches, apparently having been thrown from a passing train. Curious, he opened the suitcase and stumbled back when he discovered what was inside.

When police arrived and opened the suitcase, they found the body of Lars Bense wrapped in a plastic bag and old newspapers.

An autopsy revealed that the boy had been severely beaten with a blunt object, stabbed several times in his upper body, and sexually abused.

The suitcase was tragically unremarkable—an ordinary, mass-produced piece of luggage. The brown pressboard case was a generic model sold in countless shops across East Germany at the time. Nothing distinguished the scruffy, battered suitcase as unique, making it impossible to trace its origin. It could have belonged to anyone.

The indistinct plastic bag offered no clues either. It was an unbranded, clear plastic bag like millions used in East Germany to package various household items. Nothing about the bag's design, color, size, or shape distinguished it as unique.

The only thing left in the suitcase were the crumpled-up newspaper pages. It was a standard edition sold at hundreds of newsstands throughout the city. However, one chilling detail caught an investigator's eye—a completed crossword puzzle in the pages, filled out in green ink.

Unlike the generic bag and case, this puzzle presented an opportunity. The distinctively colored handwriting could potentially be matched to a killer. Where other physical evidence failed to identify Lars' murderer, these cryptic answers scribbled casually across a page might provide the key.

Each person's penmanship has unique characteristics that develop over time. The longer an individual is out of school, the more their handwriting flows directly from the brain to the hand, bypassing engrained styles. Experts call this "brain writing."

The green-inked scrawl of the crossword held telltale hints about its author—the slant of the letters, spacing between words, and shapes of punctuation. These subtle, ingrained details weren't exactly a fingerprint, but it was their best chance.

Upon closer examination, the green-inked handwriting had highly distinctive traits that experts determined could only come from one person. While completed in capital letters, it was written in a flowing, cursive style. But uniquely, wide gaps separated the different sections of the letters. Handwriting specialists claimed this irregular, as block cursive with exaggerated spaces was extremely rare.

From the horrific nature of the crime, investigators constructed a psychological profile of the perpetrator. The sexual assault and violent murder of a child indicated a pedophilic killer—one who would likely not stop at a single victim.

Profilers warned that this perpetrator would almost certainly strike again, compelled by sinister appetites. They were unsure if Lars was this killer's first victim, but they knew he would not be the last if they didn't stop him quickly.

A handwriting expert named Wiesen convinced police to start systematically collecting writing samples from Halle-Neustadt residents for comparison. If they could identify the puzzle author, they might find the killer.

Investigators agreed and put together a team to analyze handwriting samples. Handwriting experts within the police and state security services cooperated with statisticians, mathematicians, and linguists.

The hunt for the killer sparked an investigation unprecedented in scale for East Germany. A massive task force was assembled to collect handwriting samples from Halle-Neustadt's nearly 100,000 residents, going door-to-door citywide.

Officers systematically visited every apartment block and house, requesting writing samples to compare against the cryptic crossword clues. Meanwhile, investigators combed through reams of documents from social security and city registers, searching for a match. Even trash was scoured for discarded handwriting.

This exhaustive search was like finding a needle in a haystack, but the stakes couldn't be higher.

Investigators cross-referenced passport and registry lists against officers verifying occupants door-to-door, checking for unregistered residents or people who may have recently moved. Traffic police, detectives, the fire department—all departments were enlisted, united in the urgent mission.

As the handwriting search continued, investigators pursued other angles as well. The suitcase used to transport Lars became a key focus. Police proposed displaying it in a shop near where the boy vanished, hoping the shock of seeing it might jolt someone's memory—or even the killer's conscience.

Initially, this idea met resistance, with some in denial that such crimes occurred in their community. But authorities insisted, choosing a central store in the residential blocks where Lars was last seen. For a weekend, the worn suitcase was exhibited under constant surveillance.

Investigators hoped its presence might elicit eyewitness leads on who had carried it, provoke telling reactions, or lure out the killer. But the dramatic effort ultimately proved fruitless—the suitcase failed to summon critical clues from the community. Yet police knew that even long shots were worth pursuing with lives on the line.

With all other physical evidence providing generic dead-ends, the completed crossword puzzle remained the primary hope for a breakthrough. Investigators mobilized assistance from a youth group to expand the handwriting sample pool.

The children were tasked with collecting residential wastepaper from assigned city blocks. This refuse was then sorted systematically by police, searching specifically for discarded crossword puzzles that could contain the killer's writing.

After several weeks of analyzing the original crossword and the samples of thousands of collected handwriting samples, experts concluded that the handwriting most likely belonged to a middle-aged woman, not the male killer they had presumed. This breakthrough indicated that the puzzle's author and the killer could be two different individuals.

Six weeks into the investigation, detectives enlisted expert assistance from Berlin's Humboldt University Criminalistics Department. They analyzed the evidence in an attempt to determine the likely location from where Lars was first abducted, and they built a psychological profile of Lars himself. They wanted to understand how he might have reacted to a potential abductor. Would he have complied with an authoritarian adult? Trusted a familiar relative or neighbor? Or had he been lured by a younger individual offering entertainment?

Despite new expert perspectives, investigators remained convinced that the key to finding the killer lay within the handwriting. But after five months of asking for samples, they had only collected them from a fraction of the city's residents, and they were no closer to finding the killer.

Investigators then worked with the local newspaper to publish an easy-to-solve crossword puzzle, offering a prize to attract participants. The handwriting samples poured in, but there were still no matches.

Eleven months after Lars' murder, Block 398 was scheduled to collect handwriting samples. As officers painstakingly went door-to-door through the massive apartment structure, one door knock went unanswered. A neighbor explained that a woman in her 40s lived in the vacant apartment, but she was a seasonal worker who spent the winters working as a waitress in a busy cafe near the Baltic Sea.

Regardless, investigators would need the woman's handwriting and worked with officers in the area to get her sample. It was handwriting sample number 551,198.

Amazingly, the woman's handwriting bore a striking resemblance to the writing from the crossword puzzle. When handwriting experts analyzed the sample, they were 100 percent sure it was an exact match. Investigators couldn't believe that, after countless hours and more than half a million samples, they finally had a potential match.

However, by the time they had made the discovery, officials in the Baltic Sea town where she was staying informed investigators that the woman was gone. She had traveled south to Werder, East Germany, on vacation with her twenty-year-old daughter.

At 5:30 the following morning, two investigators from the Lars Bense task force arrived in Werder and knocked on the door of the woman they only identified as "Ingeborg G."

When Ingeborg and her daughter Kerstin answered the door, they were genuinely surprised to see officers there. Ingeborg explained that they had left Halle-Neustadt on January 11 that year and had known nothing about the boy's disappearance and murder. Kerstin, too, had been waiting tables out of town when the boy went missing.

When officers showed her the crossword puzzle, Ingeborg confirmed it was indeed her handwriting. When she was shown a photo of the suitcase, she recognized it immediately as her own.

After these revelations, however, Kerstin spoke up. She told officers that her boyfriend, Matthias, had been alone in their flat during that time, and he'd had access to the suitcase and the discarded newspapers.

Kerstin told officers that she had left to work in another town on January 13, but Matthias stayed behind for a few days until he met up with her again. Kerstin said her boyfriend had strange sexual fantasies involving violence, which frightened her.

Nineteen-year-old Matthias S. was arrested on November 17 at his job site. He remained calm and composed for hours during his interrogation, saying very little. However, when presented with the evidence against him, he confessed. Matthias explained that he'd fantasized about killing a child for as long as he could remember.

He told detectives that on January 15, he saw the boy walking alone through the snow toward the city center. Matthias took his opportunity, offering the boy a toy car. He then enticed Lars to follow him to his girlfriend's apartment, where he sexually assaulted him.

Afraid that Lars would expose him, Matthias knocked the boy unconscious with a hammer, put him in the bathtub, and continued beating him. He stabbed him repeatedly, stuffed him in a plastic bag, and placed it in the suitcase. He explained that he stuffed the suitcase with newspapers to soak up the blood.

Matthias then purchased a train ticket to Leipzig. During the journey, he waited until the train reached a remote, wooded area between the cities, and then he heaved the bag out of the train window.

Finally, the trial of Matthias S. began in the summer of 1982. Charged with murder and sexual abuse, Matthias testified to fantasies of killing children stemming from childhood trauma. Disturbed sexual appetites also became apparent in his testimony. The prosecution painted him as a pathological predator who was too dangerous ever to be released.

Ultimately, the Halle District Court concurred. They sentenced Matthias to the maximum penalty—life imprisonment with no possibility of parole. Additionally, his civil rights were revoked, reflecting the egregious brutality of his crimes.

After German reunification in 1990, Matthias' case was re-examined under new juvenile sentencing guidelines. Although eighteen when he murdered Lars, he would have been tried as a minor in West Germany.

So, in 1991, prosecutors applied for a retrial, which was granted. The 1992 sentencing under juvenile law imposed a maximum of ten years of detention as a minor, with subsequent incarceration in a psychiatric hospital.

After his reduced juvenile sentence, Matthias underwent psychiatric treatment until 1996. He lived in an assisted living facility for another three years before being fully released in 1999.

After his release, he did his best to live anonymously, but reports tracked him to Magdeburg, Germany, where he later had a wife and son. Matthias died at age fifty on January 15, 2013—thirty-two years to the day after he murdered Lars Bense.

CHAPTER 2
BETTER OFF IN HEAVEN

Laurel Schlemmer spent most of her early life in the quiet Pittsburgh suburbs. She grew up in McCandless, a small borough north of the city, and graduated from Allegheny High School in 1992. After high school, Laurel attended Grove City College, a small Christian school close to home, where she earned a degree in Elementary Education.

Her first teaching job out of college was at Eden Christian Academy near her home in McCandless. She next moved to the Fox Chapel School district, then Kerr Elementary School. Her coworkers at the school where she worked and the members of her church congregation saw her as kind-hearted, sweet, and loving. She was always ready with a comforting word or a helping hand. Laurel was a woman of faith, and her deep belief in Christian teachings guided her actions.

Laurel first met her husband, Mark Schlemmer, on a Christian singles online dating website in the early 2000s. They were both devout Christians, and Mark worked as an actuary at Highmark Health. The two fell in love quickly; by 2005, they were married.

Immediately after the wedding, they settled into a charming two-story colonial home on Saratoga Drive in McCandless. The neighborhood was affluent, and their home was filled with love, faith, and the promise of a shared future. The couple became long-time members of the North Park Church congregation, where Laurel had been attending Bible studies since her twenties. Their faith was integral to their lives, shaping their every action and decision.

However, beneath the surface, Laurel was grappling with a growing unease. Mark's staunch opposition to birth control and his desire for a large family was at odds with her own feelings. Laurel had no interest in having children, but she found herself unable to voice her concerns, not wanting to go against her husband's wishes. This internal conflict would simmer beneath the surface, a silent storm brewing in her heart.

Despite her reluctance, Laurel and Mark Schlemmer welcomed two sons into their family within the first few years of their marriage. The first, Joshua, was born in 2007. The second son, Daniel, was born the following year.

Once filled with the laughter and joy of two people in love, their home was now brimming with the delightful chaos that children bring. However, the arrival of the children also brought new challenges for Laurel.

Daniel was diagnosed with Tourette syndrome, a neurological disorder characterized by repetitive, stereotyped, involuntary movements and vocalizations called tics. Laurel became a stay-at-home mom, and this added a layer of complexity to the already demanding task of parenting. Laurel found herself navigating the intricacies of raising a child with special needs—a challenge she had not anticipated.

Despite her love for her children, Laurel struggled with the demands of motherhood. The constant care required for her young sons, especially Daniel, was overwhelming. She found herself torn between her desire to be a good mother and the reality of her situation. The responsibility of caring for two young boys was a heavy burden to bear.

Yet, Laurel persevered. She was a woman of faith and leaned on her beliefs to guide her through these challenging times. She continued to attend Bible studies at the North Park Church, seeking solace and strength in the word of God. However, the strain of her circumstances began to show, and those around her could not help but notice the change.

September 5, 2009, was a warm, sunny day in Ross Township, just north of Pittsburgh. Laurel had some errands to run that Saturday afternoon, so she packed the boys in the car and drove to the Ross Park shopping mall. She parked her car in a sun-drenched spot in the parking lot, leaving Daniel, who was just a toddler at the time, strapped in his car seat.

As the minutes quietly slipped away, a drastic change occurred inside the car. Outside, the ambient temperature was a comfortable 80 degrees, but the car's glass windows acted like a greenhouse, trapping the heat and raising the temperature inside significantly. The sunlight streaming through the windows was absorbed by the car's interior, converting to a heat that was impossible to escape. The inside of the vehicle reached a sweltering 112 degrees.

Luckily, a concerned passerby noticed the distressed child alone in the vehicle, his tiny face flushed from the heat. Recognizing the potential danger, they quickly dialed 911. Within minutes, the local police arrived at the scene, their sirens cutting through the usual hum of the mall parking lot.

The officers immediately noticed the toddler in the backseat, his face red and sweaty. They worked quickly using a specialized tool to unlock the car. As the door swung open, a wave of hot air rushed out, making it clear how dangerous the situation had been for the young child.

Daniel had been in the car for more than twenty minutes, but it was clear that any longer could have had severe consequences. Officers quickly checked him over and found, to their relief, that he was unharmed.

Laurel returned from shopping and saw police officers surrounding her car and her son being comforted by emergency medical technicians. Despite the potential severity of the situation, Laurel Schlemmer was allowed to leave with only a citation and a small fine.

Despite the challenges of raising two boys and the strain it put on Laurel, Mark wanted to have more children. He saw the joy and love in their family, even amidst the chaos. Laurel had her doubts, but she eventually agreed. So, in 2011, they welcomed a third child, a boy they named Luke. Despite

Laurel's difficulties, they believed their growing family was worth all the challenges.

The burden of raising three young boys was taking its toll on Laurel. Joshua, the eldest, seemed to have an angelic charm, always finding a soft spot in his mother's heart. However, dealing with Daniel had always proven to be a difficult task for her. Luke, currently in the throes of his "terrible twos," presented a whole new level of challenge for the already worn-out mother.

On April 16, 2013, Laurel, Luke, and Daniel visited her parents' home in nearby Marshall Township, Pennsylvania. After visiting with the boy's grandparents, Laurel took Luke and Daniel outside. In a quiet moment away from watchful eyes, she tied the boys' hands and feet with twine. The children, trusting their mother, likely didn't understand the significance of what was happening. Laurel carefully positioned the boys on the ground behind her van. With a solemn look, she pressed her forefinger to her lips, gesturing for silence, and softly whispered, "Shh."

With her young sons restrained and positioned behind the vehicle, Laurel climbed into the van's driver's seat. Igniting the engine, she shifted the vehicle into reverse and slowly rolled backward over her boys. Shockingly, she pulled forward again and repeated the action three times. Laurel then calmly exited the van, detached the binding twine from her sons, and called 911.

The aftermath was a scene of horror. Both boys were severely injured. Daniel, who already had the challenges of Tourette syndrome to contend with, suffered internal injuries. Luke had broken bones and was unable to walk. Both boys were rushed to the hospital.

When questioned by the police, Laurel insisted that the incident was unintentional, and she was under the impression that the boys were still inside the house with their grandparents. An inquiry was initiated, but Child Protective Services classified the incident as an accident. Consequently, no legal charges were filed against her.

Nearly a year had gone by, and the enormity of Laurel's actions bore heavily on her conscience. Despite the absence of significant consequences for her actions, the burden of guilt was overwhelming. In late March, she confided in her husband, Mark, expressing her desire to admit to the police that she had deliberately caused harm to their children the previous year. She felt the compelling need to confess that it wasn't an accident.

Mark, however, firmly advised against speaking to the authorities. He understood that such a confession would inevitably result in Child Protective Services intervening and potentially taking their children away. Instead, he encouraged her to place her trust in her faith, reassuring her that things would eventually find a way to resolve.

April 1, 2014, dawned like any other day in the Schlemmer household. The sun rose, casting a warm glow over their two-story colonial home on Saratoga Drive. Laurel watched from the sidewalk as her oldest boy, Joshua, got on the school bus. She and his two younger brothers waved as the bus drove away. Lauren said goodbye to the other mothers at the bus stop, then walked back home with three-year-old Luke and six-year-old Daniel.

Laurel spent the morning with Luke and Daniel, their home filled with the young boys' innocent laughter and playful chatter. As the morning wore on, Laurel decided it was time for the boys to have their bath. While the boy's grandmother watched television downstairs, Laurel walked upstairs and filled the bathtub with water. The sound of the rushing water echoed through the house.

Soon afterward, Laurel led Luke and Daniel to the bathroom. The boys, trusting and unsuspecting, followed their mother. They stepped into the bathtub, the water enveloping them. Then, in a moment that would forever change their lives, Laurel crawled into the tub fully clothed, held the boy's faces down in the water, and sat on top of them.

As the boy's arms thrashed, Laurel remained calm. Once their movement ceased, she tenderly lifted each child, towel-dried them, combed their hair, and carefully laid them on the bathroom floor. Laurel then removed her wet clothes, placed them in a garbage bag, walked into the study, and called 911.

While speaking with the emergency operator, a faint tremor could be detected in Laurel Schlemmer's high-pitched voice. Yet her interaction, which spanned five minutes, was marked by an eerie calmness and extreme politeness.

> "I, uh, let my six- and three-year-old sons play in the bathtub a little bit before their bath this morning, and, uh, I was, and then I went to, to

> the restroom and, um, took longer than I should have or planned and then I came back. They're unconscious. I think that they've, they've drowned in our bathtub."

When the operator asked if the boys were breathing, Laurel replied, "It doesn't look like it, sir," even though she was in another room. The operator then asked if she had performed CPR, but she admitted she didn't know how. Just before paramedics arrived, the operator asked if anything was in their mouths. Laurel replied, "Just water."

Emergency services arrived quickly, rushing the boys to the hospital. Luke succumbed to his injuries within an hour of arrival, despite their best efforts. Daniel, however, clung to life, his condition critical.

When detectives questioned Laurel, she admitted to drowning her two youngest sons, telling them she heard "crazy voices" in her head that told her to push the boys underwater.

Laurel was driven by a misguided belief that her sons were autistic. She told investigators that she could be a better mother to their older brother if the other two boys weren't around. She believed Luke and Daniel would be "better off in heaven."

She explained that her younger sons felt "foreign" to her and were not as easy to raise as their older brother, Joshua.

Laurel Schlemmer was charged with the murder of her son Luke and the attempted drowning of Daniel. Yet, there was an increasing likelihood that the attempted drowning charge would escalate to another count of murder.

Daniel, just six years old, was in a coma, sustained by life support for four harrowing days. However, the lack of oxygen had inflicted irreparable damage to his brain. Sadly, on April 5, his fight for life came to an end.

While awaiting trial, Laurel was instructed not to have any contact with her surviving son, Joshua. However, her husband, Mark, consistently ignored this court order and facilitated visits between Joshua and Laurel.

The non-jury trial of Laurel Schlemmer began three years after the tragic events that claimed the lives of her two youngest sons. The courtroom was filled with palpable tension as the prosecution and defense prepared to present their cases.

The prosecution painted a picture of a mother who, driven by her distorted belief that her two sons were autistic and that she could be a better mother to their older brother if they were "in heaven," had taken the lives of her own children. They presented evidence of the events of April 1, 2014, as well as the attempted murders from the previous year, building a case of premeditated murder.

The defense, on the other hand, presented a different narrative. They portrayed Laurel as a woman overwhelmed by the pressures of motherhood and her husband's desire for a larger family. A key witness for the defense was a psychiatrist who testified that Laurel had tried to be an ideal Christian and loyal mother, but she felt overwhelmed by her circumstances. The psychiatrist also testified that Laurel's ability to form the intent to kill was significantly impaired and substantially diminished. The defense argued that she was found to have suffered significant dissociation, meaning she lost touch with herself and functioned as though she was disconnected from her body.

However, before a verdict could be reached, a jail psychiatrist declared Laurel mentally incompetent to stand trial. A judge ruled that Schlemmer was unfit to stand trial after doctors reported she suffered from delusions and believed she followed God's orders when she killed her sons. She was sent to a state mental hospital for treatment.

In June 2016, doctors determined Schlemmer's competency had been restored after more than a year of treatment. Her trial was scheduled to start in January 2017.

In May 2017, Schlemmer pleaded guilty but mentally ill to two counts of third-degree murder, child endangerment, and tampering with evidence. She was sentenced later that year to fifteen to forty years in prison for each murder, meaning she could spend up to eighty years in prison. Her son, Joshua, will be almost forty before she's eligible for parole.

CHAPTER 3
THE GROOMER

Kayleigh Haywood was a typical fifteen-year-old girl from the United Kingdom. She had dreams and aspirations like any other teenager. She cherished her family and friends and envisioned attending college, exploring the world, and eventually starting a family of her own. Like her friends, she was captivated by social media, often engrossed in her phone and sharing regular updates about her life.

However, everything took a drastic turn on October 31, 2015, when she received an unexpected Facebook message from an unfamiliar man.

> "Hi, how are you? I've seen your picture. You're very pretty."

Within minutes of receiving the initial message, Kayleigh found herself captivated. Twenty-seven-year-old Luke Harlow appeared to be an intriguing young man.

Kayleigh and Luke both initially lied about their ages. Kayleigh claimed she was nineteen, and Luke told her he was a year younger. However, Kayleigh quickly admitted that she was only fifteen years old. But this didn't deter Luke, and he continued to shower her with attention and compliments.

Despite the twelve-year age difference between them, she felt a surge of excitement that someone older was showing an interest in her. The flattery continued.

> "Have you got a boyfriend? Oh, you're so pretty. How come you haven't got a boyfriend?"

> "Oh, I'd like you to be my princess. I'll treat you right. I'll be your boyfriend."

> "I'll buy u a present yeah.. Cause I love ya ;) xxxx"

Luke's Facebook profile seemed harmless enough. His tagline read as "Luke Funtimes Harlow."

Over the following thirteen days, Luke and Kayleigh were glued to their phones, exchanging messages. At Luke's insistence, Kayleigh kept the conversations hidden from her family. They both knew her parents would never approve of their fifteen-year-old daughter chatting online with a twenty-seven-year-old man.

Despite being aware that it was wrong, Kayleigh couldn't help but believe she was embarking on a loving and reliable relationship with a man who genuinely cared for her. Someone who knew her like no one else did. Luke made countless promises, showered her with flattery, and gradually manipulated her emotions. The rapid and robust nature of online communication allowed him to gain Kayleigh's trust within a matter of days.

When she and her parents had trivial arguments, he sympathized with her and did his best to turn her against her parents. Of course, he steered most of their conversations subtly toward sex. He encouraged her to discuss her previous sexual encounters with him and expressed his desire to have her exclusively. He managed to profoundly influence her psyche in a remarkably short period.

Luke Harlow began discussing the idea of her visiting him, promising to buy drinks and host a fun party. The allure of his flattery drew her in, and she eagerly expressed her interest in coming over to meet him.

After two weeks of intense online chatting and telephone calls, a web of emotions entwined their hearts, making Kayleigh believe she had stumbled upon a loving and trustworthy connection with this older man.

Luke invited her to his house, and they agreed on a date. Friday, November 13. An air of excitement and danger swept over Kayleigh. Luke had painted a picture of a cozy movie night, a simple meal, and the allure of a vodka-induced adventure. She was torn between the thrill of this potential rendezvous and the nagging feeling that she was venturing into forbidden territory. She knew her parents would never allow it.

Ordinarily, Kayleigh wouldn't lie to her parents, but she believed she knew better. Though he was older, Luke was charming. It would be a harmless lie. The magnetic pull of Luke's charm was impossible to resist.

That night, Kayleigh told her parents she was sleeping over at her friend Katie's house. Butterflies fluttered in her stomach as she realized she would have to lie to Katie, too. Guilt swept over Kayleigh as she told Katie she had been looking forward to staying over, but at the last minute, changed plans to stay at her aunt's instead. She felt horrible deceiving her parents and friend, but her longing to meet Luke overpowered her better judgment.

As the sun dipped below the horizon that Friday evening, Kayleigh asked her father, Martin, to drop her off ten minutes from their home at Ibstock Community College, telling him she would meet Katie there. Instead, she walked twenty minutes to Luke Harlow's apartment and met him for the first time.

Saturday morning, Kayleigh's mother, Stephanie, received a message from her daughter's phone asking if she could stay at Katie's house another night. Knowing she was safe with her friend, Stephanie agreed.

As the Sunday morning sun painted the world in hues of gold, a sense of unease tugged at Katie's heart. Awakening to the light, she noticed a text message on her phone from Kayleigh. Chillingly, it read only one word: "Help."

Her heart pounding, Katie immediately replied, "What do you mean?" Right away, she received a reply, "I meant hello."

Katie assumed the message was just a simple mistake. Confident that Kayleigh was safe at her aunt's house, she didn't give it another thought.

All through the rest of that Sunday, an odd silence enveloped Kayleigh's family and friends. Her usual, frequent posts on Facebook and other social media platforms were absent—a strange departure from her typical behavior. Despite their unease, however, her family reasoned she must be preoccupied with her friends.

Later that day, fate intervened. A local man stumbled upon a shattered, white cell phone lying on a remote country road near Ibstock. Despite the severe cracks on the screen, the phone miraculously powered up. The man scrolled through her contact list and called the last number dialed, which happened to be Kayleigh's friend, Katie.

Katie received the call, and her heart sank as she realized the discovery's significance. Katie's phone had been found nowhere near her aunt's house. Without wasting a moment, she dialed Kayleigh's mother, knowing something was terribly wrong.

Stephanie was utterly taken aback when Katie explained that Kayleigh wasn't with her, and her phone had been found smashed on a rural road. With no trace of Kayleigh's whereabouts on social media and no one having had any recent contact with her, the gravity of the situation dawned on the family. They realized they had no choice but to involve the police.

Under the direction of Detective Chief Superintendent David Sandall, the police launched their investigation. Their initial focus was scrutinizing Kayleigh's messages, social media interactions, and posts. As the investigation unfolded, a crucial revelation came to light: Kayleigh's iPad in her bedroom was synced with the same messages from her phone. They quickly realized she had been in extensive communication with a man named Luke Harlow through Facebook.

Astonishingly, they had exchanged over 2,600 messages within a mere two weeks. Harlow had lavished her with attention and compliments, and their interactions had led to plans of meeting on the day she vanished. They were particularly alarmed to discover Harlow had insisted on keeping their relationship hidden from others. It was a textbook example of child grooming.

> "Got you all to myself now babe. You have to give me kisses whether you want to or not!"
>
> "We need to have drinks soon babe, so I can get you drunk and take advantage. xxx"
>
> "I'll make you take your clothes off first. I'd be too tempted to do naughty stuff if you was in my bed naked ;) xxxxx"

Luke Harlow was swiftly apprehended and slapped with kidnapping charges. However, despite his arrest, there was still no trace of Kayleigh, and he adamantly maintained his innocence, professing to know nothing about her mysterious disappearance.

From Kayleigh's phone records, they knew she had been happy and content that Friday and into Saturday. She sent a selfie to a friend, told another that she had watched a movie, and sent various text messages.

Inside Harlow's home, police found evidence that Kayleigh had been there. Her phone charger was still plugged into the wall, and her other belongings were still in the house. Harlow told police that he knew she was underage and that it was wrong, but he didn't care.

Harlow had placed the mattress directly in front of the television in the living room, and he claimed he and Kayleigh had watched movies together all day on Saturday. When they ran out of vodka, he ran next door to his neighbor, Stephen Beadman's house. Beadman had a car, and the two men drove to town to buy more alcohol.

Harlow told detectives that when they returned, he invited Beadman to his house and introduced him to Kayleigh. After all three drank an enormous amount of vodka, Harlow claimed he went to bed, and when he woke up on Sunday morning, Kayleigh and Beadman were gone.

When police arrested Stephen Beadman, they couldn't help but notice the severe scratch marks that marred his face. The apparent signs of a struggle were immediately alarming and heightened the investigators' suspicions.

Investigators weren't sure what really happened on Saturday night, but they knew that after 9:00 p.m., Kayleigh, an obsessive user of Facebook and social media, never used her phone again.

When investigators went through Harlow's online accounts, they quickly realized he was a serial groomer. Many times in the past, he had lured underage girls to his apartment. During the two weeks he had groomed Kayleigh, he was simultaneously grooming two other girls. One was fifteen, another thirteen. Both girls believed that Luke Harlow was their boyfriend. His messages to the girls read:

"If I kidnap you, I'm keeping you."

"Having sex with drunk, unconscious girls is my favorite. I wish I could kidnap you for Xmas, but I would probably be arrested and sent to prison."

Although he admitted to grooming young girls, he insisted he had no idea what had happened to Kayleigh.

During a three-day interview with detectives, Stephen Beadman consistently provided false information and attempted to mislead the detectives. He denied any knowledge of what happened to Kayleigh. Beadman maintained that all three had consumed a substantial amount of vodka, causing him to black out. He had gaps in his memory. He could only recall that he had tried to kiss her, but she rejected his advance and ran out of the apartment.

Meanwhile, police and search crews frantically searched the area for Kayleigh Haywood.

As investigators diligently pursued every lead provided, more distressing evidence came to light. A red bra was discovered in a field and promptly recognized by Stephanie

Haywood as belonging to Kayleigh. The investigation progressed into the subsequent days, Monday and Tuesday, when more of Kayleigh's clothing was located in a field across from Sence Valley Forest Park.

Detectives learned that Stephen Beadman worked as a landscape gardener and had a storage locker. When they searched his storage locker, they found more of Kayleigh's belongings: her handbag and a top.

During questioning, Beadman claimed that he had injured his face while working at a farm, but when detectives searched the farm, they found a bag containing Beadman's clothing caked with Kayleigh's dried blood.

After three days of lying to detectives and having the evidence pile up against him, Beadman eventually began giving more details of what had happened that night.

Beadman had indeed tried to kiss her and was rejected, but there was far more to the story. Beadman had removed most of her clothes, and Kayleigh had run out of Harlow's apartment into the cold winter night, carrying her phone and wearing nothing but her top. She was scared to death. She made it less than fifty feet from Harlow's front door before Beadman wrestled her to the ground. He then dragged her across the road to Sence Valley Forest Park, where Kayleigh's phone was later found.

Beadman took her into the park's parking lot, where he raped her. He then forcibly walked her out of the park and through a plowed farm field, to an area where an old, unused railroad crossed a small pond.

Kayleigh had been beaten and raped, then walked more than a mile into a cold, desolate area. She must have known her fate. Kayleigh took an opportunity when she saw a pile of old bricks near the railroad. She quickly grabbed a brick, smashed Beadman in the face, and ran.

But wearing no shoes, Kayleigh was no match for the twenty-nine-year-old Beadman. He chased her down and beat her repeatedly in the face with a rock, killing her.

Police found Kayleigh's body on November 18, 2015, six days after she had disappeared. She was only found after Beadman gave the general location of her body. She was covered with defensive wounds all over her body, and an autopsy revealed she had been subjected to a horrific sexual assault. The injuries to her face and head were so severe that her parents were not allowed to see her. She was later identified using dental records.

The case was taken to court in June 2016. Stephen Beadman pleaded guilty to raping and murdering Kayleigh, while Harlow pleaded guilty to grooming and sexual activity with a child. Both men, however, denied false imprisonment. Still, the jury realized that a girl doesn't willingly run from an apartment, unclothed, into a freezing November night, and they were both found guilty of falsely imprisoning Kayleigh.

Luke Harlow was sentenced to twelve years in prison for meeting a child following sexual grooming, two counts of sexual activity with a child, and false imprisonment. Stephen Beadman was sentenced to life in prison with a minimum term of 35 years for the false imprisonment, rape, and murder of Kayleigh Haywood.

Five years later, in April 2021, Stephen Beadman died from oxygen deprivation to the brain and cardiac arrest while in prison. His death was not treated as suspicious.

In the aftermath of the heart-wrenching incident, Kayleigh's family established "Kayleigh's Cause" to advocate for raising the minimum age for social media website usage to 16. They joined forces with the police to produce a poignant short film titled "Kayleigh's Love Story," intended to raise awareness about the perils of engaging with strangers on the internet. The film skillfully reenacted some of the crucial events from the last fourteen days of Kayleigh's life and has been viewed by thousands of school children nationwide, garnering millions more views online from across the globe.

CHAPTER 4
THE WRONG WIFE

Located in southeast Portland, the Oregon Culinary Institute was a renowned institution where aspiring chefs and restaurateurs honed their skills. The institute boasted a fully operational restaurant, drawing locals with its student-prepared dishes and affordable prices.

At the helm of the institute's culinary training was Chef Daniel Brophy. An Oregon native, Daniel had dedicated 45 years to the food industry, with two decades focused on teaching. He had been imparting his knowledge at the Oregon Culinary Institute for the last ten years.

Daniel earned a degree in Biology from the University of Sioux Falls, South Dakota. Beyond his culinary expertise, he was a marine biology enthusiast, a certified master gardener, and a connoisseur of mushrooms. Oregon's forests were his favorite foraging grounds.

Daniel was passionate about organizing field trips, spear-heading student projects, and engaging with the community through talks. Widely adored by his students, Chef Brophy was the very embodiment of the institute's spirit.

On June 2, 2018, a seemingly ordinary Saturday, Dan began his day as he always did. He reached the institute early, preparing for the day's classes. At precisely 7:22 a.m., he deactivated the alarm, unlocked the school's doors, and made his way to the primary cooking space, Kitchen One.

Within a short span of less than ten minutes, another staff member arrived at the institute. Like Dan, she was there to set things in motion for the students who'd be coming in soon. However, nothing could have prepared her for the scene she was about to encounter.

Upon entering Kitchen One, she was met with a chilling sight: Dan Brophy lay motionless on the floor, his face turned upward, a bullet wound evident in his chest. Without hesitation, she dialed 911, her heart racing as she grappled with the horrifying reality.

As the sirens wailed and the emergency medical teams rushed in, the institute slowly filled with students, each one unaware of the tragedy that had just unfolded.

Dan Brophy, at 63 years old, was no more. The two bullet wounds—one in his chest and the other in his back, both directly targeting his heart—were evidence of a deliberate act. The scene was eerily calm, reminiscent of a calculated mafia assassination. Everything was in its place; no items were missing, even though there were valuables clearly visible. It was as if someone had coldly and methodically executed him.

The lack of security cameras in the school complicated matters. There was no DNA evidence, witnesses, or signs of a struggle. It was a detective's nightmare.

Three hours after the discovery, detectives contacted the one person they believed needed to know immediately: Dan's wife. They phoned her, urging her to come to the institute as quickly as possible. Nancy Brophy, who lived in Beaverton, roughly a 15-minute drive away, arrived at the institute at 10:47 p.m.

Detective Posey approached Nancy with a heavy heart, choosing his words carefully. "I just want to let you know that we believe it's Dan that has been killed."

Nancy responded with a hint of resignation,

> "Yeah, I kinda got that when everybody gave me the sad-sack look. All I can think about is, 'Oh my God'. Here's the terrible thing: Even if you find who shot him, it's not going to bring him back. And I want him back. That's the part I want! I don't care about who shot him; I just want him back. I don't want him dead."

The raw pain in her voice was palpable. Yet, as the minutes ticked by, Nancy's demeanor began to shift. She seemed to find a way to cope, even resorting to humor in the face of such a tragic situation.

Trying to proceed with the investigation, Detective Posey gently said, "We just need your permission to search through his truck and go through that."

Without missing a beat, Nancy quipped, "Sure, and clean out the trash. He's a pig." The unexpected lightness in her response caught everyone off guard, starkly contrasting the grim atmosphere surrounding them.

Dan and Nancy's relationship spanned nearly a quarter of a century, with nineteen of those years as a married couple. With Dan at sixty-three and Nancy five years his senior at sixty-eight, their bond was undeniable. While Dan's culinary prowess made him the primary earner, Nancy's professional journey was more eclectic, hopping from one job to another throughout their time together.

Born and raised in Texas, Nancy was an alumna of both the University of Houston and the University of Indiana. Her first marriage was to a police officer, but when that fell apart, she relocated to Portland. It was there, in the early 90s, that her path crossed Dan's. At a different culinary institute, their shared passion for food ignited a connection. Although Dan was married with a son at the time, fate had other plans. When his marriage eventually ended, he and Nancy decided to tie the knot.

Nancy's professional endeavors saw her managing a catering business for a while, and later, she worked for a pension company. However, her heart always yearned for something more creative. In 2011, she finally heeded that call and embarked on a full-time writing career. Her niche? Steamy romance novels infused with action and suspense. With evocative titles like "Hell on the Heart," "The Wrong Lover," "The Wrong Brother," "The Wrong Cop," and "The Wrong Husband," her stories predominantly revolved around the thrilling world of Navy SEALs. And lots of sex.

Dan and Nancy were the epitome of a perfect couple to all who knew them. Their bond seemed unbreakable, with no visible cracks or tensions. They were two peas in a pod: always together, always in sync.

In her grief, Nancy took to Facebook to share the heart-wrenching news of Dan's demise. Her post read:

> "For my Facebook friends and family, I have sad news to relate. My husband and best friend, Chef Dan Brophy, was killed yesterday morning. For those of you who are close to me and feel this deserved a phone call, you are right, but I'm struggling to make sense of everything right now. There is a candlelight vigil at Oregon Culinary Institute tomorrow, Monday, June 4th, at 7 p.m. While I appreciate all of your loving responses, I am overwhelmed. Please save phone calls for a few days until I can function."

The community came together for the vigil, mourning the loss of a beloved figure. As the investigation into Dan's death progressed, the police found themselves at a dead end. Dan was a man without enemies, and the idea of someone wanting him dead was baffling.

However, a curveball came three days into the investigation. Nancy made a peculiar phone call to detectives that would shift the direction of their inquiries. She asked the lead detective for an official letter stating she wasn't a suspect in her husband's murder, intended for her insurance company.

Taken aback, the detective responded, "Why would you need that?"

Nancy explained, "Because they don't want to pay if it turns out that I secretly slipped down to the school and shot my husband."

The detective, clearly surprised, replied, "Well, we never would do something like that. I've never heard of that being done."

Nancy, sounding exasperated, said,

> "This is such a stupid little policy. I can't believe they're making me jump through the hoops like this. Cause it's only $40,000. And, as my sister said, 'You know, usually when they do that, it's for millions.' And I said, 'Yeah, we weren't insured for millions.'"

While Nancy had gone out of her way to make the conversation seem innocuous, it raised eyebrows with investigators. The request was unusual, making the detectives wonder if there was more to the story than met the eye.

While Nancy had been quick to downplay the insurance policy's value, emphasizing the modest sum of $40,000, she conveniently omitted that multiple other policies were in play. Combined, these policies amounted to a staggering $800,000. This revelation added a new layer of complexity to the case, introducing a potential motive.

As detectives delved deeper into the investigation, their first step was to comb through Dan and Nancy's residence, hoping to unearth any clues that might shed light on the circumstances surrounding Dan's death.

The discovery of the Glock handgun was significant. It was the same type of gun that had killed Dan. Nancy had been forthright about its existence, explaining its purchase at a gun show as a safety measure for Dan's mushroom foraging expeditions. She was adamant that the gun had remained untouched since its acquisition, pointing to the zip tie around the trigger and the orange chamber plug as evidence of its pristine condition.

However, the investigator's examination of the weapon told a different story. The gun's barrel was indeed unused, but it was misaligned on the weapon's frame, suggesting it had been tampered with or possibly even disassembled and then reassembled.

The barrel and slide's positioning was slightly off, not fitting snugly against the frame as expected from a brand-new, unused firearm. Also, the zip tie around the trigger was present, as Nancy had mentioned, but it had been cut.

This discrepancy raised several questions. Why would an untouched gun show signs of tampering? Was Nancy's account of the gun's history accurate? And most importantly, could this very Glock 17 have been the weapon used in Dan's murder? The investigation was taking a turn, and the detectives knew they were onto something crucial.

Another discovery of a "ghost gun kit" in the house added another layer of intrigue to the investigation. Ghost guns, by their very nature, are designed to be elusive. Without serial numbers, they leave no traceable footprint, making them a favored choice for those looking to operate outside the law. The mere presence of such a kit, especially in a household without any apparent ties to criminal activities, was perplexing.

Nancy's explanation for the kit was as unexpected as the discovery itself. She claimed it was purely for research purposes—a tool to aid her in crafting a compelling narrative for her next book. She explained that the protagonist of this story would utilize a ghost gun, and she wanted firsthand knowledge of the assembly process to lend authenticity to her writing.

While it wasn't uncommon for writers to immerse themselves in their subject matter for the sake of realism, the detectives couldn't help but be skeptical. The timing, combined with the other discoveries and inconsistencies, made them wary. Was Nancy's explanation genuine, or was it a convenient cover for something more sinister? The detectives knew they had to tread carefully, ensuring they didn't overlook any detail, no matter how small. The puzzle pieces were slowly coming together, but the bigger picture remained elusive.

Three months into the investigation, detectives stumbled upon a chilling piece of evidence. While researching Nancy's background, they found an article she had written seven years before Dan's murder. The blog post's title was as startling as its content: "How to Murder Your Husband."

The article's opening lines were particularly unsettling:

> "As a romantic suspense writer, I spend a lot of time thinking about murder and, consequently, about police procedure. After all, if the murder

> is supposed to set me free, I certainly don't want to spend any time in jail. And let me say clearly for the record, I don't like jumpsuits, and orange isn't my color."

Her candid discussion about the challenges of committing a perfect murder was eerily prescient.

> "The drawback is the police aren't stupid. They are looking at you first. So you have to be organized, ruthless, and very clever."

In the post, she explored various motives for murder, including financial gain, infidelity, and abuse. Her analysis was disturbingly thorough, suggesting a deep contemplation of the subject.

She also discussed potential murder methods in her blog post. Knives, she wrote, were a "personal and close up" method, but they left "blood everywhere," making them messy and potentially incriminating. Poison, often stereotypically considered a woman's weapon, was dismissed as too easily traceable.

Interestingly, she also discussed guns as a method of murder. She described them as "loud, messy, and requiring some skill." This analysis was particularly chilling, given that Dan was killed with a Glock handgun, a weapon that Nancy and Dan had purchased together.

Perhaps the most haunting line from the post was her reflection on the human capacity for violence:

> "I find it is easier to wish people dead than to actually kill them," she mused. "I don't want to

> worry about blood and brains splattered on my walls. And really, I'm not good at remembering lies. But the thing I know about murder is that every one of us have it in him/her when pushed far enough."

The discovery of this blog post added a new dimension to the investigation. While it was not direct evidence of guilt, it certainly painted Nancy in a different light. The detectives now had to grapple with a question: Were these merely the musings of a fiction writer, or was it a window into the mind of a potential murderer?

Initially, the lack of security cameras at the Culinary Institute was a setback for the investigators. However, they were determined to leave no stone unturned. They expanded their search, hoping that nearby establishments or street cameras might have captured something—anything—that could provide a lead.

Their diligence paid off. After sifting through countless hours of footage, a pattern emerged. A gray Toyota Sienna minivan was seen repeatedly circling the vicinity of the institute before and after the crucial six-minute window: the time between when Dan disarmed the alarm and when his coworker stumbled upon his lifeless body.

While not clear enough to identify the driver or capture the license plate, the footage revealed a distinct feature: a scrape over the rear driver's side fender wall. This detail was significant. Nancy owned a gray Toyota Sienna which bore the same distinctive scrape upon inspection.

Confronted with this evidence, Nancy's account of her whereabouts on that fateful morning became inconsistent. Initially, she claimed to have been at home in bed. However, when pressed, her story shifted. She then asserted that she had driven to a park to write, using the solitude to focus on her work. Yet, she claimed no recollection of the morning's events, attributing her memory lapse to a "memory hole." She described it as a form of retrograde amnesia, a condition where traumatic events can lead to memory loss.

While trauma-induced amnesia is a recognized psychological phenomenon, the timing and circumstances made detectives skeptical. The gray minivan, the scrape, and Nancy's changing alibi combined to cast a long shadow of doubt. The investigation was heating up, and every new piece of evidence seemed to draw a tighter circle around Nancy.

On September 5, 2018, the net finally closed around Nancy Brophy. She was arrested in connection with Dan's murder. The evidence against her was mounting, and each discovery painted a more incriminating picture.

Upon her arrest, a chilling detail emerged. Nancy's iPhone had a page bookmarked, ominously titled "10 Ways to Cover Up a Murder." The article contained advice that seemed eerily relevant:

> "The best time to commit a crime is in the very early hours of the day when most people are asleep."

This aligned with the timeline of Dan's murder, with her vehicle being spotted leaving the vicinity at 7:29 a.m., a mere seven minutes after Dan had disarmed the alarm.

The prosecution meticulously built their case as Nancy awaited her trial behind bars. The narrative they were constructing was one of financial desperation and cold calculation. Contrary to her initial claims, investigators soon discovered the $800,000 that Nancy stood to gain from life insurance policies on Dan's life. This starkly contrasted the couple's financial struggles, which had begun in 2014 and worsened by 2016, when they defaulted on their mortgage payments.

Yet, amidst these financial woes, the couple's expenditure raised eyebrows. Although they couldn't pay their mortgage, they were shelling out over $1,000 monthly on life insurance premiums and had recently acquired a Glock handgun for $1,500.

However, the most damning evidence came from Nancy's computer. Records showed that she had purchased a barrel and slide for a Glock 17 handgun on eBay, costing her $335. Thus, Nancy could have swapped out the original barrel and slide, used the modified gun to commit the crime, and discarded the eBay-purchased parts. She could have then reassemble the Glock with its original components, making it appear completely unused.

This theory explained the anomaly detectives had noticed with the Glock's barrel and frame alignment. The pieces of the puzzle were falling into place, and the image they formed was one of premeditation and deceit. The prosecution was confident they had a strong case against Nancy Brophy.

Nancy's trial began in April 2022, three and a half years after her arrest. The judge, however, did not allow the defense to bring up her blog entry, "How to Murder Your Husband." He reasoned that it was written too long ago, and it didn't exactly describe the crime. And, after all, she was a writer.

Her defense team attempted to introduce doubt into the narrative, suggesting that a homeless man, also seen on security footage around the time of Dan's murder, could have been the perpetrator.

In a surprising move, Nancy decided to testify in her own defense. Whether she hoped to appear as an innocent older woman or believed she could outwit the court with her intelligence, her decision to take the stand proved a misstep. Her demeanor during the cross-examination was marked by contempt, and her responses were disjointed and inconsistent.

When questioned about the Glock's misaligned barrel, she casually admitted to having "played with it." The prosecutor pressed her, "Did you ever remove the slide and barrel?" to which she responded, "Oh sure, I played with it." This admission was a revelation; she had never disclosed this to the police.

As for the additional slide and barrel she had purchased on eBay, she offered no explanation for its whereabouts.

The prosecution argued that Nancy's original plan was to swap the slide and barrel from the ghost gun onto the Glock she had purchased at a gun show, kill her husband, and then switch everything back, rendering the murder weapon untraceable. However, when she realized the ghost gun parts wouldn't fit, she purchased a slide and barrel from eBay that she knew would work.

When asked why she had purchased the extra barrel and slide, she calmly responded,

> "If there would have been a trigger, I would have purchased a gun trigger. I was fascinated with gun pieces at that point."

The fact that she hadn't disclosed the purchase of the slide and barrel to detectives, combined with their mysterious disappearance, raised suspicions. The prosecution suggested that she knew the shell casings at the crime scene could never be traced back to the Glock because she had used a separate barrel and slide.

When asked about the missing parts, she claimed ignorance, saying,"I have no idea where that slide and barrel is." The prosecutor pointed out the irony of her inability to locate the alleged murder weapon, to which she retorted, "I see nothing ironic about this case at all."

Far from helping her case, Nancy's testimony only strengthened the prosecution's narrative of a calculated, cold-blooded murder. Her contemptuous demeanor, inconsistent responses, and the mounting evidence against her painted a damning picture. The trial was far from over, but Nancy's own words seemed to be her worst enemy.

Throughout the trial, a total of 102 witnesses were called, none of whom testified that the relationship between Dan and Nancy was anything other than loving. However, the prosecution focused on the incriminating evidence against Nancy, particularly the surveillance footage of the gray minivan circling the crime scene.

When questioned if she believed it was indeed her in the surveillance video, Nancy reluctantly admitted, "You know, I do, I do. But I would say that it took me a while to get to that stage." Still, she had no recollection of it. When pressed further about her presence near the crime scene during the critical window of time, she defensively retorted,

> "That's your version of what happened. That is not my version. I think your case is held together with, real frankly, Band-Aids."

As the trial progressed, more evidence came to light that seemed to contradict Nancy's claims. Despite her assertion that she had never purchased ammunition, her internet search history revealed queries on "How to load a Glock." Furthermore, investigators learned she had visited a public shooting range that didn't require check-ins just a few months before the murder.

Nancy's claim of retrograde amnesia was also called into question. Her memory loss conveniently affected only a tiny window of time, specifically around the period of the crime.

The problem with that claim was that she hadn't been informed of Dan's murder until three hours later. Although she claimed the memory loss was due to trauma, it seemed to have magically chosen the few specific minutes around the murder rather than the time that she had actually experienced the trauma.

Furthermore, the prosecution pointed out that during her initial 40-minute interview with the police, Nancy didn't ask any questions about Dan. Additionally, Dan was murdered on a Saturday—the only day he would be alone during a six-minute window. This detail suggested that the killer had intimate knowledge of Dan's schedule, something a stranger wouldn't have known.

While the judge didn't allow the jurors to hear about Nancy's blog post "How to Kill Your Husband," he permitted broader questions about her writing. Taking advantage of this, the prosecutor asked, "As a writer, is it true that you spend a lot of time thinking about murder?"

Nancy replied, "Oh yeah. When you're writing romantic suspense, somebody's dying."

The prosecutor continued, "You also consequently think about police procedure quite a bit. Is that right?"

Nancy, clearly agitated, replied, "Yes and no. I mean, I have wrote that, and I know what you're quoting me on."

He then asked her, "If there was one thing that you know about murder, is it that anyone is capable of doing it?"

She confidently quipped back,

> "I absolutely believe that. I don't think that people murder willy-nilly. But going back to my case, where is the motivation? You know, an editor would laugh and say, 'I think you need to work harder on this story. You have kind of a big hole in it.'"

With that, the prosecution ended the cross-examination.

The prosecution had one final witness to call to the stand: Andrea Jacobs, Nancy's former cellmate while she was awaiting trial. Her testimony added a new layer of intrigue to the case.

Andrea recounted a conversation they had about Dan's murder. According to Andrea, Nancy had described the murder, holding out her arms to show how far away the gun was when he was shot.

When asked if Nancy had ever admitted to her involvement in the murder, Andrea recalled a telling slip of the tongue. According to Andrea, Nancy had started to say "I" about the murder but quickly switched to "it." This subtle shift in language suggested a possible admission of guilt.

Ultimately, Nancy's own words proved to be her downfall. Had she chosen to remain silent, the evidence against her, largely circumstantial, might not have been sufficient for a conviction. However, her decision to testify, coupled with her inconsistent and contemptuous responses, undermined her defense. Her demeanor on the stand and her seeming inability to provide coherent, consistent answers painted a picture of guilt that was hard for the jury to ignore.

On May 25, 2022, Nancy Brophy was found guilty and sentenced to life in prison. However, she will be eligible for parole after serving 25 years, when she's ninety-two years old.

CHAPTER 5
THE CHAMPIONS

The Champion family has a deep-rooted history in the region northwest of Nashville, Tennessee, with their presence extending for more than two centuries. In the 1950s, Boyd and Doris Champion decided to put down roots in the quaint town of Cadiz, Kentucky, just across the state border. They purchased a farm there, establishing a new chapter in the family's long history in the region.

Their first-born son, Lindsey, came into the world in 1952. As he grew up, he attended the local Trigg County High School, where he met Joy Allen, a fellow student who would become the love of his life. Their high school romance blossomed, and upon graduation, they decided to make their commitment official by getting married.

Both Lindsey and Joy were ambitious and driven to further their education. Joy enrolled at Murray State University, where she pursued a degree in elementary education. She was a dedicated student and graduated in 1976, ready to make a difference in the lives of young children. On the other hand, Lindsey chose to attend Western Kentucky University, where he studied mathematics and business finance. He graduated in 1974, equipped with the knowledge and skills to pursue a successful career in finance.

After completing their respective degrees, the couple returned to their hometown of Cadiz and purchased a farm, continuing the family tradition. Lindsey found employment at the local Farm Credit Services office in Hopkinsville, where he quickly rose through the ranks. His hard work and dedication eventually earned him the position of director, where he played a crucial role in supporting local farmers and the agricultural community.

Joy, with her passion for education, began teaching at Trigg County Elementary School. She was a beloved teacher known for her dedication to her students and ability to inspire a love for learning. Throughout her 30-year career, she touched the lives of countless students and left a lasting impact on the community. Recognizing her educational contributions, the Cadiz-Trigg County Chamber of Commerce honored her with the prestigious Educator of the Year award.

Together, Lindsey and Joy Champion became pillars of the Cadiz community, contributing to its growth and development through their respective careers and commitment to making a positive difference in the lives of those around them.

Together, Lindsey and Joy Champion built a cozy home on the edge of their farm on Old Dover Road in Cadiz. The location was perfect, with Lindsey's sister living just across the road, adding to the sense of family and community.

However, life was not without its challenges for the Champions. They faced the heart-wrenching pain of three miscarriages, which cast a shadow over their dreams of starting a family. By 1978, they had nearly given up hope of having a child naturally, and they decided to adopt. That's when they welcomed Ryan, a three-month-old baby with fiery-red hair that matched Lindsey's, into their lives.

Just as they thought their family was complete, life had another surprise in store for them. Four years after adopting Ryan, Joy discovered she was pregnant. Nine months later, their joy doubled with the birth of their daughter, Emily.

As they grew up, Ryan and Emily displayed contrasting personalities. Ryan was outgoing and loved being the center of attention, often playing the role of the class clown. On the other hand, Emily was more focused and serious about her studies. Emily's dedication to academics paid off in high school, when she was voted most likely to succeed and graduated as a salutatorian. Her achievements earned her a full-ride scholarship to Western Kentucky University. Later, she transferred to Auburn University, where her family's strong interest in horses influenced her decision to pursue a career in veterinary medicine. Emily's exceptional academic performance led to her early admission into veterinary school as a junior, marking a rare accomplishment. She eventually became a horse veterinarian working at Delta Down Racetrack.

Ryan, meanwhile, chose a different path. He served in the military for nearly a decade—an experience that shaped his character and outlook on life. After his service, he returned to the area and settled in Oak Grove, about 30 minutes from Cadiz. Ryan found work as a handyman, taking on remodeling and construction projects.

For Lisa Champion, Lindsey's sister, October 26, 2014, started like any other ordinary day in Cadiz. However, shortly after 11 a.m., the tranquility of the rural area was shattered by the sound of gunshots. While gunshots were not uncommon in the area, the frantic pounding on her front door minutes after the shots immediately signaled that something was terribly wrong.

On her front porch stood her nephew, Ryan Champion, his wrists bound with duct tape. In a state of panic, Ryan screamed for his Aunt Lisa to call for an ambulance. Lisa quickly dialed 911, and after making the call, she cut the duct tape from Ryan's wrists. As they ran toward her brother's house across Old Dover Road, she asked Ryan where the rest of the family was. But as she approached the front door, Ryan stopped her with a chilling warning:

> "You don't want to go in there. They're all dead."

When police arrived, they were confronted with a gruesome sight. Inside the home, they found the motionless bodies of sixty-two-year-old Lindsey, sixty-year-old Joy, and thirty-one-year-old Emily. Each had suffered a fatal gunshot wound to the head, and their bodies were discovered in different rooms of the house.

The family had recently come back from church and were preparing lunch. A pot of soup continued to bubble on the stove, a stark and eerie contrast to the violence that had abruptly shattered the ordinary scene.

The police, however, were about to encounter another surprise. In the kitchen, they discovered a fourth body lying on the floor, also with a gunshot wound to the head. The man had a unique, large, black birthmark on his right eyebrow and forehead, which gave the appearance of an abnormally large eyebrow. It looked almost like a solid-black tattoo across his forehead. Identification in his pocket revealed his name to be Vito Riservato, but the police were at a loss as to who he was or what his connection to the Champion family might be.

Ryan was clearly in shock from the events that had transpired. He sat beneath a tree in the front yard of his parents' home, mumbling incoherently and unable to respond to questions. Concerned for his well-being, he was quickly rushed to the hospital for evaluation and care.

The small town of Cadiz had a limited police force, ill-equipped to handle the complexities of a quadruple homicide investigation. Recognizing the need for additional resources and expertise, the local police immediately called in the Kentucky State Police to assist with the case.

Initially, investigators considered the possibility that Vito Riservato, the unidentified man found dead in the kitchen, may have been involved in a romantic relationship with Emily. However, after speaking to Emily's friends, it became clear that Riservato was not someone Emily would have dated. The connection between Riservato and the Champion family remained a mystery, and investigators were determined to uncover the truth.

Just discharged from the hospital, Ryan was finally physically able to speak with investigators about the harrowing attack that left his family dead. When asked if he knew who Vito was, Ryan confirmed that Vito was the perpetrator who had abducted and murdered his loved ones. Ryan went on to explain to detectives that he had managed to overpower Vito and shoot him in self-defense before Vito could take Ryan's own life.

Ryan revealed that he had only recently met Vito a few days prior when he was introduced as a potentially helpful hire for a remodeling project Ryan was undertaking. Additionally, Ryan mentioned Vito's connection to his girlfriend, Ann Plotkin—Vito was romantically involved with Plotkin's daughter.

Detectives remained puzzled about Vito's possible motive for killing Ryan's family. They pressed Ryan for more details, asking him to clarify his relationship with Vito, offer any insights into why Vito might have wanted to harm his family, and recount the events that transpired on the day of the murders.

Investigators took Ryan back to the Champion residence, where he walked them through and re-enacted the events of that fateful day.

When speaking with detectives, Ryan revealed why he ultimately chose not to bring Vito on for the remodeling project. Just a few days prior, Ryan had invited Vito to the house while he did some laundry. While Ryan was upstairs, he overheard Vito making sexual advances toward Emily, Ryan's sister, who was visiting from Louisiana. Ryan immediately asked Vito to leave, feeling uneasy about his behavior around Emily. However, the disturbing incident made Ryan question whether Vito could be trusted as a hire for the remodel. So, despite Vito's potential to help with the work, Ryan decided it would be best not to involve him after witnessing his advances on his sister.

Ryan expressed to the investigators that he had been troubled by Vito's fixation on Emily and was concerned for her safety. He mentioned that he had returned to his parents' house early that Sunday morning, bringing a gun from his truck to teach his sister how to defend herself.

Ryan recounted that he had taken the gun inside the house and demonstrated to Emily how to load it, disengage the safety, and properly aim. After showing her, he placed the gun on the kitchen counter.

Ryan revealed that Vito had returned to the house that morning while Ryan was visiting with his sister Emily. Vito entered, wielding the gun he found sitting on the kitchen counter. First restraining Ryan with duct tape, since he posed the most significant physical threat, Vito then taped Emily's hands to neutralize any resistance.

With the two siblings bound, Vito shockingly began trying to woo Emily using what Ryan described as laughably cliché romantic overtures. Vito even lay on the floor beside her, speaking softly as she recoiled from his advances.

The situation took a terrifying turn when Lindsey and Joy Champion pulled up on the long driveway, arriving home from church around 11 a.m. Seeing the parents return sent Vito into a panic. He rushed outside, leaving Emily and Ryan alone, still bound in tape. Desperately, the two siblings struggled to get free—but their hopes were shattered by the sudden crack of a gunshot from outside.

Ryan claimed that after the first shot rang out, he thought it was just a warning. However, three more deadly shots then followed in quick succession. Vito burst back into the house and chillingly executed Emily with two clean shots to the head, not saying a word.

Seeing the emptied gun, Ryan seized his chance as Vito scrambled to reload. He recalled grappling with Vito until he finally wrested the weapon free just as Vito reloaded. Ryan fired once, killing Vito with a single bullet to the head.

Ryan Champion spoke to local television stations, recounting a shortened version of the story he had told the police, in which Vito Riservato had single-handedly killed his entire family. However, when Vito's roommates saw the news coverage of the murders, they immediately felt that something was off about Ryan's account.

Vito Riservato lived twenty miles away in Hopkinsville with several roommates, all of whom came forward with critical insights about the man painted as a killer.

They described Vito as a gentle soul: nonviolent and incapable of the savage crimes Ryan pinned on him. Vito had a young child with a woman in Louisville he visited frequently, cherishing his role as a doting father.

In the days prior, Vito had cryptically told his roommates that his money troubles would soon vanish. He let slip he was offered $30,000, but he brushed off their questions about the job with a casual "don't worry about it."

Vito's roommates took his comments in jest. To their knowledge, Vito had never possessed a firearm and feared guns. They knew he lacked even the basic understanding of how to handle a firearm.

Given that the victims had been shot in the head, investigators started to doubt if Vito could have been the shooter, considering he had no familiarity with firearms. In contrast, Ryan, who had a decade of military service under his belt, was well-versed in using guns. Detectives started to speculate whether Ryan had promised Vito $30,000 in exchange for murdering his family.

When Ryan recreated the crime scene at the house, he provided a detailed account of how Vito had shot Emily twice in the head and then needed to reload the gun. However, Ryan's explanation didn't align with the evidence. The shell casings and live rounds scattered throughout the house and outside indicated that the gun would have needed to be reloaded two shots earlier than Ryan had claimed. Ryan's version of events was becoming increasingly inconsistent with the evidence.

Three days after the murders, Ryan was called in for another round of questioning. During this session, detectives confronted him with the discrepancies in his account regarding when Vito had to reload the gun.

Ryan's response was,

> "If he had to reload before he ever came back up... He couldn't have because he didn't have any.
>
> I'm not doubting what y'all are saying at all. As a matter of fact, especially when you explained it, it makes perfect sense. And I know y'all know your business, but I also know what I remembered.

> The only logical explanation that I see is that I'm missing time, and that's not a normal thing people do."

Detectives quickly realized that Ryan's credibility was in tatters. He had been caught in a lie. What had started as a straightforward interview had now escalated into an interrogation. Despite two more hours of questioning, they still lacked sufficient evidence to charge him.

However, days later, just before his family's funeral, Ryan Champion was taken into custody and charged with four counts of capital murder and one count of capital kidnapping.

From behind bars, Ryan reached out to a local radio station, proclaiming his innocence and urging his friends to step forward and vouch for his character. Among those who responded to his plea was his girlfriend, Ann Plotkin. Ann spoke to the police and television reporters, asserting that Ryan was a generous and kind-hearted man who would willingly give the shirt off his back to help others.

As investigators examined the phone records of both Ryan and Vito, they noticed a third phone number that had been in contact with both of them. The number belonged to Ryan's girlfriend, Ann Plotkin.

Text messages among the three phone numbers revealed that Ann Plotkin had been serving as a go-between for Ryan and Vito. The messages also indicated that Ryan and Vito had been acquainted for much longer than the few days Ryan had initially stated. Over 100 messages suggested that the trio conspired to carry out the murders.

Security footage revealed that the three had met at a local Waffle House the day before the murders.

It became evident that Ryan had employed Vito solely to set him up as the fall guy for the murders. It appeared that Ryan had promised $10,000 for each person killed. However, it was unclear whether Ryan had changed his mind about paying or if he had never intended to pay Vito from the outset, meaning he had always planned to kill him as well.

Ann Plotkin was aware of the impending murders and took no action to prevent them. As a result, she was arrested and charged with complicity to commit murder, having played an active role in orchestrating the killings.

Throughout the pre-trial phase, Ryan persistently claimed he was innocent. Yet, the mounting evidence against him, including phone records, security camera footage, and statements from Vito's roommates, told a contrasting story.

Nonetheless, in December 2016, just two months before his trial commenced, Ryan Champion entered a guilty plea to all charges, opting to do so to evade the possibility of receiving the death penalty.

After entering his guilty plea, Ryan received a life sentence without the chance of parole. He is currently serving his sentence at the Eastern Kentucky Correctional Complex, located in West Liberty, Morgan County.

Similar to Ryan, Ann chose to enter a guilty plea. She faced three counts of complicity to murder, highlighting her substantial involvement in the planning and execution of the crime. For her part in the murders, Ann received a 22-year prison sentence—a testament to the gravity of her actions.

In 2019, Ann Plotkin sought early medical release due to a terminal illness, but her request was turned down. She died the following day.

CHAPTER 6
THE SCREWDRIVER KILLER

It was a typical, sweltering summer day in June 1957 as George Davies read through the "Jobs Wanted" section of the Waterbury, Connecticut newspaper. As he thumbed through the pages, an ad caught his eye. It read, "French girl desires light housekeeping or mother's helper."

Perfect, he thought. Davies, however, had no intention of hiring the girl. He had much more devious plans in mind.

The following morning, seventeen-year-old Gaetane Boivin left a note for her mother saying she was responding to an ad for a new job opportunity.

When Gaetane failed to return home that evening, her family's worry turned to panic. By morning, with still no word from the girl, the frantic Boivins contacted the police to report her missing.

When officers arrived, they tried to reassure the worried parents that their daughter had likely just run off with a boyfriend.

Having recently immigrated from Quebec with their nine children, the Boivin family spoke minimal English. They were unaware of the police's tendency to assume missing girls had run off with boyfriends.

The Boivin family searched for the girl on their own, but their search was futile.

Only four days after Gaetane's disappearance, another young girl went missing in Connecticut.

On the morning of Monday, May 13, 1957, Virginia Doucette, just twelve miles away in Bristol, helped her nine-year-old daughter, Brenda Jane, get ready for school. Brenda wore an orange floral blouse and skirt, and she carried a handmade, green, sleeveless sweater that her grandmother made for her.

Brenda headed out at 8:15 a.m. to walk the twenty minutes to Mountain Fall Elementary School.

Along her usual route, Brenda turned onto Allentown Road, planning to stop at the home of her friend and classmate Judy Petrozza. But Brenda never made it to Judy's house that morning. Judy had stayed home from school that day with no one to walk with.

Troublingly, neither Judy's mother nor Brenda's teacher contacted the Doucettes when she didn't show up that day. Caught up in her regular routine, Virginia Doucette figured Brenda would walk through the door at 4 p.m. as always.

But 4 p.m. came and went without any sign of the girl. It wasn't until forty-five minutes later that the awful truth dawned on the Doucettes—Brenda had never arrived at Judy's home or the school. Alarmed, they called the Bristol police to report their daughter missing.

Bristol police officers, firefighters, and neighbors swiftly formed search parties to look for Brenda. But just three hours after she had vanished, her body was discovered in the bushes off Beacon Heights Road, a secluded, dead-end street.

The nine-year-old's clothes were ripped from her body, and her sweater was twisted tight around her neck. She had been viciously stabbed twenty-two times with a rectangular object, likely a screwdriver. An autopsy showed that six wounds pierced her heart. The medical examiner determined Brenda had died around 8:30 a.m., just fifteen minutes after leaving home.

The Doucettes' home was a mere 1.4 miles from Mountain Fall Elementary School, just shy of the 1.5-mile cutoff for bus transportation. With busing unavailable, Brenda had been forced to walk that day—a decision her parents blamed for the tragedy. They pointed fingers at the school district's rigid busing policy, claiming it had cost their daughter her life.

The lead investigator dispatched officers with bloodhounds to search the countryside for the murdered girl's belongings—her lunchbox, the money she had brought for milk, her watch, and the suspected murder weapon, a screwdriver.

But heavy rains had washed away other potential evidence like footprints, tire tracks, and scents, erasing leads before police could find them.

Within twenty-four hours, Bristol police questioned approximately fifty registered sex offenders in the area. However, each person they interviewed had a solid alibi.

A week after the murder, the flag at Mountain Fall Elementary School was raised back up from half-mast, although a cloud of grief still hung over the town.

A rookie officer in his first months as a probationary detective was determined to prove himself on the high-profile case. Reviewing the questioning of potential suspects, he noticed a slight inconsistency in the statements of one thirty-eight-year-old registered sex offender, George Davies.

The detective and a state police sergeant paid a visit to the home of George Davies. When he answered the door, the detective immediately recognized him—he had arrested the slender, good-looking man five years prior for child molestation.

"Hello, George!" the detective exclaimed as the smile washed away from Davies' face.

When Davies learned the officers had come to pick him up for further questioning in the Doucette case, he insisted his alibi eliminated him as a suspect.

However, he reluctantly agreed to go to Bristol police headquarters once again. But first, he asked—would they excuse him while he went to the bathroom?

Davies stalled for time, keeping the detectives waiting longer than expected. When they went to check on him, they found him unresponsive in a back bedroom, having intentionally delayed them to swallow six sleeping pills in a suicide attempt.

The officers hurried Davies to the hospital to have his stomach pumped, and they placed him under police watch. After twenty-four hours, he was deemed healthy enough for discharge and was promptly arrested for breach of peace.

Despite extensive interrogation, Davies held firm that he had been in Hartford on the morning the Doucette girl was murdered.

Davies insisted police could verify his alibi by looking at the job application he'd filed at a Hartford typewriter factory.

But he was bluffing—company records revealed he'd applied several days prior to the murder. Davies was scheduled to start work the morning of Brenda's death at 7 a.m., yet never showed up.

With his alibi shattered, Davies continued to deny any knowledge of the crime, threatening again to end his life if harassed further. Eventually, however, he broke under pressure and admitted to killing the girl.

In his confession, he stated he was driving around randomly that Monday morning when he spotted the young Brenda walking alone. He quickly drove ahead of her, pulled over, and placed a jack under the front bumper.

When she got close, he asked her for help. He told her to grab a screwdriver from the glovebox so he could loosen the hubcap. Though initially hesitant, Brenda leaned into the car, believing he genuinely needed help. That's when he shoved her inside, slammed the door, and sped off.

As she screamed, he forced her head down onto the seat and held her there. By the time they reached Beacon Heights Road, she was crying again. In a panic, he stopped the car, reached over, and strangled her. She gasped for air before going limp.

> "She sounded like my second wife, Nan, when she screamed," Davies told detectives. "I wanted to shut her up like I want to shut up my wife when she starts these tantrums."

Davies went on to explain that he had pulled the girl from the car and stabbed her repeatedly with the screwdriver in a frenzied attack. He said he felt an urge to hurt someone and slammed the screwdriver with all his might, sometimes missing her entirely in his rage.

After pulling off her sweater and tying it tightly around her neck, he shoved her body into the bushes and drove off.

Davies then tossed her green lunchbox into a storm drain and threw the bloody screwdriver from the window of his car. He later disposed of her wristwatch in a public restroom trash can.

Shortly after Davies confessed to the murder of Brenda Doucette, Gaetane Boivin's body was discovered by a hunter off Greystone Road near the Mattuck Forest, about 3 miles from her home.

Autopsy results showed the seventeen-year-old had been strangled and stabbed 50 times. The medical examiner noticed the same rectangular wounds. She, too, had also been murdered with a screwdriver.

Investigators knew Davies was behind the killing and immediately confronted him. He didn't put up a fight and promptly confessed, "Yeah...I did it."

Davies admitted to calling Gaetane after seeing her advertisement in the newspaper, picking her up at 9 a.m. as arranged before driving away from her home. When he reached over and tried to kiss her in the front seat of his car, she pushed him away. Angry at her rejection, Davies pulled the car over, put his hands around her neck, and strangled her. He claimed it took five to ten minutes of choking her for her to lose consciousness. Davies then carried the young girl's body into the woods, dropped her on the ground about three-quarters of a mile from the road, and repeatedly stabbed her in the chest with a screwdriver.

"The image of Nan was clear in my mind. I was pretty nervous thinking about my wife," Davies told detectives.

After disposing of the girl's watch and wallet, he went to his parents' home feeling very lonely, explaining to detectives that his wife had left him again—for the sixth time in the past year.

When his wife, Nan Davies, heard about his confession, she stormed,

> “George can die in the electric chair for all I care! If the police hadn't caught up with him, I might have been his next victim!”

Gaetane’s mother told reporters,

> “Never any pity for him. We just hate him. It is entirely up to the law to take care of him, but don't let him come out again among the people. Don't let anything happen in another house as it happened here!”

A psychiatrist who had treated Davies stated that execution was the best option for him, saying,

> "There is no doubt he knew what he was doing like most pedophiles. He should be treated not as a patient but as a criminal."

The doctor believed Davies was fully aware of his actions and deserved the death penalty rather than treatment.

Davies blamed his crimes on having an overprotective foster mother, growing up in the Depression era, his two failed marriages, and his sexual desires.

He was adopted when he was eighteen months old by loving and devoted parents. He worked in the Civilian Conservation Corps as a mechanic and factory operator. When he married his first wife, Gertrude, his foster parents let them live in a family-owned bungalow. They had four kids and were seen by neighbors as nice and quiet people.

However, in 1952, Davies' deviant criminal nature was exposed when he was arrested for molesting two young girls, ages nine and ten, in Wolcott, Connecticut. He pleaded guilty and was sentenced to one to two years in state prison for the disturbing crimes. His wife subsequently divorced him and retained custody of their four children—two boys and two girls.

While incarcerated, Davies underwent evaluation by psychiatrist Dr. Daniel Sayers, who dismissed him as simply "an erotic character" who was not "suffering seriously" mentally.

Davies was released on parole on August 8, 1953, after serving only ten months of his sentence.

Davies soon became a person of interest in another case from mid-July 1952—the vanishing of ten-year-old Connie Smith from a summer camp fifteen miles outside Thomaston. Connie was the cherished daughter of affluent ranchers Helen and Peter Smith and the grandchild of a former Wyoming governor.

The night before her disappearance, Connie fell off a tent platform and was given an ice pack by the camp nurse. The following morning, she informed her tentmates that she was returning it to the infirmary, but she never returned.

Some speculated that amnesia had set in from her fall. Others believed Connie decided to pay a visit to her nearby grandparents. The camp gatekeeper spotted her walking north on Indian Mountain Road toward Lakeville, Connecticut.

Along her route, residents of two homes gave Connie directions to Lakeville. Multiple drivers passed her walking on the road, with one who witnessed the girl trying to hitchhike on Route 44 just outside of town. After that, she disappeared without a trace.

Connie's family searched for her tirelessly from that day forward, but the effort to find the vanished child never ceased.

Following his release on parole, Dr. Sayers informed Davies of his requirement for additional psychiatric treatment. In October 1953, Davies sought the services of another psychiatrist. During his sessions, he expressed his distress over his divorce. However, after attending only three appointments, he canceled further visits.

On June 3, 1956, Davies married Fernanda Reese (Nan) from Torrington, Connecticut. Nan had been married before and had a son from her previous marriage. The three moved into a trailer behind Davies' foster parents' home in Thomaston. However, Nan believed that the marriage was not a happy one.

> "He was oversexed. He wouldn't work. He wouldn't pay his bills. And he would beat me up every time we got into an argument. He's got a terrible temper," Nan said.

At a point when Davies and Nan were separated, he remembered his former psychiatrist, Dr. Staneslow, and visited him on February 5, 1957. He expressed his distress over his troubled marriage and received a series of four electric shock treatments during that month. When Nan returned shortly afterward, she reconciled with him.

However, by April, his mood had plummeted once more. Nan had left him again, and conflicts had arisen with his parents. Once again, he turned to Dr. Staneslow, seeking solace for his difficulties. This time, he expressed his desire to get a separate apartment.

Less than a month later, on May 9, he killed Gaetane Boivin.

Three days after was Mother's Day, and Davies brought Nan a bouquet of flowers with a note that read, "To my loving wife whom I'll never see again."

The following day, he killed Brenda Doucette.

The day after that, he paid another visit to Dr. Staneslow. However, the doctor held reservations about the extent of Davies' depression, perceiving that it might not be as severe as Davies portrayed it to be.

Davies was captured on May 29. In less than two hours, the New Haven County grand jury had indicted him for the Boivin and Doucette murders.

The trial of George Davies began on October 11 of that year. Despite the trial extending for six weeks, the state's argument remained concise and straightforward. Testimonies were given by witnesses, who attested that strands of Brenda's hair had been discovered in the defendant's car. Furthermore, the prosecutor introduced the prisoner's confession as evidence.

Davies stepped onto the witness stand to demonstrate his state of insanity. He openly confessed to both murders and affirmed the accuracy of his statements to the police. Throughout his testimony, he refrained from mentioning the victims by name and spoke in an emotionally detached manner.

He acknowledged possessing an "ugly temper" and recounted episodes of losing control. He told the court of a specific incident where he impulsively stole a car registered under his foster mother's name and intentionally crashed it into a tree due to his anger. He said he didn't even remember what he was mad about.

Various psychiatrists presented contrasting opinions about Davies' mental state during the trial.

Dr. Bernard A. Rogowski labeled Davies as a psychopath. His diagnosis implied that Davies had the potential for impulsive and irrational actions that deviated from normal judgment.

In contrast, Dr. Sayers, who evaluated Davies in 1952 and 1957, found no indications of disturbed thinking during his examinations.

Dr. Staneslow's testimony added another layer to the debate. He suggested that Davies possessed the cognitive capacity to resist his impulses to kill and could distinguish between right and wrong. According to him, Davies chose to commit the murders to cover up his deviant abuse of the girls. Two other psychiatrists supported Staneslow's viewpoint.

Yet another psychiatrist testified with a completely different point of view. Ultimately, these contrasting psychiatric perspectives shaped a complex portrait of Davies' mental state, leaving the jury to grapple with his culpability.

The public defender asserted that Davies was "one of the saddest and most tormented men I have ever seen." He implored that Davies' actions were never driven by intention, deliberation, or premeditation, and he asked the jury to spare his life.

In contrast, the prosecution demanded the death penalty. Ultimately, the jury's decision arrived after nearly five hours of deliberation. They agreed with the prosecution and sentenced Davies to death.

Over the next two years, Davies became one of the most troublesome prisoners in the Wethersfield State Penitentiary.

He sometimes showed remorse and begged to move up his execution day. Other times, he was frightened and depressed. He threatened suicide repeatedly, once stealing a shard of glass and slashing his wrists. After that, he was placed on twenty-four-hour watch.

In April 1959, he confessed to more killings—one of a woman in Wolcott and another in Watertown.

Then he confessed to the murder of Connie Smith, the girl who went missing near Lakeville.

"Yeah, that's the girl. Although it isn't a good likeness," he told detectives when shown a photo of Connie Smith.

Davies was escorted from prison to a river near Litchfield, where he pointed to a spot on the sandy banks and told investigators he had buried Connie's body there seven years earlier.

If Davies were indeed telling the truth, recent flooding would have likely washed away her body. However, investigators still wanted to try. Using bulldozers and power shovels, investigators dug twelve feet into the river's shores but found nothing.

Detectives believed Davies was lying about killing Connie. Years earlier, he had confessed to killing another young woman, twenty-six-year-old Jean Martin, but police records showed she died of diabetes and alcoholism.

Jean's mother, however, believed him.

> "My daughter was murdered by George Davies. I just know it. They were seen together often. They were out together that night. She didn't die of diabetes and alcoholism like they say. Why was it her body was found on one side of the road and her purse and belt on the other?"

But detectives had stopped believing his confessions.

In an interview just before he was put to death, Davies admitted,

> "It was all a lie about Connie Smith. I raised the hopes of the girl's parents once before, and I don't want to do it again. I don't want to go with this lie on my conscience."

George J. Davies died in the electric chair on October 20, 1959.

CHAPTER 7
TENNESSEE

Danvers, Massachusetts, home to around 27,000 residents, boasts a storied past and is sprinkled with various landmarks and well-liked tourist spots. However, the town is perhaps most famously recognized for its former name, Salem Village, and its association with the infamous Salem witch trials of 1692.

Colleen Ritzer felt a calling to become a teacher from a young age. In her early twenties, she pursued this passion by accepting a position at Danvers High School, where she taught algebra.

Her enthusiasm for teaching and learning was contagious, and she often began her classes with motivational quotes or images. Colleen was also very active on social media, sharing puzzles and games to aid her students' learning. People noted that she always made time to assist anyone struggling with their studies.

Philip Chism, a 14-year-old student in Colleen's class, had recently moved to Massachusetts from Tennessee due to his parents' ongoing divorce. Although he was new to the school, Philip had succeeded in making some friends and had joined the soccer team. He was known to be quiet and courteous, with a particular interest in history. He had even approached his history teacher to request a transfer to an honors history class for a more challenging experience. However, Philip was an average student who occasionally failed to turn in his homework assignments, and his request for a class change was declined.

On Tuesday, October 22, 2013, as was her routine, Colleen showed up at the high school before 7 a.m. That day was designated as "Dress Like Your Friend Day." In keeping with the theme, Colleen wore a purple shirt and black pants, coordinating with her friend and fellow math teacher, Sarah.

Philip Chism was present at the school as well. Earlier in the day, he had performed well on a quiz about Machiavelli and Louis VIII. At 1 p.m., Philip went to his math class, taught by Colleen Ritzer, which was the final period of the school day. His demeanor was typical, although he appeared slightly more reserved than usual. Until then, the day had seemed like any other at Danvers High School.

When class was over at 1:55, Colleen invited any students who needed extra help to stay afterward. Only two students opted to remain: a girl named Autumn and Philip Chism.

Autumn was busy with a project on the chalkboard while Colleen spoke to Philip. Autumn overheard their conversation and noticed that when Colleen mentioned Tennessee, his demeanor changed. He was visibly upset at her mention of his former home, and he started muttering to himself.

Colleen noticed this and quickly changed the subject, but it didn't seem to make a difference.

Colleen momentarily left the room to speak with her friend Sarah in the hallway. While Colleen was in the hall, Autumn spoke to Philip, who seemed fine. His speech had cleared, and he appeared to be in a normal mood again.

After their conversation in the hallway, Sarah asked if Colleen needed to return to her classroom, and Colleen replied that Autumn was working on a project on the chalk-board, but she wasn't really sure why Philip was still there.

Colleen then returned to the classroom and let Autumn and Philip know she would be leaving soon. As Autumn left the room, Colleen spoke to her at the classroom door. Autumn told Colleen that she was an excellent teacher and a wonderful person. When Philip heard this, his demeanor shifted again; he appeared visibly upset and irritated at the comment.

Once Autumn had left the room, only Colleen and Philip were left inside. Most students had already left for the day, with just a handful still lingering in the halls before the final bell at 3 p.m. Colleen left classroom A209 and headed to the second-floor girls' bathroom.

At 6:30 p.m. that evening, a distressed Diana Chism reported her fourteen-year-old son missing. He hadn't returned home from school, and his coach confirmed that he hadn't been at soccer practice that afternoon.

Three hours later, at 9 p.m., Sue Ambrozavitch, the principal of Danvers High School, emailed the entire school faculty and staff, notifying them that a student was missing.

As soon as she received the email, Sarah called Sue. Colleen's parents had just contacted her, asking if she knew anything about where their daughter might be. Colleen was missing, too.

Colleen lived with her parents, who had grown increasingly worried when she failed to return home at her usual time. She typically arrived home between 3:30 and 4 p.m., but hours had passed with no sign of her. Her father, Tom, had already driven the route between their home and the school, searching for any trace of his daughter. He had noticed that her car remained parked in its usual spot at the school, but there was no sign of Colleen anywhere around the school grounds. The family's anxiety was mounting as the minutes ticked by, and the absence of their beloved daughter weighed heavily on their hearts.

As the hours wore on, the worry for both the missing teacher and student intensified. Danvers High School had long since been closed for the day, and there seemed to be no plausible explanation for their continued presence on the school grounds. The unsettling silence and absence of any news only heightened the sense of unease that had settled over the families.

Sarah also shared with Sue a detail that seemed too significant to be mere coincidence: Philip had been a student in Colleen's last class of the day. The fact that both were now missing at the same time raised alarm bells. The connection between their disappearances seemed too strong to ignore, adding another layer of concern to an already distressing situation.

Sue, joined by a few other teachers, hurried to the school to look for Colleen and Philip, but their search yielded no results. Colleen's classroom seemed untouched. Her personal items were gone, but her car was still in its regular parking spot, adding to the growing sense of unease. The puzzle pieces weren't fitting together, and the teachers couldn't shake the feeling that something was terribly wrong.

At 11:20 p.m., having received no news from their daughter, the worried Ritzer family formally reported Colleen missing to the Danvers police.

Investigators swiftly requested Colleen's cell phone provider trace the location of her phone. The last known location of her phone was approximately a 24-minute walk from Danvers High School.

They also traced the location of Philip's phone, which was found to be near the Hollywood Hits Theater, a local cinema. When the police arrived at the theater, Philip was nowhere to be seen, but while searching the nearby area, police found both Philip and Colleen's smashed cell phones.

The search for Colleen and Philip intensified, with efforts focused both within the school and the surrounding area. In a troubling turn of events, Colleen's purse was found near the school. However, it was empty when examined, devoid of all its contents, including her cards and identification.

As the search of the school persisted, investigators came across an ominous clue—the second-floor girls' bathroom floor was dotted with dark red stains.

At 12:30 a.m., now into October 23rd, police were alerted to a solitary pedestrian walking along the southbound lane of Route 1 North at Salem Lane in Topsfield.

Officers from Topsfield Police Department responded swiftly, and they soon recognized Philip Chism walking alone along the busy road. During a pat-down search, they found he was carrying a knife.

Philip was taken into custody and brought to Topsfield Police Station, where officers thoroughly searched his backpack. Inside, they found a box cutter smeared with blood, as well as Colleen's credit cards, keys, and driver's license. They also discovered underwear, which would subsequently be identified as Colleen's.

When confronted about the items in his backpack, Philip initially explained that he had innocently come across them at a Stop & Shop and had merely picked them up. However, he quickly changed his story, asserting that he had taken them from a car. When the officers inquired about the origin of the blood on the box cutter, Philip finally conceded, saying, "The girl."

He calmly told the police she was in the woods, and she was beyond help.

Philip was taken to the Danvers Police Station, where his mother eventually joined him. Those present observed a noticeable change in his demeanor once she arrived. He asked to speak with the officers privately, without his mother present. After his conversation with detectives, he was officially placed under arrest.

As Philip was being questioned at approximately 3 a.m., a few hours into the interview, a tragic discovery was made.

The body of Colleen Ritzer was found in a wooded area near the school. She had been strangled, stabbed sixteen times, her throat was slit, and she had been brutally raped. Naked from the waist down, her top had been pulled up and her bra down. Next to her body was a handwritten note saying, "I hate you all."

Colleen's body was posed in what was referred to by police as a sexually suggestive position, and she had been violated with a tree branch that was still inside her.

Approximately 20 yards from her body, investigators found a large, wheeled recycling bin, along with bloodied gloves and clothing.

The high school and its surrounding area were equipped with over 100 security cameras, and investigators began the arduous task of reviewing all the footage. The recordings would soon uncover a profoundly unsettling and horrifying sequence of events. The video surveillance gave investigators a detailed timeline of Colleen's tragic death.

Just before 3 p.m., Colleen Ritzer was seen on camera leaving her classroom and heading to the second-floor girls' bathroom.

Seconds later, Philip Chism slipped out of the classroom. He had already changed from the red sweatshirt he had been wearing into a light blue hoodie. He glanced down the hallway in both directions and checked something in his left pocket. He then went back into the classroom only to re-emerge seconds later. He then pulled the hood over his head and headed up the stairs, toward the girls' bathroom.

As he approached the bathroom door, he hesitated momentarily as if he was listening for something, removed a box cutter knife from his pocket, put on a pair of white gloves, and entered the bathroom.

Although no cameras were in the bathroom, investigators pieced together a likely sequence of events. It was believed that Philip Chism entered the bathroom and overpowered Colleen. He then sexually assaulted her before he stabbed and slashed her sixteen times with the box cutter. Colleen's death was ultimately attributed to strangulation and sharp force injuries to her neck. However, some investigators speculated that she may have died in the bathroom, while others believed her death occurred later. It is possible that Philip strangled her first, but the exact sequence of events remains uncertain.

Eleven minutes after Chism entered the bathroom, a female student walked in. A half-wall partially obstructed her view, but she later told investigators she saw a bare buttock. Although she noticed a darker skin tone than her own, she didn't realize it was male and assumed it was just another student changing clothes. Respecting their privacy, she turned around and left. She hadn't heard any cries for help or Colleen bleeding out on the floor.

Moments after the girl left, video footage showed Philip leaving the bathroom carrying Colleen's pants over his arm. He walked down the stairs and left the building.

A mother of another student, who was waiting in her car outside the school, spotted Philip as he exited the building, crouched behind a bush, and changed his clothes. When he emerged from the bushes, he was wearing a white T-shirt.

Philip then walked back into the building and went back into Colleen's classroom, where he changed back into his red sweatshirt. He grabbed his backpack and the bags Colleen had brought to school that day.

He dumped Colleen's bags into a recycling bin on the first floor, then climbed the stairs to the second floor.

The video showed Philip as he neared the bathroom where Colleen's body was located. Before entering the bathroom, he suddenly stopped, turned on his heel, and began walking the other way. He had just caught sight of his friend Ramsey on the second-floor landing. Earlier, Philip had agreed to meet Ramsey at the soccer field but hadn't shown up.

Philip tried to ignore him and walked away, but Ramsey called out to him, asking what he was doing. Philip made up an excuse and said he was looking for something, but Ramsey couldn't help but notice he looked scared and was dripping with sweat.

Philip urged Ramsey to go to the soccer field and wait for him, assuring him that he would join him there shortly. He then quickly jogged down the stairs, but Ramsey trailed behind him. Ramsey watched as Philip pulled a large, wheeled recycling bin toward the elevator.

Ramsey again asked what he was doing, but Philip again avoided the question, telling him to go to the soccer field; he would meet him there later.

As Ramsey walked away, video cameras showed Philip wheeling the recycling bin into the elevator. He rolled the container into the girls' bathroom on the second floor and placed Colleen's body inside.

Philip wore a black ski mask as he wheeled the bin out of the school and into a wooded area behind the school. He removed Colleen's body and placed it against a fence. He then sexually assaulted her with a three-foot-long tree branch, sexually staged her body, and covered her with sticks and leaves. Investigators believed he cut her again with the box cutter, slicing her throat. Some investigators believe she died at this point.

Before leaving the scene, Phillip dropped a handwritten note that read, "I hate you all."

Video cameras then showed Philip returning to the school without the recycling bin. He entered the school, changed out of his bloody jeans, and briefly went into the second-floor girls' bathroom again.

He then left the school again and returned to the woods for another twelve minutes.

When he returned to the school, security cameras showed that he had spoken to a friend about a church youth group. Shortly afterward, just before 4:30, he left the school for the final time with Colleen's cell phone, wallet, and underwear in his backpack.

Philip walked to the Hollywood Hits Theater and purchased a ticket to see the movie Gravity. After the movie, he shoplifted a hunting knife, used Colleen's credit card to buy a hamburger at Wendy's, and began walking along the busy shoulder of the Route 1 highway toward Topsfield.

When police picked him up on the highway and asked where he was coming from, he said, "Tennessee."

Philip Chism was charged with murder, aggravated rape, and armed robbery. He was held without bail. Despite the substantial evidence against him, including his partial confession, Philip pleaded not guilty.

In Massachusetts, individuals aged fourteen and older who are charged with murder are automatically subject to trial as adults. Consequently, Philip faced trial as an adult for the murder charge while being tried as a youth offender for armed robbery and aggravated rape.

While he was awaiting trial, Philip attacked a youth services worker. He followed her into a locker room, where he choked and beat her before other workers intervened. The worker suffered injuries to her back, face, jaw, and neck. He was charged with attempted murder and faced a separate trial.

Philip's trial for the murder of Colleen Ritzer began in 2015. His defense attorneys did not contest the fact that Philip had killed Colleen. Instead, they argued that he had done so during a psychotic episode, which they claimed was triggered by Colleen's mention of the word "Tennessee" to him.

On these grounds, the defense requested that the jury find Philip not guilty by reason of insanity. Defense attorney Denise Reagan pointed out that Philip's family had a history of mental health problems, and it was likely that he had been affected by these issues from an early age as well.

A psychiatrist who took the stand on behalf of the defense also suggested that Philip likely suffered from early-onset schizophrenia, which could have contributed to his actions.

However, a doctor who testified on behalf of the prosecution countered that Philip was not psychotic and that his symptoms were inconsistent with such a diagnosis.

Tests performed by the prosecution's doctors indicated that he was attempting to fake severe mental illness. They claimed that, although he may have shown some signs of distress and emotional disturbance, these signs weren't enough to impair his ability to distinguish between wrong and right.

Moreover, the prosecution argued that it was clear that Philip had premeditated the attack, as evidenced by the fact that he had brought a ski mask, gloves, a change of clothes, and a box cutter to school that day.

Philip's defense attorneys also vigorously argued for his acquittal on the charge of sexual assault in the woods. They contested the medical examiners' findings, asserting that they believed Colleen had already died when the assault with the tree branch occurred. They argued that, based on this belief, Philip should be acquitted of that particular aspect of the crime.

In Massachusetts, life sentences without parole for juveniles have been deemed unconstitutional. Separate rulings by both the U.S. Supreme Court and the Massachusetts Supreme Judicial Court have established that Philip could not be sentenced to life without the possibility of parole for the murder charge due to his age at the time of the crime.

Ultimately, the jury rejected his insanity defense, and in 2016, Philip Chism was convicted of the murder of Colleen Ritzer. For the murder charge, he received a life sentence with the possibility of parole after twenty-five years, the maximum sentence allowed given that he was only fourteen years old at the time of the crime.

He was also sentenced to forty years plus one day in prison for armed robbery and another forty years plus one day for rape. The sentences will run concurrently, meaning that, technically, Philip will be eligible for parole when he reaches the age of fifty-four.

Philip Chism was placed in a state juvenile detention facility and remained there until his eighteenth birthday, when he was transferred into the state prison system.

Colleen's funeral drew a crowd of over 1,000 people who came to pay their respects. Additionally, hundreds of students and teachers took part in various vigils and community events to honor and celebrate her life.

Colleen's family created the Colleen E. Ritzer Memorial Scholarship to honor her. Since its inception in October

2013, the scholarship has awarded nearly $400,000 in college scholarships to more than eighty aspiring teachers.

Philip Chism's mother reached out to the Ritzer family and said:

> "Words can't express the amount of pain and sorrow these past two and a half years have been. However, there is no one who has suffered more than the Ritzer family. My utmost esteem, prayers, and humble respect are with them today as they continue their journey to heal."

In his victim's impact statement, Tom Ritzer said:

> "It makes me sick to know that I walk the same halls as her killer. It makes me sick to know I drove by her in the woods and drove home. A dad's job is to protect his family; I didn't protect Colleen. A dad's job is to fix things; I can't fix this."

CHAPTER 8
DEATH IN THE CORNFIELD

Tucked into the farmlands northwest of Toledo, Ohio, near the Michigan border, was the quaint village of Metamora, home to just over 500 residents. Endless seas of corn blanketed the landscape, stretching as far as the eye could see down the sleepy, rural roads. For the farming families that called this tucked-away corner home, life moved at an easy pace in the summer of 2015. With the warm season in full swing, the villagers relished the idyllic, pastoral setting surrounding them. Though just a tiny speck on the map, Metamora provided a peaceful respite for its residents amidst the vast Ohio farmlands.

After their summer vacation, the Joughin family arrived back home to Metamora. Twenty-year-old Sierah Joughin was on her summer break before starting her junior year of university. With ambitions to see the world, she eagerly awaited studying abroad that coming fall.

Keen to make the most of the sunny Ohio summer, Sierah set out on her new, purple bicycle on the afternoon of July 19,

2016. She pedaled seven miles from her family's Metamora farm to the home of her boyfriend, Josh Kolasinski, hoping to meet up with him when he finished work.

Sierah and Josh whiled away a lazy July afternoon together. Childhood sweethearts, they had been a couple for seven years, enjoying a classic small-town romance.

As the sun sank lower in the sky around 6:30 p.m., Josh wanted to escort Sierah safely home for the seven-mile bike ride back. Though daylight stretched for hours ahead, he dutifully accompanied her on his motorcycle as she pedaled down the rural roads. While he rode, he filmed a quick video of them—smiling with happy faces—and posted it on Snapchat.

Confident and strong-willed, Sierah insisted Josh turn back after a few miles—she could manage the rest herself through the seas of corn. She promised to call later that night.

At 9:30, Sierah's mother, Sheila, pulled into her driveway, surprised to see Sierah's bedroom light on but her daughter nowhere in sight. Sierah was conscientious—if she'd planned to stay with a friend, she would have let her mother know.

Just then, the phone rang—it was Josh. With anxiety in his voice, he explained how they'd parted ways hours ago, but he hadn't heard from Sierah since. Alarm bells went off for Sheila. It wasn't like her daughter not to check-in. Dread mounting, she knew something was wrong.

Calls to Sierah's phone went straight to voicemail, and texts went unanswered.

Josh and Sheila mobilized quickly, climbing into their vehicles to retrace Sierah's likely route home along the rural backroads. Sierah's family members also joined the search, combing the lonely stretches of pavement surrounded by cornfields for any sign of the missing young woman or her purple bike. However, their frantic hunt through the night yielded nothing.

Josh and the family posted on social media to see if any of her friends had heard from her, but Sierah had simply vanished. Options exhausted and dread mounting, Sheila placed a call to the police to report her daughter missing.

The Fulton County Sheriff's Department sprang into action to look for the missing girl, but they soon realized their rural force was too small to mount an effective search. By the early morning, they had called in the FBI to assist—manpower and resources were urgently needed to find Sierah.

Law enforcement, drones, helicopters, and cadaver dogs flooded the area to canvass the lonely country roads for clues. Officers knew every minute could count in finding the missing girl as they raced against time.

Examining every angle, investigators noticed a crucial detail in the Snapchat video posted by Josh—Sierah was wearing a Fitbit watch. They swiftly obtained data from both her Fitbit and smartphone, showing her last-known location on County Road 6. This was around the same area where Josh said they'd parted ways. The digital footprint from her devices gave authorities a new, focused search zone along the rural route.

By late morning, investigators uncovered the first heart-stopping clues. About halfway between Josh's house and Sierah's, a section of corn along the rural road showed clear signs of a violent struggle. Stalks were trampled and matted, and there was a strong smell of gasoline. A few feet beyond, officials discovered Sierah's distinctive, purple bicycle abandoned in the rows of corn. The handlebars and seat were stained reddish-brown. Nearby were more ominous finds: her earphones and sunglasses, a pair of men's sunglasses, a screwdriver, automotive fuses, and a blood-stained sock. Investigators found a blood-stained kitchen towel one thousand feet north along the road. But while the evidence painted a frightening picture, there was still no trace of Sierah herself. It was obvious she had been abducted.

Closer inspection of the area revealed a single row of tire tracks going into and out of the trampled area of corn. While not distinctive enough to determine a make and model, investigators knew they were from a motorcycle. Less than twenty-four hours after Sierah vanished, suspicion fell on her boyfriend, Josh. He was the last to see Sierah before her disappearance, and he rode a motorcycle similar in width to the telltale tracks left at the scene.

While the long-time couple seemed to have a loving relationship, investigators had to explore every angle. Though it was difficult to imagine him harming his devoted girlfriend of seven years, officials knew looks could be deceiving if someone had a darker side. But within minutes of interviewing Josh, it was clear he wasn't involved in her disappearance. He had a solid alibi for the time just after he left Sierah.

During questioning, however, Josh revealed another potential clue—he had seen a large, white van acting strangely near where Sierah went missing. As he and the family frantically looked for Sierah after she vanished, the van crept along the rural road. When Josh approached on his motorcycle, it sped away. Josh remembered a partial license plate number, which police traced to a local woman.

Detectives brought the woman in for an interview, and she told investigators that she had believed the young man on the motorcycle was trying to run her off the road that night, so she'd sped away.

A search of the van and luminol tests for blood inside came up empty. Clearly, the woman wasn't involved, and the van was a dead end.

A potential break arose when a local man came forward after noticing a black motorcycle helmet on County Road 6 the night Sierah vanished. Unaware of the missing girl at the time, he had briefly stopped to grab the helmet and throw it in the back of his truck, thinking little of it. But when he later heard the news of Sierah's disappearance, he took a second look at the helmet. His heart skipped a beat when he saw a reddish smear resembling dried blood. He immediately called the police, and the FBI sent the helmet for DNA testing.

FBI agents went door to door in the sparsely populated area around County Road 6, asking if anyone had seen anything suspicious on the night Sierah went missing. On July 21, they knocked on the door of James Worley, who lived at 10627

County Road 6, just a few hundred yards from the abduction site.

Worley's property had a small house, a machine shop, a small barn, and a large barn. Fifty-seven-year-old Worley was friendly and polite as he welcomed the three FBI agents into his home. To the agents' surprise, Worley freely admitted that the motorcycle tracks and the items found at the scene were his.

He told them that around 5:45 that evening, he was riding his motorcycle when it broke down on County Road U, just before the Michigan state line. He said he finally got the motorcycle running again, but as he was riding home, it broke down again on County Road 6. While pushing the motorcycle home, he said he spotted two bicycles in the nearby cornfield—one blue, one light gray.

Worley said he pushed his motorcycle into the cornfield and considered riding one of the bicycles home, then changed his mind. Instead, he pushed his motorcycle out of the corn again, continued pushing it home, and arrived home at around 10 p.m.

He told FBI agents that somewhere along the route home, he lost his helmet, sunglasses, fuses, and a screwdriver, but at no time did he see anyone else or the missing girl. But one thing stood out right away to agents: Worley had fresh scratch marks on his arms and bruises on his legs.

Immediately, the agents knew they might be face-to-face with the abductor. Worley's admissions lined up with evidence and location, but they lacked any definitive link to Sierah. They would need to unravel his account and seek evidence before drawing conclusions.

Though odd in his responses, Worley had been friendly until he was told that they had found his motorcycle helmet. He immediately asked if he could get it back, but the agents told him it was evidence, because they had found a bloody palm print on it. Worley's demeanor changed drastically. He became paranoid and accused the agents of trying to set him up.

> "So you guys wanna dig a hole and throw me in it. My past is whatever you have on record."

When Worley mentioned his past, the agents' ears pricked up. What had he done in the past? When they asked if he had been swabbed for DNA in the past, he freely admitted he had. In 1990, twenty-six years earlier. Worley claimed he had done time in prison for growing marijuana. While that was true, it was a lie of omission. Marijuana wasn't the only reason he had spent time in prison.

Still, Worley seemed confident and talkative, inviting agents to look around his house. The home itself was messy but ordinary. However, when the FBI agents made their way to the large barn, Worley seemed more concerned. As they walked into the barn, Worley nervously said,

> "Don't worry, there's no secret hatches."

One end of the barn was filled with large hay bales, but when agents began moving those bales, they revealed a large, green storage crate. Knowing they needed a warrant to look further, Worley stopped them as they opened the lid. Inside, agents briefly saw several plastic Ziploc bags filled with clothing, but Worley told the agents they would have to leave.

The FBI had already sought a search warrant. They shortly had one in hand and continued their search.

Inside the green crate were plastic bags filled with women's clothing, mostly lingerie. The contents of each bag were written in black pen: Lace bra, panties, skirt, white beach dress, daisy dukes, white romper, black lace dress, pink teddy, leggings, thongs, go baby. Other items were in the crate, such as sex toys, rubber gloves, rope, a clothesline, and adult diapers.

When an agent asked why he had these strange items, Worley got defensive.

> "Dude, these aren't strange at all. What's wrong with that? That's you in *your* head. I give out lingerie and stuff like that."

Worley claimed that he often gave lingerie to women he dated. However, that didn't explain the rope, rubber gloves, and adult diapers.

When agents continued moving hay bales, they discovered they were stacked in such a way that they hid a small room between them. A large, inflatable air mattress lay between the bales, and restraints were nailed to the wall.

In another area in the barn, dirt on the floor bore fresh rake marks. The neat, parallel lines indicated that the area had been smoothed over recently. Nearby, a rake was propped innocuously against the wall. Curious, agents brushed the dirt aside and realized a rug was hidden beneath the ground. When the carpet was removed, it revealed a wooden hatch.

This was exactly what Worley had jokingly told the agents they wouldn't find.

Opening the hatch unveiled a chilling sight—a large chest freezer hidden below ground and carpeted inside.

Damp straw and debris were clustered along the bottom of the freezer. The interior was marred with ominous, dark splotches. A powerful smell of ammonia emanated from within. Investigators knew these could be grim signs of attempts to conceal human remains. The cold container seemed specially prepared for preserving a body out of sight.

Worley had an excuse for everything. He claimed the freezer was only for storing his stash of marijuana, and the mattress was an old one that his invalid mother used to sleep on. He said, "The only DNA you'll find on that thing is my mother's."

As investigators continued their search, they found zip ties, a ski mask, two sets of handcuffs, more rope, duct tape with hair still stuck to it, a trash bag with more adult diapers, and a pair of pink women's underwear with blood on them.

Inside the machine shop, investigators found his motorcycle with dried blood on the handlebar grips, more handcuffs, handcuff keys, more adult diapers, more zip ties, and a bottle of bleach.

A more thorough search of his home revealed muddied and wet clothing, as well as more adult diapers. His computer history was analyzed and showed recent searches for "hitch-hiker," "hogtyed [sic] teen," "bound," "beaten down teens," "forced teens," "stranded and forced," and "rough pick-ups."

In his trucks, investigators found zip ties, hair strands, dried blood, duct tape, a ski mask, and pepper spray. There were also several areas on the floorboard that had been cleaned with bleach.

Worley, again, had excuses. He claimed all the items they had found were for a pornography business he planned to start. But detectives didn't believe a word of what he was saying, and they arrested him for the abduction of Sierah Joughin.

Prosecutors believed they had enough evidence to charge James Worley with murder, even without a body. At 6:30 that evening, however, within hours of Worley's arrest, they found Sierah Joughin.

Late that afternoon, a farmer walking through his field found a matted-down area of corn and a mound of freshly dug soil. He knew it looked like a grave and called the Sheriff.

Just 200 yards from the abduction site, investigators unearthed the body of Sierah Joughin. She had been buried at the bottom of a shallow grave. Her hands were handcuffed behind her back, and her ankles were tied together with duct tape. A large, yellow, cone-shaped dog toy was secured to her mouth with a shoelace. She was not only wearing a lace, white, cloth top similar to the ones found in Worley's barn but also an adult diaper. She had a large laceration on her forehead and a contusion on her leg.

Sierah had died of asphyxiation due to the size of the dog toy in her mouth. She couldn't breathe, and the toy was put in her mouth with such force that it broke her teeth.

DNA from Worley's motorcycle helmet tested positive as belonging to Sierah, as did several items in his barn, including the air mattress, pink panties, duct tape, and paper towels.

The attack had been a crime of opportunity. Worley had no way of knowing that Sierah would be riding her bike that day. Yet, he seemed prepared, having duct tape, rope, and ski masks at the ready. Investigators wondered if there were more victims.

When they looked into his background, they got their answer. When Worley said he had been in prison in 1990, he didn't mention that he had gone to prison for kidnapping.

On July 4, 1989, twenty-six-year-old Robin Gardner rode her bicycle down a rural road in Whitehouse, Ohio, just nineteen miles from Metamora. She heard a truck coming up behind her and expected it to pass, but the next thing she knew, the truck had hit her. She flew from her bicycle and into the ditch.

When James Worley got out of the truck, he asked if she was okay before he hit her over the head from behind with a hammer. He then put a screwdriver to her throat, handcuffed one of her wrists, and dragged her toward his truck.

Robin fought against him, but he screamed at her to stop fighting or he would kill her. Worley got her into his truck and then attempted to get both of her hands behind her back, but she was able to break loose.

Luckily, a passing motorcyclist saw the struggle, stopped to pick her up, and drove her to safety.

Robin suffered a skull fracture and concussion from the blow with the hammer, but she was able to identify Worley as her attacker.

Worley tried to tell police that he had accidentally hit her with his truck; he only handcuffed her because she was hysterical, and he was trying to calm her down, but they didn't buy his story for a minute.

Worley was charged with abduction, found guilty, and sentenced to six-to-ten years in prison. Sadly, he was released on good behavior after serving only three years.

For his crimes against Sierah Joughin, James Worley was charged with two counts of murder, two counts of abduction, four counts of kidnapping, two counts of felonious assault, two counts of aggravated robbery, one count of possessing criminal tools, one count of gross abuse of a corpse, one count of tampering with evidence, and two counts of having a weapon while under a disability.

Two years later, at trial, Worley pleaded not guilty and played the part of the innocent victim. After six hours of deliberation, he was found guilty on all counts.

At his sentencing hearing, Worley spoke for forty-five minutes, claiming his innocence and that the FBI had set him up. During his ramblings, many of Sierah's family members walked out of the courtroom in protest.

Worley's defense requested a life sentence; the judge said that if he believed there was a remote chance of his innocence, he would give him a life sentence. Instead, he sentenced him to death.

James Worley is scheduled to be put to death on May 20, 2025.

Though nothing could compensate her daughter's loss, Sierah's mother, Sheila Vaculik, found some small closure in a wrongful death suit against Worley. Awarded his property, she called it a "dark piece of land" and had the barn demolished.

After the trial, Sierah's family and other activists argued that insufficient information was available to law enforcement and residents about convicted violent felons in their communities. If a system had existed to warn the public of local offenders, Sierah's death might have been prevented.

In response, an advocacy group started a petition for a violent offender registry in Ohio, gathering over 13,000 signatures. This momentum led legislators to draft "Sierah's Law"—a bill to create a database of offenders convicted of crimes like murder, kidnapping, and abduction.

In late 2018, after advocacy from Sierah's mother, the reworked bill unanimously passed the legislature and was signed into law.

CHAPTER 9
THE FIFTH NAIL

It was a typical, rainy day in the Pacific Northwest on May 16, 2005, when a 911 call came into the Kootenai County, Idaho, emergency dispatch center. The caller reported a suspicious, white pickup truck that he didn't recognize parked on his property in the area of Wolf Lodge. As the 911 operator gathered more details, the caller looked inside the truck and noted a few items on the front seat: a small toolbox and an axe.

Later that morning, the 911 operator received another call from the same man. This time, the man was frantic, and it was clear something horrible had happened. The man explained that he went to his neighbor's door to hire their son to mow his lawn, but when he got to the door, he noticed blood smeared near the doorknob. Lots of blood. When he pounded on the door, no one answered.

The 911 caller owned the house, which he rented to forty-year-old Brenda Groene, her thirty-seven-year-old boyfriend Mark McKenzie, and Brenda's three children from a prior marriage: thirteen-year-old Slade, nine-year-old Dylan, and eight-year-old Shasta.

Sheriff's deputies rushed through the rain and drove down the long, muddy driveway to the rural Wolf Lodge home. As they approached, they peered inside the family's parked vehicle and noticed a hunting rifle lying on the front seat and bullet holes in the back windows.

Continuing toward the house, blood stains on and around the front door came into view. Deputies also noticed a large amount of blood mixed into a pool of rainwater in the grass beside the front porch. Deputies pounded on the locked front door, but they heard only barking dogs inside the house.

The officers rushed to the back door to find it wide open, and one of the dogs was quickly subdued. The other, however, was terrified and hiding inside the home.

Once inside the kitchen, an officer made a gruesome discovery—the body of a teenage boy, Slade, was lying face down on the floor. His hands were bound behind his back with duct tape, and more duct tape had been wrapped around his head.

Another victim lay in the area between the kitchen and living room. Face down was the body of a fully-dressed adult woman, Brenda. Her hands were cuffed behind her back using three heavy-gauge zip ties in a style similar to law enforcement. Duct tape was also used to restrain the woman's ankles and feet.

As they continued further into the house, deputies found another body. A male victim, Mark, lay face down in the living room. Dressed only in shorts, he had been bound with zip ties around his wrists and ankles.

All three victims were dead. When they searched the rest of the home, they found a few guns upstairs but no more victims.

One of the officers was familiar with the family that lived at the Wolf Lodge home and knew Brenda had two additional young children, but the officer assumed—hoped—they were visiting their father at the time.

As investigators searched the rest of the property for clues, police received a call from Steve Groene, the father of the three children living in the home with their mother and her boyfriend. Steve was desperate for any scrap of information about the horrific incident.

Steve, however, confirmed the investigators' worst fears. None of the children were with him. All three of his children should have been at the home that night. But with only one teenage victim found inside, it meant the two younger children, nine-year-old Shasta and eight-year-old Dylan, were missing.

An Amber Alert was quickly issued for the two missing children, and the residents of both Idaho and Washington were made aware to be on the lookout.

As forensic investigators searched the house for clues, they found a large blood smear on the back door and droplets inside and out. They saw numerous dried blood stains inside the house, some containing grass clippings from the freshly mowed lawn.

Prominent, red smears on the swinging kitchen doors suggested someone drenched in blood had passed through them. The glass coffee table was shattered, leaving fragments strewn about. Moreover, there seemed to be blood everywhere—on the furniture and walls, trailing down the hall to a bedroom, and massive amounts soaked into the bedding.

While no blood was found upstairs, detectives did uncover a single plastic zip tie matching those on the victims.

It became apparent that Slade initially had duct tape over his mouth, which had slipped or been pushed down to around his neck. He also had red stains on the bottoms of his bare feet, suggesting he had walked through blood at some point during the attack.

He had suffered severe blunt force injuries to his head and body, indicating he was ultimately beaten to death. Slade's head lay at the feet of his mother, Brenda.

Brenda had been gagged with duct tape, and her head had been beaten so severely that she couldn't be recognized. She was eventually positively identified using her tattoos.

Unlike the other two victims, Mark had no duct tape on his body but similarly showed severe blunt force wounds crushing his skull. Investigators also suspected a bloodied person had moved over him at some point, based on distinct blood droplet patterns on his body.

Most horrifying was the revelation that the murder weapon was a framing hammer—each blow left a circular injury with cross-hatched imprints.

Authorities remained focused on finding Dylan and Shasta, treating it as a dangerous predator abduction case. The Kootenai County Sheriff's Office requested assistance from the FBI and other resources to locate the missing children.

Over the next several weeks, the entire country held its breath as the search for Dylan and Shasta unfolded in real time on national television. Desperate for answers, the children's father, Steve, even contacted a psychic to aid in the search, but to no avail. Several leads from friends, family, and locals also failed to yield results.

Finally, on July 2nd, nearly two excruciating months after the murders, authorities got the call they'd been waiting for. A waitress and a customer at a local Denny's restaurant claimed to have seen a girl matching Shasta's description come in with a tall, slender man. Both were certain it was her. The man was described as around 6'3" with dark, curly hair and wearing a hat.

Authorities arrived to find forty-two-year-old Joseph Edward Duncan III from Fargo, North Dakota, with the little girl. She was finally safe.

Investigators soon discovered Duncan had a lengthy criminal history, including several outstanding warrants for sexual abuse, being an escape risk, and more. According to reports, he had been committing violent crimes since he was fifteen, when he raped a nine-year-old boy at gunpoint. By the time he was seventeen, he had been sentenced to twenty years in prison for a crime against a fourteen-year-old boy. Duncan told his prison therapist that by the time he was sixteen, he had raped thirteen younger boys.

Duncan was released on parole in 1994 after serving fourteen years. Then, in March 2005, he was charged with another crime against two boys. After a doctor friend had posted his bail, Duncan vanished without a trace—until now.

Investigators also learned Duncan had stolen a red Jeep Cherokee from an Enterprise Rent-A-Car in St. Paul, Minnesota.

Even before leaving the Denny's, Shasta quickly confirmed that Duncan was the man who had brutally murdered her family.

She was transported to a nearby hospital for treatment. Officers contacted her father, Steve Groene, who raced to be beside his daughter. Joseph Duncan was immediately taken into custody, but one question remained—where was Dylan?

Investigators soon uncovered surveillance footage from a convenience store in nearby Coeur d'Alene, Idaho, but the video only showed Duncan and Shasta. Dylan wasn't with them.

Detectives then visited Shasta in the hospital, where she recounted what had happened that harrowing night at their Wolf Lodge home.

Shasta said she was abruptly woken on the night of May 16 by her mother, who told her an intruder was in the home. She went to the living room, where her whole family had been ordered onto the floor, bound, and held at gunpoint. Shasta identified the intruder as Joseph Duncan—a man she and her family had never seen before.

Duncan tapped Shasta on the head and put his fingers to his lips, making a "shush" sound. He then picked her up and carried her outside. Duncan laid her on the grass in the backyard and told her he would kill her if she made a sound. A few minutes later he brought Dylan out, and the two children lay silently on the grass. Duncan then turned around and went back inside the house.

Shasta heard Mark shout in pain just after Duncan re-entered the home. Unaware of what was happening inside, she saw her brother Slade walk out of the house, but he was acting strangely and stumbling around in the yard. Next, she recalled being loaded with Dylan into a truck, driven to a nearby property, and transferred to the stolen, red Jeep.

Shasta said Duncan drove them to a campsite deep in the woods of Montana. Occasionally, he would slap the children and chain them to trees when he needed to leave.

He also made them drink water that had been dosed with small, white pills, but she didn't know what it was.

Shasta also described Duncan forcing them to write letters to their father, giving hope of a safe return. Dylan's letter read, "We know what happened to Mom."

At one point, Duncan chained Shasta to a tree and took Dylan away. They were gone for hours. When Dylan returned, he was severely injured, and Shasta learned that he had been taken to a cabin where Duncan had tortured him.

Shasta told detectives that Duncan forced her to watch a horrific video of Dylan with his hands tied behind his back. Duncan suspended him from a noose tied to a beam in the cabin's ceiling. Duncan could be heard taunting Dylan in the footage, shouting,

> "The devil is here, boy! The devil himself likes watching children suffer and cry!"

The video showed Duncan lowering Dylan to the ground after he lost consciousness and reviving him. He then promised to take him to the hospital, but he never did. At one point, Duncan eerily sang the Lord's Prayer in a shrill, high-pitched voice. As he uttered the words "Thy will be done," Duncan interrupted himself and screamed at God,

> "Can this be your will? You put people on this Earth to do this? How can you let me do this? God, where are you? Show yourself!"

Shasta then described to the detectives that, during another incident, Duncan reached into a cooler to pull out a beer, but instead, a sawed-off shotgun that he had stored inside the cooler fired, killing Dylan.

Shasta wasn't sure if Duncan had intentionally fired the gun or if it was an accident. He then carried Dylan's lifeless body outside and burned him in the campsite's fire pit.

After Dylan's death, Duncan told Shasta that she needed to choose how she wanted to die. He said he could either shoot her or he could choke her to death with a rope. Shasta told detectives she chose to be strangled, assuming it would take longer, giving her more time to talk him out of it.

Luckily, she was right. He put a rope around her neck and began to tighten it when Shasta remembered Duncan had earlier mentioned his nickname was "Jett." She begged him, "Please don't kill me, Jett."

When Shasta spoke his nickname, it was as if she had unlocked something deep within Duncan's psyche. Overflowing with emotion, he loosened the rope from her neck and broke down weeping. He then sobbed, "When you call me that, I can tell you really care about me." Once he composed himself, Duncan packed Shasta into the Jeep and drove toward Coeur d'Alene.

As he drove through Coeur d'Alene with Shasta, they stopped at the local Denny's, where people recognized Shasta and called 911.

Shasta explained to detectives that just before they went to the Denny's, Duncan told her that she had taught him how to love, and he had decided not to kill her; instead, he said he was bringing her back to her father.

Before the interview concluded, Shasta gave one more piece of information that stunned detectives. She said that Joseph Duncan told her this wasn't his first time. He'd murdered others in the past.

A forensic team began examining the Jeep Cherokee Duncan was driving, and they found evidence on the exterior suggesting it had recently driven on dusty, brush-filled back-roads. Inside, they noted several normal items like brochures, camping gear, and a laptop. However, they also uncovered more sinister objects—rolls of duct tape, several lengths of rope, and video production equipment.

Investigators also found a sawed-off shotgun wrapped in duct tape, a handsaw, and a bag of plastic zip ties matching the type used on the victims.

Location data on a camera memory card led investigators to a potential search area in Montana. On July 3rd, just one day after Shasta's rescue, investigators located a remote cabin that seemed to match the one in Duncan's recordings.

Despite extensive searching, Dylan's remains were nowhere to be found initially. However, the FBI lab continued examining the camera equipment and uncovered extremely graphic videos shot inside the cabin, showing his brutal torture of Dylan.

Two days after Shasta's rescue, FBI agents combing the mountains in Saint Regis, Montana, found Dylan's remains.

On the day Dylan's body was recovered, Joseph Duncan asked to speak with a prison chaplain. He wanted to confess that he had killed three people in a house and wanted the Lord to forgive him.

Four days later, he finally sat for an interview with Kootenai County detectives about the Wolf Lodge murders.

Detectives learned Duncan had kept a secret online blog called "The Fifth Nail" that he started in 2004.

In a post just days before the attack, Duncan wrote that he wanted to harm society as much as possible. In chilling foreshadowing just months before torturing and murdering a child, Duncan argued that criminals should not be punished but offered amnesty and counseling instead.

During his interrogation, Joseph Duncan explained to detectives that he randomly drove by the Wolf Lodge home and saw Shasta and Dylan outside playing in the yard.

Then, he decided to return to the house under the cover of night.

He said he arrived at around 2:30 a.m. and watched the home from afar. He boasted of measures he had taken not to leave evidence. He used oversized, disposable shoes to leave misleading footprints and gloves to avoid leaving fingerprints. He claimed he used night vision goggles as he crossed the large, open field in front of the house.

Duncan said he was very quiet, knowing there were dogs inside. Once confident everyone was asleep, Duncan stood on a chair outside Shasta and Dylan's window, ready to snatch them from their beds. Suddenly, one of the dogs entered the room, sniffed around, and looked directly at him through the window.

The dog growled, and Duncan jumped off the chair and ran to the fence, thinking, "shit, he made me." Duncan claimed he patiently waited for another hour but had an internal struggle. He did his best to look for excuses not to go through with it.

He then put the family's fate up to chance—as if it were just a coin toss. He told himself,

> "If the door is unlocked, I'll go in. If it's locked, I'll leave."

The door was unlocked, and Duncan walked in carrying the sawed-off shotgun. Surprisingly, the dogs did not react as he walked in.

Wearing a mask and hat, he was startled to see Brenda asleep on the couch. He froze momentarily, waiting to see if she moved, but she lay there unaware.

He walked past her and was heading down the hall, toward Slade's room, when the dogs charged him. Duncan claimed he swung the shotgun toward the dogs, ready to fire, but the dogs scampered off. However, the noise had woken Brenda, who still lay on the couch and seemed to be looking directly at him.

In the dark, Duncan couldn't tell for sure if her eyes were open or closed. He walked up to her and harshly whispered, "Where's your husband?" to which she looked at him with a confused expression. She said that he wasn't home. Duncan then said, "The man," and Brenda understood he was talking about her boyfriend, Mark.

Duncan then quietly but forcefully escorted Brenda up the stairs. When Brenda shook Mark awake, he woke to see a shotgun in his face. Duncan said he was strangely overcome with emotion at the sight of his face, but he composed himself and used zip ties to restrain them both.

While attempting to restrain them, Duncan dropped one pair of zip ties, which investigators later found.

However, Mark was a large man, and the zip ties wouldn't fit. Instead, he walked them downstairs and had Brenda tie Mark's wrists and ankles.

Duncan then asked if they had any guns. He intended to make them assume he was only there to steal the weapons—not abduct the children. He knew they would do anything to protect the children, but they wouldn't fight as hard to save the guns.

Duncan instructed Brenda to wake the children while Mark lay face-down and immobilized on the floor. Duncan then bound Slade, Brenda, and Mark with duct tape to further ensure they didn't move.

Duncan explained to detectives that he couldn't believe how easy it all was.

His story then aligned with Shasta's account. He took the two children outside and set them in the grass.

Then, using a framing hammer, Duncan removed Slade's ankle tape, walked him outside but out of the view of the children, and violently struck him on the head. Assuming he had killed the boy, Duncan went back into the house.

Duncan commanded Brenda to stand up, but with her feet bound, she was unable to stand. He took the framing hammer and attempted to use the claw end to cut the duct tape around her ankles, but he inadvertently slipped, pulled the hammer up, and struck her in the face. He then told detectives that Brenda's face was so damaged that he only killed her out of mercy. He continued striking her in the head.

He then turned to Mark and struck him in the head. Shasta heard him cry out in pain before he fell silent.

When Duncan went back outside, he was shocked to see Slade still walking around in a daze. He yelled at the children to stay put as he ran after Slade, eventually catching up with him and striking him in the head and shoulders until he collapsed.

Before he left, Duncan returned to the house, but he told detectives he was surprised to hear both Brenda and Mark still making gurgling sounds.

Either to avoid looking at them or to prevent blood spatter, Duncan covered them with a blanket and continued beating them in the head until he was certain they were dead.

Duncan insisted the killings were mercy killings and had nothing to do with rage. He claimed that he was only putting the family out of their misery.

Duncan packed Shasta and Dylan into Brenda's truck and drove them a short distance to where he had parked the stolen Jeep Cherokee. This explained why the neighbor had found the unfamiliar truck on his property and called 911.

Duncan claimed that as they drove off, he saw Slade standing in a daze in the front yard again, but he didn't stop because the sun was coming up. He said he washed and disposed of the hammer, but he refused to tell detectives where.

Slade eventually made his way into the house and died at his mother's feet. Slade was also believed to be the source of the blood droplets on Mark's body.

After his arrest, a former landlord of Duncan's in North Dakota handed over a document he had left behind titled "Autobiography of Ed Duncan." It appeared to have been written when he was a teenager in prison. In it, he spoke of his deviant desires and psychosexual undertones. In the 101-page document, he said that in the 1980s, he dressed in drag, took photos of himself as his alter-ego "Jazzy Jet," and gave them to male admirers.

It was upon looking further into his background that investigators learned Duncan had spent fourteen years in prison for raping a boy at gunpoint and was paroled in 1994.

In 1996, he spent more time in jail on drug charges but was paroled after only a few weeks.

Not long after his release, ten-year-old Anthony Martinez was abducted at knifepoint while playing with friends in Beaumont, California. Despite extensive searches in the weeks that followed, the little boy remained missing.

Tragically, Anthony's body was discovered in April 1996 by a park ranger, showing clear signs of violent assault. As with the Wolf Lodge victims, he had been bound with duct tape. Despite a partial fingerprint and suspect sketch, Anthony's case went cold.

However, after Duncan's arrest in Idaho, authorities linked the evidence to Anthony Martinez's case.

On July 12, Joseph Edward Duncan III was charged with three counts of murder and kidnapping. Shortly after Shasta's rescue, he also confessed to murdering Anthony in 1997.

However, that wasn't the only past crime tied to Duncan—he also confessed to killing two young girls in Seattle in July 1996 by beating them to death.

Based on the details, authorities believed he was referring to nine-year-old Carmen Cubias and eleven-year-old Sammiejo White, who disappeared near Duncan's home at the time.

Their skeletal remains were found seventeen months later, but with scarce evidence, the case quickly went cold until Duncan's shocking confession.

On October 16, 2006, Duncan pled guilty to the Wolf Lodge murders and kidnappings, immediately receiving three consecutive life sentences without parole.

In August 2008, a federal grand jury recommended the death penalty after seeing the horrifying thirty-three-minute video presented into evidence. The footage depicted nine-year-old Dylan screaming as a nude Joseph Duncan sexually, physically, and verbally abused him.

Later that year, a judge handed down three additional life sentences.

On April 5, 2011, Duncan pled guilty to killing Anthony Martinez. He received two more life terms.

Despite confessing to the deaths of Sammiejo White and Carmen Cubias, Duncan was never charged, likely due to insufficient evidence.

After over fifteen years in prison, Joseph Duncan's twisted saga finally came to an end on March 28, 2021. The serial killer and pedophile responsible for such horrific murders died from a terminal brain tumor at age fifty-eight.

His passing marked the close of a case that shocked the nation with its depravity and cruelty. For the families of Duncan's innocent victims, his death brought about a small measure of justice and finality after so many years of anguish. However, the deep scars from his unspeakable crimes will forever remain for those left shattered in his wake.

CHAPTER 10
TONY THE PERVERT

Hartlepool is a seaside port town in northern England with a history dating back to the seventh century. Three-year-old Rosie Palmer lived on Henrietta Street in a quiet Hartlepool neighborhood just a few hundred yards from the coastline of the North Sea.

On the last day of June 1994, John Thornton picked up his step-daughter, Rosie, from nursery school, and immediately after coming home, Rosie ran off to play with her neighborhood friend. But at 3:30, Rosie heard the familiar jingle of the ice cream van in the distance and rushed home to get some money from her father.

When Gary Amerigo, who had driven the ice cream van in the area for years, arrived in front of Rosie's house, she stood by herself with her flaming-red hair and anxiously waved for him to stop. Although Rosie didn't quite have enough money for the giant ice pop she wanted, he didn't have the heart to tell her no. He handed it to her with a smile and continued on his usual route.

An hour later, John Thornton went out of the house and was surprised to see that Rosie wasn't in the front yard. He walked to the neighbor's house where she had been playing earlier, but she wasn't there either.

John gathered together with Rosie's mother and several neighbors to search the area around their homes, but little Rosie had vanished. Panicked and losing hope, they called to report her missing at 8:45 p.m.

Immediately, police launched a search party. Tracker dogs were sent to follow any scent of the girl, and officers went door-to-door through the neighborhood to search for clues.

Teams searched all along the nearby beach, through industrial buildings, warehouses, and abandoned structures, and beneath piers—anything within walking distance. But there was no sign of the girl.

As night fell, the dogs lost the scent of Rosie, and officers continued to search with flashlights through the night. The next day, helicopters searched from above while coast guard boats checked along the shoreline. Volunteers throughout the city passed out flyers and assisted in any way they could. Officers continued their door-to-door searches and asked residents to fill out questionnaires with any helpful information.

One door police knocked on was that of thirty-two-year-old Shaun Anthony "Tony" Armstrong, who lived just a few houses away. They first spoke to Tony Armstrong on July 1, the day after Rosie went missing. Armstrong opened the door and told police he hadn't seen the girl, and they quickly moved on to the next house.

Rosie had been missing for almost forty hours on July 2 when police stepped up their search of the immediate neighborhood. Officers knocked again on doors and conducted cursory searches of every home within a small radius of Rosie's. Again, Tony Armstrong opened his door to the police, and this time, he allowed them to search his home. But they again moved along when they found nothing out of the ordinary.

When questioning a nearby shop owner, however, the man mentioned that he had first heard about the missing girl from a customer at about 4:30 on the day she went missing. The customer said he was going to help with the search.

Officers were confused. Rosie hadn't been reported missing until after 8:00 p.m. Even her father didn't know she was missing until 4:30. When police asked who had mentioned it to him, he replied, "Tony the Pervert," referring to Tony Armstrong. The shop owner said he also noticed what looked like blood on Armstrong's hand. When he asked what had happened to his hand, he claimed a dog had bitten him, but there was no injury—just blood.

Other neighbors had also noticed strange behavior from Armstrong on the day Rosie went missing. Witnesses said he had walked into the ocean fully clothed and flailed his arms erratically.

Shaun Anthony "Tony" Armstrong was born on June 30, 1962, just fifteen miles north of Hartlepool. He had lived in the area his entire life.

Tony Armstrong was unemployed and had struggled for years with alcohol and prescription drug addiction. Although he had been investigated for alleged sexual offenses against children in the past, he was never formally charged. His criminal record, however, showed several other arrests.

In 1993, a year prior to Rosie's disappearance, Armstrong had been diagnosed with a personality disorder and a psychopathic personality. His psychiatric consultant wrote a letter describing him as "vulnerable" and stating he needed housing assistance. The letter allowed Armstrong to receive government assistance to rent the house just around the corner from Rosie.

However, reports from his social worker noted that Armstrong would likely be a risk to any child he came into contact with.

Neighbors often noticed him strangely wandering the area and acting oddly. Many had heard rumors of his diagnoses and his prior accusations of sexual offenses, which earned him the nickname "Tony the Pervert."

On July 3, when investigators learned that Tony Armstrong had mentioned Rosie was missing before she was reported missing, they rushed to his apartment to speak to him again.

This time, Armstrong had noticeably changed. He was no longer cooperative, helpful, and polite. Instead, he was shifty and on edge. He looked worried, and detectives knew something was wrong. Armstrong was arrested on suspicion alone while investigators conducted a full forensic search of his apartment.

This time, investigators discovered the body of Rosie Palmer stuffed in a plastic garbage bag and hidden in a cupboard.

Her shorts and underwear were found in a separate bag nearby.

Rosie had been severely sexually assaulted and mutilated. Due to the condition of the body after being hidden for days, the medical examiner was unable to definitively determine or confirm a cause of death. Rosie's body showed signs of additional violence, mutilation, and harm beyond sexual assault, but specific details were not provided. The attack appeared to have been prolonged and brutal.

Despite the body being found in his cupboard, Tony Armstrong denied any involvement and did his best to feign mental illness. He was willing to plead guilty only to manslaughter due to diminished responsibility.

A crafty crime journalist, Bernard O'Mahoney, who was covering the story, had another plan. O'Mahoney posed as a woman and wrote letters to Armstrong while he was being held awaiting trial. The two exchanged letters back and forth over time, and O'Mahoney gained his trust.

Eventually, Armstrong replied to him,

> "Yes, I'm responsible for the crime, but please don't tell anybody."

O'Mahoney immediately passed the letters on to police, which helped seal Armstrong's fate. His plan of claiming mental illness had fallen through, and he quickly changed his plea to guilty of murder.

On July 27, 1995, after almost a year in custody awaiting trial, Armstrong appeared at Leeds Crown Court, where he pleaded guilty to the murder of Rosie Palmer.

During the hearing, Rosie's family members confronted her killer, calling him a monster who shattered their lives. They demanded maximum punishment.

The judge declared his actions as appallingly evil and stated he represented a significant risk to society. As a result, he was sentenced to life in prison. In 1995, however, it was common practice for judges to issue a life sentence without setting a minimum number of years before parole eligibility. The judge likely felt the severity of the crime warranted an indefinite life sentence.

In May 2006, however, after over a decade behind bars, Shaun Anthony Armstrong's original sentence underwent a standard review at the High Court to determine if his eligibility for a minimum term should be revised.

Upon review, a judge determined that by current guidelines, the assault and murder of a young child would likely warrant a life sentence with a minimum term of sixteen years. The new judgment made Armstrong eligible for parole in 2010.

As Armstrong's parole date approached, Rosie's mother, Beverley Yates, became active in trying to prevent his release. She oversaw a campaign launched in March 2010 petitioning for Armstrong to be required to sign the Sex Offender's

Register if he was ever released, despite him not being convicted of a specific sexual offense.

She pushed for new rape charges to be brought against him that could justify requiring him to register as a sex offender.

Although she was unsuccessful in bringing new charges against him, Armstrong's parole was ultimately denied.

Armstrong was denied parole for a second time in 2022 and will be up for parole again in 2024, but Rosie Palmer's mother is ready to fight if necessary.

CHAPTER 11
THE ICE CREAM KILLER

Estibaliz "Esti" Carranza was born on January 14, 1978, in Mexico City, Mexico. She grew up in a typical working-class neighborhood with her parents, Armando and Consuela Lopez, and her two older brothers.

While Esti's mother stayed home caring for the children full-time, her father worked as an investigative journalist and author. He published several moderately successful books on Mexican culture, traditions, and shamanism. His investigative journalism, however, featured exposés on government corruption that put the family at risk.

By all accounts, Esti had a turbulent childhood plagued by her father's controlling and abusive behavior. Armando was known to have a volatile temper. Neighbors often reported loud arguments and sounds of violence coming from the Lopez home.

Esti later described living in constant fear of her father's strict rules and expectations. She said he demanded total obedience and would lash out at the slightest perceived offense. Even something as minor as spilling a glass of milk could provoke rage.

The abuse deeply impacted young Esti. She later recounted that she began having vivid fantasies of killing her father as early as age seven. These thoughts brought a sense of comfort and control when she felt powerless against his attacks. However, the violent visions remained solely in her imagination throughout her childhood.

The family's life in Mexico City changed forever when armed government forces raided their home one frightening night. Esti was just five years old at the time, but the trauma of seeing uniformed men with guns storming in stayed with her.

After this terrifying invasion of their family's sanctity and safety, Esti's father decided it was time to flee Mexico. He had angered influential people with his writing and feared further retaliation from the government.

In 1983, the family packed up what they could and made the journey across the Atlantic to Barcelona, Spain. Esti's father hoped the European city would provide new inspiration away from the oppressive Mexican authorities he battled against.

Starting over in Spain represented a fresh start for the struggling but resilient family. However, adjusting to an unfamiliar new home would prove challenging, especially for young Esti.

The pressures of the international move only exacerbated her father's abusive tendencies. He demanded perfection from the entire family, critiquing their behavior constantly. Esti bore the brunt of his criticism—her childhood memories from this time mostly involved efforts to avoid her father's wrath.

In Barcelona, the family struggled financially, and Esti's father became dismissive, wanting the children to be "seen and not heard."

According to her brothers, Esti changed dramatically after arriving in Spain. They remember her transforming from a lively, outgoing child to an anxious, withdrawn girl who flinched at sudden movements. She was reluctant to bring friends home out of fear of provoking her father's anger toward them.

As early as age ten, Esti had dreams of becoming a mother. By her teens, she had become obsessed with having children of her own.

As she grew older, Esti found refuge in school and her studies. She worked hard to maintain excellent grades, hoping academic success would satisfy her demanding father. Esti discovered a passion for languages, becoming fluent in Spanish, English, German, and French.

However, despite her efforts to appease her father, he remained cold toward her. The constant stress and trauma of walking on eggshells around him caused Esti to retreat further into dark fantasies of fighting back. According to later psychological assessments, these violent thoughts became an obsession and coping mechanism. As a result, she struggled to fit in with her new surroundings.

Whenever her father lashed out, Esti would imagine sneaking into his bedroom at night to stab him to death. Other times, she planned elaborate poisoning plots. These lurid revenge fantasies brewed stronger as she entered her teenage years, though she never acted on them.

At nineteen, Esti finally moved out to attend the University of Barcelona, where she studied economics at her father's urging. It was there that she began dating an older student named Ernesto. He noticed Esti's beauty and intelligence right away and pursued her aggressively. Flattered by the attention, the couple soon fell in love.

After nearly five years together, Esti thought she had finally found the man who would marry her and give her the life and children she desperately wanted. But Ernesto abruptly ended the relationship. He told Esti he never saw a future with her.

The sudden rejection ignited Esti's desire for revenge—the same feelings she had for her father. She fixated on plans to cut the brakes on Ernesto's car. Luckily, she didn't follow through.

Eager to begin a new chapter, twenty-five-year-old Esti left Spain in 2003 and moved to Germany. She had studied German in school and wanted to gain fluency in the language. Esti also hoped distance would help relieve the pain of the break-up.

She first worked as an au pair for a family in Munich. Caring for the two young children allowed Esti to immerse herself in German culture and language, as well as embrace her love of children. After her contract ended, she moved to a small village and got a job at the local ice cream shop.

Compared to her traumatic upbringing and volatile relationship, Esti found immense satisfaction in serving ice cream with a smile. She enjoyed the peaceful, idyllic life in her adopted German village. It was the happiest and most secure Esti had felt since she was a little girl.

In the spring of 2002, a frequent customer named Holger Holz entered the ice cream shop. Holger worked as a refrigerator salesman and always stopped in after his shift for a cone.

Although he was fourteen years older than Esti, she immediately noticed his animated energy and outgoing demeanor. The two struck up friendly conversations night after night. Holger made her laugh with amusing stories of his life in Germany.

Before long, they began dating and quickly fell into an intense romance. Holger's adventurous, quirky spirit was a stark contrast to the men Esti had known. His attentiveness made her feel truly loved and valued for the first time.

Holger, however, was a follower of Hari Krishna and didn't believe in sex before marriage. He wanted to get married as soon as possible.

Holger proposed after only three weeks of dating, and Esti enthusiastically accepted. After they married, the couple relocated to Holger's hometown of Berlin to start their new life together.

In Berlin, Esti held various service jobs as a waitress and cashier to help support them while Holger continued his work. At first, she was overjoyed by their wedded bliss. But deep inside, Esti knew she had made a mistake in marrying Holger.

As she expected, Holger's charming personality soon morphed into something more sinister. He began exerting major financial and emotional control over Esti's life.

Holger demanded she turn over all the tip money from her waitressing job. He also took away her passport and other vital documents, threatening to destroy them if she tried to leave. Additionally, Holger allotted Esti a tiny budget while he splurged on firearms, video games, and other frivolities.

Plus, her dreams of starting a family had been crushed. Because of his belief in Hari Krishna, he believed sex was only for procreation, and he wasn't ready to have children.

Behind closed doors, his mental and physical abuse intensified. He called Esti derogatory names and sometimes got physical when angered. She described him grabbing, shoving, and slapping her around their apartment.

Esti initially attempted to rationalize Holger's behavior and dismiss the red flags. She told herself he was just stressed about finances and would get over this angry phase.

Holger then proposed to Esti that they should move to Vienna, Austria, and open an ice cream shop. She had experience working in an ice cream shop, and he'd spent his life working with refrigerators. It made perfect sense. Esti believed that with this new scenario, maybe they could finally start a family.

Esti and Holger moved to Austria and opened the Schleckeria ice cream shop, and for a few months, it seemed that Holger had changed. But it soon became evident that Holger still relished his power and control over her.

Feeling trapped yet again with an abusive partner, Esti fell into a deep depression. Holger spent barely any time in the shop while she doubled her hours, and their sex life had been reduced to zero. It seemed that her dreams of starting a family were slipping.

According to psychologists, it was a perfect storm of circumstances that pushed Esti back into the obsessive, homicidal thoughts from her youth. The daily degradation stripped away her last shreds of agency and identity.

In 2007, frustrated with her marriage, Esti began having an affair with Manfred Hinterberger, an ice cream machine salesman who, like Holger, was fifteen years her senior.

It wasn't long before Esti had had enough of Holger, and she told him she wanted a divorce. Surprisingly, he agreed but refused to move out of their home. Frustrated, Esti's demented thoughts of death resurfaced.

In April 2008, after finishing a double shift, Esti came home to find Holger glued to the television playing a gory first-person shooter video game. He barely acknowledged her arrival.

Seeing him distracted, Esti reached for the Beretta pistol Holger kept hidden in a kitchen cabinet. She walked up behind the sofa and shot him directly in the back of the head at point-blank range. As Holger's limp body slid to the floor and blood pooled around him, Esti put another bullet through his temple.

After ruthlessly executing Holger, Esti knew her work was far from finished. She now faced the gruesome task of permanently disposing of his remains in a way that could never be traced back to her.

Her first instinct wasn't well thought through—cremation. She dragged Holger's corpse to the center of the living room and poured schnapps over the body, hoping to incinerate the evidence. But after setting it alight, the small fire soon extinguished itself, leaving the body only partially charred.

When smoke set off fire alarms that brought fire crews to the apartment, Esti somehow quickly lied that she had burned some fish she was cooking. The firefighters miraculously believed her bold deception and left without further investigation.

With plan A having failed, Esti desperately needed a new way to make Holger's body disappear for good. She dragged his body to the empty bathtub and bought an electric chainsaw. Meticulously, she used the buzzing blade to slice off Holger's head, then his limbs, and finally to cut the torso into smaller pieces.

Esti then took empty plastic ice cream tubs from her shop and filled them with the dismembered remains, temporarily storing them in her freezer.

Over the course of several nights, Esti made over a dozen trips carrying the loaded ice cream tubs down to the street, where she called for a taxi.

Assuming they were full of ice cream, the taxi driver helped Esti load the heavy tubs, unaware they were full of body parts. One by one, Esti transported the tubs to the large freezers in the cellar of her ice cream shop.

Over the next several nights, Esti meticulously mixed up batch after batch of concrete, relentlessly encasing each of Holger's severed body parts in concrete inside the tubs.

She arranged the tubs neatly, sprinkled air freshener throughout the cellar to mask any smells, and left them encased in frozen concrete alongside actual ice cream ingredients, with no one any the wiser.

Satisfied the concrete buckets would keep Holger hidden indefinitely, Esti set to scrubbing away every trace of blood and gore from her home. She then disposed of the murder weapon. By the time she finished, it was as if nothing had ever happened.

When friends and neighbors inquired about Holger, she insisted their relationship had gone sour, and he had abandoned her and moved to India. Friends who knew him didn't question her story. It was believable.

Holger's remains were neatly hidden, and his disappearance was plausibly explained away. Other than her neighbors' occasional complaints of a foul smell, Esti had gotten away with his vicious murder. However, her bloody vengeance was far from over.

With her husband out of the way, Esti was free to continue her relationship with Manfred Hinterberger, who ran a small ice cream machine business.

It wasn't long before the couple moved in together. Compared to volatile Holger, Manfred came across as patient and gentle. Esti hoped she had finally found a loving, respectful partner who could someday give her the family she wanted so badly.

At first, the relationship seemed healthy and supportive. But, like Holger, Manfred eventually revealed his true nature to be just as selfish and cruel. He insulted her appearance, made her change herself to win his affection, and, worst of all, refused to give her children.

Manfred started demanding Esti get plastic surgery because he found her physically unattractive. He said her nose was too large and her lips too thin.

Additionally, Manfred refused to have children with Esti because he already had sons from a previous marriage. Her lifelong dream of starting a family was crumbling once again.

For two years, Esti desperately tried to get Manfred to love her how she needed to be loved, but when he told her he wanted to have an open relationship, she knew it was over. However, despite denying his request, she soon realized he was seeing other women anyway.

Feeling betrayed and robbed again, Esti descended back into darkness. The only scenario that she imagined could free her from endless abuse was Manfred's death.

Again, Esti had had enough. She had sacrificed everything already for her dream of a family—even committing murder —and she would not let another man ruin it for her.

On the night of November 21, 2010, Esti slipped sedatives into Manfred's evening tea until he fell into deep unconsciousness. Once she confirmed he was asleep, she retrieved a revolver she kept beneath her bed and shot Manfred four times in the back of the head at point-blank range.

Repeating her eerily precise methods, Esti dragged his body to the bathtub and sawed apart Manfred's corpse. She then packed the parts into plastic ice cream tubs, encased them in concrete, and concealed them in the cellar beside Holger's remains.

Just like before, she scrubbed the murder scene thoroughly to eliminate any evidence. But this time, friends became suspicious. They knew she and Manfred were unhappy, but he wasn't the type to leave her and disappear without telling his friends or sons. Not wanting to raise suspicion, she filed a missing person report.

Esti's performance was so convincing that Manfred's own friend Roland comforted Esti in her apparent grief. Within months, the two were dating, and Roland had moved into the apartment.

On June 6, 2011, a pipe burst at the hair salon next door to Esti's ice cream shop. To fix the broken pipe, they needed to get into the cellar of her shop.

Esti was getting nervous. The thought of workers so close to the buckets of bodies in her cellar haunted her. Convinced she would soon be caught, she withdrew her life savings and disappeared.

Esti's assumptions were correct. While plumbers worked on the pipes in the cellar, they stumbled upon an ice cream tub with a bit of leg sticking out of the concrete. They immediately called the police, who found both dismembered bodies. Investigators quickly identified the corpses of Holger and Manfred, but Esti was long gone.

A frantic search for Esti began. Teams tracked down and interviewed her friends, hoping someone might know where she went. However, she had vanished without a trace, knowing she would immediately be the prime suspect.

Investigators monitored airports, train stations, and roads leading out of Austria. They were convinced Esti would attempt to cross one of the nearby international borders to avoid arrest.

For two anxious days, Austrian police came up empty in their search for the suspected murderer among them, but then they got a break. A witness reported spotting a woman matching Esti's description arriving by taxi at Vienna Airport soon after the bodies were found.

Police rushed to the airport to review security footage and passenger records. They confirmed that Esti had entered the airport and purchased a ticket to Paris, but she then got spooked and backed out before boarding the flight. It seemed she realized authorities would be waiting for her arrival in Paris.

This sighting, however, confirmed Esti was on the run within Austria. But where had she gone next? Investigators now feared she had slipped across the southern border into Italy. Austrian police coordinated with Italian border agencies and police to expand the manhunt efforts south.

After following up on dozens of tips, Italian police finally apprehended a woman fitting Esti's description in a small coastal town four days after the bodies had been found. She did not resist arrest. Austrian police transported her back to face her horrific crimes.

On June 10, 2011, authorities arrested Esti outside Udine, Italy. Under harsh interrogation, she quickly confessed to both murders and the grotesque dismemberment of the bodies. The physical evidence found at the ice cream parlor supported her graphic confession.

While awaiting trial in prison, Esti gave birth to a baby boy in 2012 after becoming pregnant by her boyfriend, Roland. She finally got the baby she so desired, but the child was taken from her after the birth to be raised by relatives.

Deemed an extreme danger with little chance of rehabilitation, Estibaliz Carrenza stood trial in November 2012. The prosecution proved that the murders were premeditated and especially heinous, given the intimate relationships involved. With overwhelming evidence against her, the court swiftly sentenced her to life imprisonment with no possibility of parole.

While serving her life sentence, Esti wrote a book about her crimes. She penned the memoir herself in prison and titled it "Meine zwei Leben: Die wahre Geschichte der Eislady," which translates to "My Two Lives: The True Story of the Ice Lady."

In the book, Esti provides her chilling firsthand account of the murders, her attempts to cover up the crimes, and the events that led to her capture. Proceeds from book sales are being put into a fund for her young son.

Esti hoped detailing her crimes in the memoir would provide some financial support for the son she would never get to see grow up. While some felt the book rewarded Esti's atrocities, she maintained it was her way of taking responsibility and atoning for the lives she took.

In a highly unusual move in 2017, Austrian prison officials transferred Esti from the women's facility to an all-male prison. The stated reason for the shocking transfer was that she was deemed "too dangerous" to remain housed with other female inmates.

CHAPTER 12
MISSING IN MISSISSIPPI

In the late 1980s, Robert Hearin Sr. was one of the wealthiest men in Mississippi. At an early age, he had invested in the oil and gas industry, and he was now co-owner of Mississippi Valley Gas Company, Mississippi's largest gas distribution company.

He was also a major investor in Trustmark National Bank (the second-largest bank in Mississippi at the time), a shareholder in Lamar Life Insurance Corporation, and acted as president of School Pictures, Inc., a company that sold franchises to take and publish school photos for yearbooks.

At seventy-three years old, Robert Hearin had done exceptionally well for himself, amassing an empire worth well over $100 million. He and his seventy-two-year-old wife, Annie Laurie Hearin, lived in a luxurious mansion on Woodland Drive in Jackson, Mississippi. Robert had met Annie while attending the University of Alabama, and they had married in 1940.

On the morning of July 26, 1988, Annie hosted a bridge club party at their home, as she did every Tuesday. The group played bridge, discussed the week's events, and ate blueberry ice cream cake. When they were finished, the last guest left the house at around 2:30 p.m. A half-hour later, their housekeeper went home for the day and left Annie alone in the house.

When Robert arrived home at 4:30 that afternoon, he was surprised that Annie wasn't in the house. He checked the back garden, the master bedroom, and the kitchen, but she wasn't there. He then checked the garage and found that her car was still there. However, when he returned to the living room and saw Annie's shoes and purse still in the house, he knew something was wrong.

Annie was frail and suffered from ileitis, a chronic intestinal disease. Without her medication, she wouldn't be able to absorb food and could possibly die within days. When Robert checked the medicine cabinet in the bathroom, her prescription medication was still there.

For the next few hours, Robert contacted their housekeeper and friends who had been with her at the bridge club party, but no one had heard from her. At 9:49 that evening, Robert contacted the Jackson police to report his wife missing.

Almost immediately after arriving at the Hearin home, investigators noticed things that Robert had not. They discovered drops of blood on the carpet and smears of blood on the front door. Later tests of the blood samples matched Annie's blood type.

Also, lying on the floor near the front door was a typed letter. The letter seemed to have been typed on an old typewriter. The letter, riddled with errors, made demands but mentioned nothing of Annie. It read:

> *Robert Herrin*
> *Put these people back in the shape they was in before they got mixed up with School Photography. Pay them whatever damages they want and tell them all this so they can no what your doing but don't tell them why you are doing it.*
> *Do this before ten days pass.*
> *Don't call the police.*
> *If any is dead, pay his children.*

Below the message, the letter listed twelve male franchise owners of School Pictures, Inc.

Just a year earlier, to avoid losses, School Pictures Inc. had sued twelve of its franchisees who had not paid their fees.

The letter had no useable fingerprints, and the paper didn't match any in the Hearin home. Experts analyzed the typeface and determined it was typed on a vintage Royal brand manual typewriter manufactured between 1912 and 1927.

The note contained several grammatical and spelling errors, which investigators believed were intentional mistakes to disguise the writer's identity.

However, one word in the letter stuck out to FBI document examiners. The word "damages" was not a word that was typically used in a note like that. It implied that whoever had written the letter may have had a legal background.

The note also demanded that Robert not contact the police, but he had already contacted the police before the letter was discovered. To be safe, the media agreed to a twenty-four-hour blackout before announcing the kidnapping. At 8:30 p.m. on July 28, Jackson Mayor Dale Danks held a televised press conference.

Although the note had mentioned nothing of his wife's safe return, Robert Hearin was willing to do anything to comply with the kidnapper's demands.

Robert hired lawyers to research the records of School Pictures Inc. and find out how much the twelve franchise owners listed in the note had lost in their legal troubles.

Trying to gain leads, they sent letters to each franchise owner listed, asking what damages they felt they were owed. Surprisingly, however, most men claimed they weren't owed anything.

Meanwhile, the FBI contacted field offices where the twelve men lived around the country to gather information on their background, finances, and potential involvement.

Investigators suspected that one of the twelve franchisees may have been the kidnapper. However, the problem with that theory was that the lawsuits against them were a matter of public record. Anyone could have looked up the names of those men.

After the press conference, two neighbors reported seeing a white van parked near the Hearin home on multiple occasions in the weeks leading up to the kidnapping.

One neighbor confronted the van driver and told police the man was agitated when asked what he was doing. Another neighbor had the foresight to write down the van's license plate number.

However, when police checked the van's registration, they discovered that the license plates had been stolen from a car at the New Orleans airport.

FBI agents in eight different states were tasked with watching the twelve men. They surveilled the subjects to determine if they took part in suspicious activities or had any unexplained absences, as well as to monitor their movements. If one of them had kidnapped Annie, they would need to provide her with food and water. But sadly, none of them seemed to act suspiciously.

Investigators continued researching the twelve men listed on the ransom note, and one name stood out: Newton Alfred Winn.

Sixty-five-year-old Winn was a lawyer from St. Petersburg, Florida, and investigators believed that if he had written the ransom note, he would have been more likely to use the word "damages" than the other eleven men on the list.

Also, the neighbor who confronted the driver of the suspicious white van parked near the Hearin home picked Winn out of a photo lineup of the twelve franchise owners. The other neighbor who took down the van's license plate number also identified Winn as the driver.

Furthermore, records showed Winn had purchased a similar white van in the weeks leading up to the kidnapping. The circumstances of the van's purchase were particularly suspicious.

When interviewed, the woman who sold the van to Winn said he had behaved strangely during the sale. She said he had insisted that his name not appear anywhere on the receipt or vehicle paperwork. Reluctantly, she left the buyer's name section blank on the paperwork. She later identified Winn as the purchaser and told investigators that he had paid cash and refused to provide any identification. Regardless of the strange circumstances during the purchase of the van, records showed it was in a repair shop at the time of the kidnapping. However, investigators then discovered that Winn had rented a similar white van during the time of the abduction.

Winn lived alone in an apartment above his office in St. Petersburg, Florida, where he worked as a civil lawyer. When FBI agents interviewed him, he claimed he had nothing to do with Annie's disappearance and gave an alibi for the day of the kidnapping.

During the initial interview, Winn told detectives he had been with a sex worker on the day of the abduction. He had no idea of the sex worker's name and didn't remember the name of the bar where he met her, but he claimed that his paralegal assistant, Don Ward, brought $100 to him at the bar so he could pay the prostitute.

Investigators then interviewed Ward, who confirmed Winn's story, but he also failed to remember the name of the bar. Winn, however, had paid for Ward's paralegal training and was working on a small salary. Detectives didn't believe his story and suspected Ward was loyal to his boss and helping to cover his tracks.

Don Ward told investigators that Winn had done business with School Pictures seven years earlier, and they had foreclosed on him. Winn had attempted to file bankruptcy three times but was denied each time, and finally, a court order was issued to seize his property. He said Winn was distraught when they took his vintage sports car. Winn told his coworkers that his business dealings with School Pictures had ruined his life.

Just three weeks before Annie was abducted, Winn received an eviction notice on his business and home. Don Ward told investigators that Winn was angry when he received the news and said he had no intention of leaving.

After interviewing Ward, investigators believed he may have been involved as well. When they pulled his vehicle records, they discovered that the white van that Winn had so-secretly purchased was in Ward's name. Winn had purchased it but had registered it in Ward's name.

Sure that Winn was the kidnapper, he was brought before a Mississippi grand jury on August 3. He denied having any knowledge about the kidnapping, and investigators didn't have enough evidence to charge him.

On August 16, Don Ward was also brought before a federal grand jury in Florida. Ward stuck to his story that he had witnessed Winn with a prostitute on the day of the abduction.

By mid-August, Robert and the FBI were losing hope. Without her medication, Annie was most likely dead or would die soon.

But on August 15, there was a glimmer of hope. Robert received a letter in the mail in Annie's handwriting. The letter was dated August 10 and postmarked in Atlanta, Georgia, on August 12.

The letter read:

> BOB,
>
> IF YOU DON'T DO WHAT THESE PEOPLE WANT YOU TO DO, THEY'RE GOING TO SEAL ME UP IN THE CELLAR OF THIS HOUSE WITH ONLY A FEW JUGS OF WATER.
>
> PLEASE SAVE ME,
>
> ANNIE LAURIE

FBI experts confirmed the handwriting was indeed Annie's, but the language was unusual. Annie typically would have used words like "basement" rather than "cellar" and "bottles" instead of "jugs." Investigators believed she was told what to write.

This also raised the possibility that if the abductor had chosen the wording, the date of the letter could have been chosen, too. Annie may have penned that letter the day she went missing. FBI profilers were all but certain that Annie Hearin was already dead.

Regardless of what investigators believed, Robert couldn't give up hope. He mailed twelve checks totaling almost $1 million to the franchisees, along with a handwritten letter begging for the release of his wife. Half of the franchise owners, however, returned the checks.

Robert Hearin did everything he was asked in the ransom note, but despite his efforts, Annie was never released.

The FBI spent the next several months looking more into Winn and his dispute with School Pictures.

In 1984, Winn was ordered by a court to pay over $153,000 to School Pictures for unpaid debts. Unable to pay the debt, US Marshals seized various items, including jewelry, other possessions, and, most significantly, his sports car.

When Robert Hearin sent the checks to the twelve franchise owners, Winn received a check for $145,000. But soon after he received it, he mailed it back with a note saying he hoped Robert found his wife safe. Investigators, however, believed that he had realized the kidnapping had gotten out of control and had returned the check to distance himself from the crime.

Two and a half months after her kidnapping, the television show Unsolved Mysteries featured the story and received a tip. Although none of the names on the list were mentioned during the broadcast, the female caller said,

> "If Newton Alfred Winn is on the list, I have some information."

When police contacted the woman and found out she worked as a psychic, they were initially apprehensive. However, they took her much more seriously when she heard what she had to say.

She said that Winn had come into her office for a consultation and confided to her about his troubles with School Pictures—as well as his plan to abduct and hold hostage the head of the company until they complied with his demands. He asked for her help, but she refused.

The FBI arranged for the psychic to meet with Winn in her office again, where she confronted him with what she had seen in the television show. She asked if he had kidnapped Annie, but he flatly denied it.

Six months had passed, and there was still no sign of Annie. The FBI then learned that Winn owned a remote cabin in Florida, but when they searched the cabin and the area surrounding it, they found nothing.

In his arrogance, Winn had sent thousands of documents to the Internal Revenue Service and told them to search for any disputed financial documents. But among all the paperwork, they found letters written back and forth between Winn and his ex-girlfriend, Marilyn Taylor, about how they had planned to kidnap and kill her husband. The letters even mentioned using an old typewriter. The letters were all too similar to what had happened in the case of Annie Hearin.

When FBI agents approached Winn's former girlfriend and showed her the evidence against her, Marilyn Taylor was quick to give up information about Winn.

When first interviewed by the FBI in February 1989, Taylor admitted that Winn had approached her in early August 1988, just after the abduction, asking her to do him a "favor."

They weren't dating at the time, and Winn had asked her to meet him in a parking lot. As she pulled up to his car, he got out and walked nervously to her window, handing her a note which asked if her car was bugged.

Once he deemed it was safe to talk, Winn paid Taylor $500 to travel to Atlanta from Daytona Beach and mail a letter for him. It was the handwritten letter written by Annie. Winn had wrapped the envelope in a gray table napkin.

His instructions were strange and precise. He instructed her not to touch the envelope or look at the address. She was to fly to Atlanta, buy plane tickets using a false name, and fly into and out of two different airports. Once at the airport, she was instructed to go into the airport bathroom and dye her hair. He told her to avoid taxis and take public transportation to a specific post office to drop off the letter. Winn was so paranoid that he asked her to wear a disguise and speak with a Scandinavian accent if she spoke to anyone.

Although Taylor told agents she had no idea what the letter was, she followed Winn's strange instructions for mailing the letter. But just before dropping it in the box, she glanced at the address and realized it was addressed to the Hearin residence.

When FBI agents showed her a photograph of the letter, she confirmed it was the one she had mailed.

Taylor told agents she had thrown the gray table napkin out of her car window on a rural road. Incredibly, FBI agents found the napkin still on the side of the road six months later.

On March 11, 1989, agents convinced Taylor to meet with Winn again. This time, she would wear a wire and try to get him to give her more information about the crime. She confronted him and told him that she had been watching the news and knew that he was involved in the kidnapping. She told him she was worried because it implicated her when she mailed the letter. But despite her concerns, Winn denied everything and said nothing to incriminate himself.

As he exited her vehicle, FBI agents arrested Winn and charged him with conspiracy to kidnap, extortion through the US mail, and perjury for lying to a grand jury.

After his arrest, FBI agents searched his office and found a vintage Royal brand typewriter similar to the one used to write the ransom note. However, when analyzed, investigators realized it wasn't the actual typewriter used. Winn had most likely planted a similar vintage typewriter in his office specifically to throw off evidence found during the investigation.

While awaiting trial, Winn refused to accept a court-appointed lawyer but said he couldn't afford to hire one, telling a judge,

> "I used to have some money. I have nothing now."

Although the judge had assured Winn that he would be appointed a competent lawyer, he chose to represent himself. Winn was a lawyer, but he had never tried a federal case.

Investigators remained suspicious of Don Ward's original statement corroborating that Winn was with a prostitute at the time Annie Hearin was kidnapped.

They believed Don Ward was lying to protect Winn due to their close professional relationship and Ward's financial dependence on Winn.

After compiling additional incriminating evidence against Ward and Winn, FBI agents paid the paralegal another visit in March 1989.

Presented with this evidence, the FBI offered Ward immunity from prosecution if he told the full truth about Winn's activities. Ward then admitted that Winn had fabricated the entire prostitute alibi story.

Under questioning, Ward finally cracked and disclosed that Winn had coerced him into deceiving the investigators. He also admitted Winn had not been working at his law office on the dates leading up to the kidnapping, contrary to the alibi.

Ward told investigators that when Winn received the $145,000 check from Robert Hearin, he said, "This is not what I wanted." Winn had wanted his life back. He wanted his car and property returned, not the money.

The trial of Newton Alfred Winn began on January 29, 1990. Both Marilyn Taylor and Don Ward testified against him.

Ward testified that Winn had paid him to take four trips to Jackson, Mississippi, from Florida to watch the Hearin house and take photographs. He testified that he had initially lied to investigators to protect his employer. However, Ward insisted he knew nothing of the kidnapping.

After three hours and forty minutes of deliberation, the jury returned a guilty verdict on all counts.

As Winn walked out of the courtroom into the sea of reporters, he was asked his thoughts on the verdict. He smirked and said, "What is there to say?"

Newton Alfred Winn was sentenced to nineteen years and seven months in federal prison. Although he wasn't convicted of murder and the body of Annie Hearin was never found, the Hearin family said they were pleased with the result.

Years later, Winn appealed his conviction, but the appeal was denied.

In 2006, eighty-one-year-old Winn was released from prison after serving over sixteen years of his sentence. Until his death six years later in 2012, Winn insisted he had nothing to do with Annie Laurie Hearin's kidnapping or death.

In November 1990, just nine months after Winn entered prison, Robert Hearin died of a heart attack at age seventy-three.

The following year, Annie Hearin was declared legally dead so that the family could settle the Hearin estate.

The remains of Annie Laurie Hearin were never found.

Online Appendix

Visit my website for additional photos and videos pertaining to the cases in this book:

http://TrueCrimeCaseHistories.com/vol12/

More books by Jason Neal

Looking for more?? I am constantly adding new volumes of True Crime Case Histories. The series **can be read in any order**, and all books are available in paperback, hardcover, and audiobook.

Check out the complete series at:

https://amazon.com/author/jason-neal

All Jason Neal books are also available in **AudioBook format at Audible.com.** Enjoy a **Free Audiobook** when you signup for a 30-Day trial using this link:

https://geni.us/AudibleTrueCrime

FREE BONUS EBOOK
FOR MY READERS

As my way of saying "Thank you" for downloading, I'm giving away a FREE True Crime e-book I think you'll enjoy.

https://TrueCrimeCaseHistories.com

Just visit the link above to let me know where to send your free book!

THANK YOU!

Thank you for reading this Volume of True Crime Case Histories. I truly hope you enjoyed it. If you did, I would be sincerely grateful if you would take a few minutes to write a review for me on Amazon using the link below.

https://geni.us/review12

I'd also like to encourage you to sign up for my email list for updates, discounts, and freebies on future books! I promise I'll make it worth your while with future freebies.

http://truecrimecasehistories.com

And please take a moment and follow me on Amazon.

One last thing. As I mentioned previously, many of the stories in this series were suggested to me by readers like you. I like to feature stories that many true crime fans haven't heard of, so if there's a story that you remember from the past that you haven't seen covered by other true crime sources, please send me any details you can remember, and I will do my best to research it. Or if you'd like to contact me for any other reason, feel free to email me at:

jasonnealbooks@gmail.com

https://linktr.ee/JasonNeal

Thanks so much,

Jason Neal

ABOUT THE AUTHOR

Jason Neal is a Best-Selling American True Crime Author living in Hawaii with his Turkish-British wife. Jason started his writing career in the late eighties as a music industry publisher and wrote his first true crime collection in 2019.

As a boy growing up in the eighties just south of Seattle, Jason became interested in true crime stories after hearing the news of the Green River Killer so close to his home. Over the subsequent years, he would read everything he could get his hands on about true crime and serial killers.

As he approached 50, Jason began to assemble stories of the crimes that have fascinated him most throughout his life. He's especially obsessed by cases solved by sheer luck, amazing police work, and groundbreaking technology like early DNA cases and, more recently, reverse genealogy.

Printed in Great Britain
by Amazon

30185338R00106

THE GIRL BEHIND THE LIGHT

D. R. Goodman

Cavenham Publications

CAVENHAM PUBLICATIONS

ISBN-978-1-7398660-0-6
ISBN-978-1-7398660-1-3

Cover design by: Deep Fuschia Ltd

CONTENTS

"DUNWICHE"

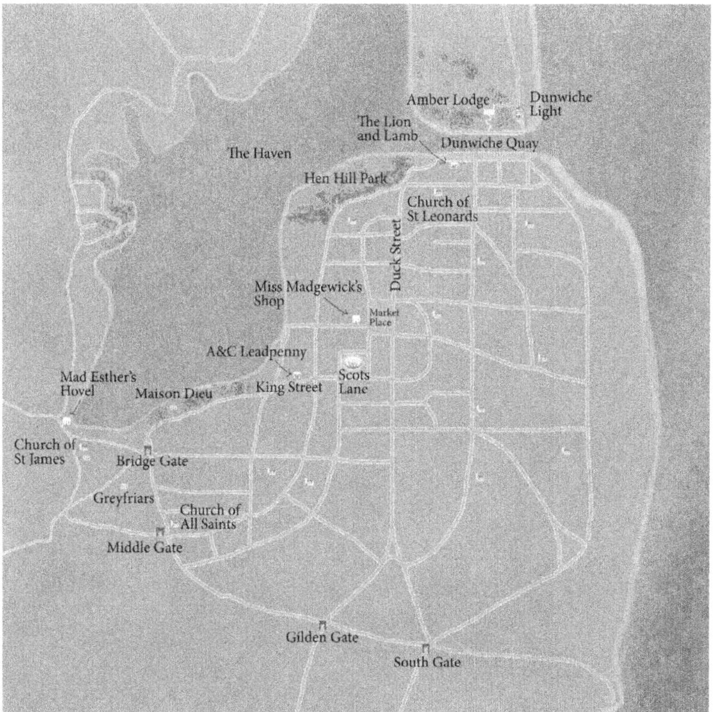
Amber Lodge
Dunwiche Light
The Lion and Lamb
Dunwiche Quay
The Haven
Hen Hill Park
Church of St Leonards
Duck Street
Miss Madgewick's Shop
Market Place
A&C Leadpenny
Mad Esther's Hovel
Maison Dieu
King Street
Scots Lane
Church of St James
Bridge Gate
Greyfriars
Church of All Saints
Middle Gate
Gilden Gate
South Gate

Chapter 1 - Daniel DeLara

20 years previously,
Dunwiche,
Englande.

All things have a reason - else they wouldn't be! The words of her mother's folklore wisdom echoed in Margaret's head as she made her way over the haven bridge and towards the front gate of Amber Lodge. Her parents had worked there for as long as she could remember, her mother as housekeeper and her father as gardener-cum-handyman.

A thunderstorm was brewing, one of many over the past few weeks. The air was stuffy and hot. There was no wind and the sky to the southeast was an ominously thick dark blue haze.

Margaret shuddered at the sight of it, her parents along with most other people would be covering the mirrors and making sure that all shiny metal objects were out of sight in case the storm demons should be attracted to them and strike the house. She wanted to be with them for her own comfort as much as theirs, but her mother had insisted she should go.

Amber Lodge was an ancient and imposing building which, together with the Customs House and the Dunwiche Light, looked south over the seaward entrance to the Haven. It stood tall, built of stone and flint with stained glass tracery windows and an entrance door of oak which had been bleached of colour by years of sun and salty air.

On the seaward side, an octagonal turret extended upwards through the corner of the library on the ground floor and the master bed chamber above, then up past the attic rooms to a glass observation room with a weather vane in the form of a sailing ship on the top. All in all, its rather stark beauty and sombre elegance suggested that it merely existed rather than had a purpose.

Margaret didn't find it at all sombre though, she knew almost every nook and cranny from having happily played there as a young child while her parents worked. She'd even been up to the turret room once and counted the church towers over the water, fourteen in all.

An elderly gentleman greeted Margaret eagerly at the heavy wrought iron gates, his voice sounding distant and strained in the still, humid atmosphere.

'Ah - you came! Good.'

'Ma sent me.' she said as she reached him.

'Did she?' He turned and raised an eyebrow as they walked up the steps and along the path 'I told her you had a free choice; So, come in, come in.'

As the two of them entered the house, Margaret wondered why he seemed rather serious, maybe it was the storm. She liked Daniel DeLara, he always had a kind word for her and he made her smile with his eccentric ways, like a kind elderly uncle. He sometimes talked about his scientific theories but she didn't really care much to hear them. Anyway, her Mother always seemed to make out that she shouldn't take notice of such things because they weren't for the likes of her to know. So she tended to just switch off and say yes or no when she thought she ought to.

The morning room of Amber Lodge was virtually unused and was kept for entertaining the very few visitors who were welcomed to the house. It had an air of faded grandeur and an initial smell of new polish but after a few minutes an old musty smell appeared underneath it. She much preferred the kitchen which was where she helped her Mother with the cleaning on Saturday mornings. Now here she was, sitting with him like an equal, being offered china tea and scones and using the best service.

They exchanged a few pleasantries, him doing his best to make her feel at ease. They discussed the weather and the oncoming storm, her parents health and the latest news in the Dunwiche Herald before he changed the course of the conversation abruptly.

He stood up, cleared his throat and gripped the lapels of his jacket uncomfortably. 'I have asked you here, Margaret, because I have decided to leave this place for good. I have not yet explained in full to your parents, as the outcome of our conversation will determine the arrangements I will have to make.' His eyes searched her face for a reaction. 'I have to leave soon but I must make sure that the house is looked after well in my absence. Your parents have done me a great service over the years but they are not able to continue for ever, and I fear that the house will need to be serviced for a long time to come.'

Margaret sat stunned, her face still not showing any emotion. She sipped at her tea.

'Do you know what a promise is?' he asked as if to a young child.

'Oh yes sir. It's when you say you'll do somethin' and then you make sure that you do. That's a promise all right, sure as eggs is eggs.'

He returned her honest simplicity with a kindly smile. 'I want you to consider an offer which could provide you with an income for life if you should decide to take it up. The fact is, that this house is very important to me and also others to come.'

He hesitated and fiddled with his ring. 'Something is wrong, very wrong. I can't quite put my finger on it. I am sure my name is wrong but I cannot remember quite what it should be and I know I would not forget under normal circumstances. But these are not normal circumstances. Names have a history, a purpose, a meaning. What does "DeLara" mean? Nothing much, I fear.'

His faded blue eyes looked sadly down at her, knowing that she hadn't the faintest idea what he was talking about. She still sat expressionless before him, hiding whatever was going through her mind. He changed his approach.

'As you know, I have been working hard to answer questions which others dare not even ask, and now, I believe my time is running out and I must move on. It may seem odd to you, that I wish to change my life, quite literally, at the age of eighty six, but my mind is made up. There is only so much that one can do in one life time, and now I feel that you should know something of the nature of my decision.'

He sat down and stared directly into her eyes 'I know you have listened politely to my ramblings on many occasions, but this time I want you to try to understand as much as you can about the situation in which we currently find ourselves. Firstly, a question. What do you know of the Great Judgement?'

Margaret flushed with embarrassment at the thought that he knew she found his ramblings rather boring but she repeated the story to him in the monotone of learned familiarity, just as she had heard it on many occasions in church and at school.

'Well, Sir. On the twenty first day of the ninth month in the year of our Lord nineteen hundred and twenty one, the seas did boil and the skies did storm and the Lord sent plague to the earth to teach us of our sins and them that were unrepentant were cast into the very pits of hell. Now we have Repentance Day where we confess our sinful thoughts and deeds to the Lord, lest we forget of it.'

'Thank you, Margaret. That's exactly what I thought you would say, but did you know that I was there? Or rather here, in this very house? Just a boy of course, and I remember it well but certainly not as you have just described it. The sea indeed was very rough and actually flooded some of the town but it certainly did not boil. Such a fantasy! Thunderstorms too had raged through the day, but these two things alone were not enough to cause such fear and awe in the minds of people.

I believe that on that fateful day reality was changed.Damaged maybe. Many people saw things that they were never meant to see, and that is why they still cling to the hope and the easy answers which the churches eagerly provide, never seeing the pieces of the story which do not fit.

Of course little things change all around us constantly and nobody ever notices, they just assume that everything is as they expect to see it and make an excuse for anything which isn't quite as it was.'

He broke off when he saw that Margaret was looking uneasy. Thoughts were fighting for space in her head and this was the type of talk that some people considered to be very dangerous. People were usually afraid to voice such opinions openly for fear of their priest or the church constables who could arrest them for it. Those same people would sometimes say that Margaret and her mother kept house for a Gildenhair and a Heathen and that they were tainted by him, but Margaret knew some things that they didn't. She knew that he kept acquaintance with people who were high up and that they kept the whole business a secret. She also knew that he had things in the house that even the Bishop held in awe.

Things from the Nonnye world.

Margaret trusted him though, and in her mind's eye a picture began to form of the hard stern faces who whispered and muttered quietly in the street, casting accusing looks in her direction but never actually calling her a sinner to her face. The picture slowly changed to the kind smile and twinkling blue eyes of Daniel DeLara. This man had shown her and her family nothing but kindness and respect, the kind of respect which earned deep loyalty. She made a decision there and then.

'Sir, I will do whatever you want me to do, I know you're a good man, and Ma and Pa know it too.'

He looked relieved and suddenly rather tired. He poured some more tea while he outlined his proposal to her, she would be allowed to move in as housekeeper and take responsibility for maintaining the house and its contents until the new owner arrived.

'I cannot think of anybody who would be more suitable to do this for me' he said. 'You are an honest and trustworthy young miss, and I am sure that you will treat the next owner of the house with patience, kindness and respect.'

He gave her a well worn note book which he said contained a list of her duties, and also some suggestions on how to make sure that anyone claiming ownership of the house was genuine.

She took it and promised to read it thoroughly, as he had requested. He also handed to her a small box which contained the keys to a metal trunk which sat in the corner of the study, with instructions that she should give it to the next owner and insist that they read the contents of a book within it as soon as possible after their arrival. This she promised to do without question.

'I have made provisions with the bank to pay you a good wage from the moment you take over from your parents until your sixtieth birthday but you must promise me something in return.'

He continued to explain to Margaret all about the arrangements he had made for her parents. This included a generous sum of money to retire with. He also explained that although she would receive a good wage for her continued service, she would be bound by her duties.

'This promise I ask you to make, is not to be taken lightly' he said. 'It will affect your whole life, and also that of your husband, should you decide to marry.'

Margaret inwardly scorned the idea of marriage. She was nineteen years old and enjoyed her free time far too much. Admittedly she liked some of the lads at the tavern but they were mostly just worthy of some taunting when they'd had too much ale. Life for Margaret had been up until now generally happy and carefree, she was fair in word and deed, and didn't stand for any nonsense from anybody. This was a great chance for her, an honour, she felt suddenly more grown up and responsible. No wonder her mother had insisted she should come, she must have known something about it all along.

After nearly three hours of conversation whilst thunder rumbled out at sea, and many more instructions and promises, Margaret took possession of the keys to the house.

'I will leave you, Margaret, with an "Always", a "Never", and a "Finally" said Daniel DeLara.

'Always remember that nothing is what it seems, not even time itself. People are scared of the things they do not understand and they label them as witchcraft, magic and the like, in order to hide their fears and ignorance.

'Never trust anyone who wants you to believe in something for the sake of it. Truth can only be established with proof and therefore does not require belief. Blind belief is for the lazy and the weak minded. Also, notice how many beliefs require the payment of money.

'Finally. Look after the cat. There will always be a cat, only one. They have many more than nine lives you know' he said with a twinkle in his eye.

'Mr. Daniel, Sir?'

'Yes?'

'Oh, er, it's nothing, nothing at all' she said.

It would have been rude to ask him, so the question of how he could be eighty six and also old enough to remember the Great Judgement over a hundred years ago would have to remain a mystery. It was time to say a final goodbye. They shook hands and then broke formality and gave each other a warm hug. She could feel him watching her as she walked to the gate, but when she turned for a final wave, the front door had silently closed. She tied a scarf over her rich dark hair to stop it blowing around in the breeze and set off over the haven bridge for home.

That was the last time she ever saw Daniel DeLara, the man who lived at Amber Lodge. That night she went down to the Lion and Lamb to celebrate with her friends. They made her wear an ashtray on her head as a crown, and tried, and failed, to get her to buy everyone a drink 'Seein' as how you're a lady of means now!' The singing and merriment went on late into the night and when she left, Margaret was feeling quite tipsy and very happy. A terse comment from a passer-by however, sobered her light and merry thoughts. It was better not to answer so she just leaned on the railings for a while to steady herself.

In the master bed-chamber of Amber Lodge, Daniel DeLara had one final check around before turning out the light and standing in the turret window. He stared out for several minutes at the moonlit roofs, the church towers and the warehouses on Havenside. *I shall miss this so much* he thought, *'tis so beautiful and yet, there is so much ugliness in the minds of so many people. So much fear. So much suspicion.*

At last he turned away and removed all his clothes. Then he picked up a basket and said goodbye to the cat before walking slowly towards the bedroom wall just as the clock of St Leonards struck twelve. As he reached it, he could hear more clocks joining in, St Katherines, St Michaels. As his feet became lighter, the sound faded away for the last time, along with all sense of time and space.

Amber Lodge was empty.

Margaret looked over the waters of the haven towards it and wondered, just for a moment, what it was that suddenly unsettled her. It looked just the same as always, she was sure that he couldn't have gone yet, but somehow, an intense feeling of emptiness washed through her mind like an ocean wave.

Reality had once again shifted, not much, but it had definitely shifted. The only person who noticed it at first was Margaret and even she did not recognise it for what it was. To her, things had changed but that was the end of the matter. He had gone and she was being very well paid to maintain Amber Lodge until the next owner arrived. How she would know the new owner was a mystery. All he had said was that she would "Know". All she knew now was that a promise was a promise and that she would try to keep it in full.

Over a period of many summers and many winters, the small shift in reality was noticed by many people. None of them saw it for what it was though, and none of them thought any more of it. As far as people were concerned, Amber Lodge was just a grand old house by the sea. Perhaps the old man who lived there had died, nobody knew, nobody asked, and over the years the house settled into a kind of equilibrium.

Time changes many things. Reality changes with time and the past becomes a series of memories which move and settle down until they fit comfortably with the present.

Margaret viewed her memories while she cleaned and dusted. In her mind, the elderly gentleman had become a professor and had loved cats. Over the years, she unconsciously made small changes to each room as odd items needed replacement, cups and saucers, plates, the rug in the hall, each one almost unnoticeable but when viewed as a whole, it was obvious that time had allowed Margaret's memories to change things to how she thought they should have been.

Reality had prepared Amber Lodge for its new owner.

Chapter 2 - The move

August last year,
Ealing,
London,
England.

James Hadleigh poured another cup of coffee from the percolator while the TV chatted to itself in the corner of the kitchen of his apartment.

This was moving day.

The idea of moving from Ealing had until recently been just a daydream for James, but a call from out of the blue had suddenly changed the dream into a reality. He had been at work when he received a phone call from his family to say that a firm of solicitors had made contact, asking specifically for him. The firm would not give details but they made it quite clear that they had news for him which would be to his advantage, and that they would even be prepared to travel to London to meet him.

Simon Perry, the man who had knocked at his door a few evenings later was full of apologies for being late, James thought he looked more like a used car salesman than a solicitor with his dark, dandruff covered suit, tight shirt collar and shaving rash. Mr. Perry explained that as a junior partner, he had been given the task of tracing James after some documents had come to light.

Apparently, some years ago, one of the original partners had died suddenly and unexpectedly. All his work at the time, was thought to have been transferred and completed successfully. Since then, the business had moved on without incident until recently when a filing clerk had noticed something odd.

A payment for routine maintenance on a house in the village of Ashwell Green in Suffolk had been made every month for many years and nobody had ever questioned it. She showed it to her boss and an investigation was started. Soon afterwards some documents were found hidden in the attic above the offices which were related, although rather obscurely, to James.

Now that they had traced him, they could lay the matter to rest and had great pleasure in being able to bequeath to him the house and an eye watering sum of money.

There were some unusual conditions in the bequest, one of them being that it couldn't be sold until he had lived there for at least two years. Mr Perry said that it was possible to get around that one if James wanted to, but that he should see the house first before making any hasty decisions.

James had been absolutely incredulous at first, then suspicious and then, after being assured several times by Mr Perry that everything was definitely in order and that there had been no mistake, he started to relax and allow himself to be excited. His life would change considerably and that, he thought, could only be a good thing.

He was fed up with the daily grind. The journey to work until now had been to walk to Ealing Broadway tube station and wait for the train, exit at Tottenham Court Road and walk in the crush to the small TV production company where he worked. He had been looking for a house but the whole process was so depressing, even outside London the prices were ridiculous. Now he found himself thrown into a life of possibilities and chances he'd never even considered before, it was as if he'd won the Lottery.

It was all so sudden. Only a couple of weeks ago he'd been wondering if he could afford to go out and also manage to pay his rent. Now he had a new house in the country and more than enough money to live the rest of his life in luxury.

The abrupt change to his fortunes however, also caused him some distress. He found himself thinking about it all the time, even at night. He woke up at four in the morning on several occasions with worries going round and round in his head, most of which were guilt. There were the dreams too, really vivid ones in which the landscape and sky constantly changed around his new house and grounds while they themselves remained exactly the same.

These dreams disturbed him because they stirred an uneasy wisp of memory from his early childhood where he used to lay in bed wondering if all the things he could no longer see were still actually there. It used to frighten him so much that he would sleep completely covered by the sheets so that he was safe from the unknown dark shapes which changed things during the night.

All in all, he didn't understand why he'd been left so much from someone he didn't know and he was sure that there had been a mistake. Surely the phone would ring and it would all be taken away just as quickly.

But the phone didn't ring. Instead he'd received papers to read through and sign. Lots of them. Eventually he came round to an acceptance of the situation although he still could not bring himself to touch any of the money. It still didn't seem right somehow.

So this was moving day. He was to leave the flat and move lock stock and barrel to the country. He took a swig of coffee and stared round at the nearly empty kitchen wondering what surprises life would throw at him next. There had to be some surprises, no one could stay the same under such circumstances. Whether they would be welcome or not, he would just have to wait and see.

A knock at the door jolted him out of his thoughts.

'James?' came a voice from outside.

'I'm coming.' He pulled himself up from the chair and answered the door.

'Wow! You're dressed already, you must be keen!' said his friend, Phil.

'Hi, Short Arse' grinned James. 'I see you're annoyingly bright for this time in the morning. Oh God, does this time really exist? - Grab a coffee and then we'll get the remains of this stuff packed up.'

They started packing the remaining books into boxes and then put them with all the other packed items. Then they turned their attention to the book cases themselves, undoing bolts and separating shelves to make them easier to get down the stairs. When James could finally face the prospect, they unplugged the percolator, washed it out and packed it with all the other last minute items.

'God, you've got a lot of junk!' said Phil as they sat waiting for the removal van to arrive.

They came at nine thirty and started loading James' home life into the back of the van while James carried out a final check in case he'd left anything.

'They will take at least a couple of hours to get from here to the turn off from the M11' James said to Phil as they left. 'Why don't I drop the keys of this place off to the estate agent and then call in and see if Emma is still O.K. for tonight?'

'Good idea, I'll meet you there.'

They parted and James made his way into town. The letting agent was ready for him, and with a few pleasantries and a handshake, he left and set off towards Emma's flat across town.

Emma, like Phil, was one of James's closest friends, they had all met as students and had formed a strong bond through playing together in a rock band. Emma had been the PVC clad, flame-haired lead singer and Phil had been the sound engineer.

James had played keyboards with them and he'd thoroughly enjoyed getting dressed up and thrashing chords out on a cheap, secondhand synth at gigs.

Things were so different now for all of them. Emma had moved on to become a rather studious archaeologist, the only clues to her recent past being a rebellious streak of red in her otherwise naturally brown hair and of course, her taste in music. Phil hadn't changed much except maybe for the little goatee beard which he now had. He was extremely intelligent and very intense, and these days taught physics at the local Academy or "School" as he still insisted on calling it.

James pressed the door buzzer and a crackly greeting came out of the metal grille in the wall followed by a rough buzzing sound as the latch was activated. He pushed the door open and went up the stairs to where Emma and Phil greeted him.

'So... Today is the big day!' she said as they all entered her flat.

'Yeah, there's no going back now' he said, jangling a set of keys in front of them.

'Are you still coming up tonight with Phil for a house-warming?'

'Oh yes! I wouldn't miss the house-warming party.'

'It's not really a party' said James 'it's just the three of us and a pizza and some beers.'

'Yeah but it's in your new house and it's exciting. I certainly wouldn't miss it, and anyway, you need to christen it properly.'

They chatted for a while over a coffee, checking directions and drawing route maps. Phil tried programming the route into his sat nav and was annoyed to find that it wouldn't accept the address and he too had to resort to paper.

James left them soon afterwards and hammered his old Renault north to catch up with the removal van. The M11 was busy at first but the traffic thinned out once he got past Stansted. He turned off at junction nine and headed along the A11 passing Newmarket and Bury St Edmunds until he reached the turning which would take him towards his new home village. The road wound its way through Elmswell and past sign posts to Badwell Ash and Great Ashfield until he found the only lane which led into, and out of, the village of Ashwell Green, where he found the removal van.

He sat behind it for a mile or so until the lane widened out and then he let them know he was there. They slowed and waved him past so that he could lead them to the house. He just managed to squeeze the car through the available gap, and with the wheels skimming the verge, he exhaled with relief as he pulled away past the van towards the next bend.

As he reached it, an ancient red hatchback hurtled into view and bullied it's way past in a cloud of exhaust smoke and dust. How he missed it he didn't know. Everything blurred for a moment and all he could remember of it afterwards was the thud, thud, thud, of a boom box and some pratt in a hoodie giving him the finger as he flashed past.

The removal men were also a bit shaken. They too, had to brake suddenly and were worried that their load may have been damaged. They made their way carefully behind James through the village, which was no more than a street of thirty or so houses, a pub, a converted victorian school and a rusting, green, corrugated iron village hall.

At the end of the village he turned into the gates of his new home and waited while the removal men parked and opened up the van. It didn't take long to unload everything, all his posessions seemed suddenly to be very small against the vast space of his new home. He stood back and surveyed the scene before him, trying to imagine it all as his own.

Chapter 3 - Ripples

The Grange was an elegant grey brick house with a slate roof and nine tall sash-cord windows spaced evenly around the front door, one directly above and four in a square on each side. It stood in at least two acres of ground and was screened from the lane by a high wall on top of which were sharp pointed spikes.

The garden was almost cut off from the outside world, mostly laid to lawn with overgrown but not completely unmanaged shrubberies and trees. A gravel drive swept round from the entrance gates to the house, widening out to pass each side of a fountain, dry and covered with ivy, and then on to the exit gates. A wisteria growing over the iron porch and up the wall had been kept trimmed enough to keep it from reaching out across the windows.

The inside of the house was bright and had an air of freshness about it once the shutters had been opened, even though it had apparently been empty for years. The high ceilinged rooms on the ground floor were each at least the size of his London flat and were still furnished, albeit slightly eccentrically.

On one side of the entrance hall was an oak panelled library complete with wheeled steps to reach the upper shelves. James lifted a dust cover to reveal a grand piano with a Moog 3C modular synthesiser standing on top of it. Another cover hid a floor-standing globe and some old scientific instruments which he did not recognise.

The room on the other side of the entrance hall had obviously once been used for entertaining. It was comfortably furnished but unlike the library, had no personal character. This room begged to be used and James immediately decided to put the TV and the games consoles in there and start to turn it into a useful living room.

One of the nicest rooms though, was the master bedroom, it had a warm atmosphere and felt fresh and inviting. The afternoon sun made the whole room glow and as if to add the perfect finishing touch, a golden ripple of reflected light played on the ceiling just above the bed.

There were some unusual things in the house too. A grandfather clock in the hall which had a twenty four hour face with a single hand pointing down at midnight or up at mid day, crudely mimicking the path of the sun. There were separate hands on smaller faces for showing minutes and seconds, the phase of the moon and also the day, date and year. Also a couple of dials with strange symbols which he didn't understand at all.

A motorbike stood at the back of the hall with a drip tray underneath it to protect the floor. James examined it and found that it was completely road worthy and taxed. Not long afterwards, a rather sheepish local man knocked at the door and announced himself as the maintenance man and gardener. He explained that the bike was his and he didn't think he would be doing any harm by keeping it there. James was lost for words and watched rather weakly as it was hurriedly wheeled outside, started and then ridden hurriedly away.

He spent the rest of the afternoon unpacking boxes, removing dust sheets and generally trying to settle in, making a mental note to change and strengthen the locks as soon as he could. He would also have to sort out the ancient plumbing in the bathroom, especially the illegal looking gas water heater which sat directly over the bath. The same would have to be done in the kitchen and scullery but apart from that, the rest of the house was in pretty good condition.

Later on, Phil and Emma arrived together with a couple of six packs, some whisky and a bottle of wine. James eagerly took them on a tour of the house and gardens, pointing out some of the unusual things he'd found in it.

Cooking was interesting. The oven was a nineteen fifties flagship model in cream enamel with big red and chrome dials on a panel which would have looked more at home as a vintage American car dashboard. It still worked though, and after a trial run in which windows and doors were hastily opened to get rid of the smell of burning dust, they managed to heat some pizzas to perfection.

They chose to eat in the smaller, brighter, more

intimate atmosphere of the kitchen rather than in the dining room, sharing the pizza slices around and keeping their glasses well topped up.

'Any chance I can catch the football results?' asked Phil, noticing that James had already installed his kitchen TV on a worktop.

'Of course' said James and handed him the remote.

The results seemed to take an age for Emma and James who weren't interested but Phil sat with rapt attention shouting at the screen. After the results, came the local news and they sat and watched a tractor being removed from a railway line and a story about a girl who had been reported missing. A snapshot was shown of her at a bowling alley with a group of friends whose faces were blurred out.

'Thirteen year old Isla Williams was last seen leaving school on Wednesday afternoon at just after three thirty' said the presenter. 'She is approximately four feet ten inches tall with light brown hair and was last seen wearing her school uniform and carrying a pink backpack'.

'They'll be looking for that backpack in a few days if she's not found' said Phil.

They sat and talked over the kitchen table for a while before retiring to the living room with a bottle of wine to watch a film. James watched most of it but he could hardly keep his eyes open by the end. It had been a very long and exhausting day. He apologised and said good night, leaving the other two to carry on talking together as he made his way gratefully upstairs.

He opened a bedroom window and took a deep breath of the fresh night air. A veil of thin cloud drifted across the sky and covered the moon, giving the landscape an eerie, shadowless appearance. He undressed with the light off, enjoying the sensation of the crisp, fresh night air on his body for a while before climbing between the sheets.

Somewhere in the distant night air an owl hooted and a gentle breeze rustled the leaves of a nearby tree. The clouds moved away and the moon-light burst through the window, reflecting watery ripples onto the ceiling. The effect was beautiful and he lay watching it for several minutes before falling into a deep and peaceful sleep.

The next morning James awoke early and went downstairs to put some coffee on for his guests. He unlocked the kitchen door and wandered out into the garden to look at the house while the percolator plopped and spat. Dew was burning off the grass al-ready, it was going to be a beautiful day.

As he walked round towards the front of the house, he started to imagine how the fountain would look after a clean up and how he could trim the foliage on the wrought iron porch without spoil-ing it. He looked at where a phone line entered the corner of the building and idly followed its path back to a pole in the lane when a thought struck him.

The reflections in his room last night did not seem right somehow. A puddle would ripple very quickly in a breeze and then, in a calm moment, become still like a mirror. The reflections on his bedroom ceiling were slow and constant. Water would have to be quite deep and wide to create a slow wavy pattern like the one last night.

Emma appeared, holding a coffee and stood with him.

'It's amazing' she said.

'Yeah, I still can't believe it's all mine... Did you sleep O.K.?'

'Yes, fine... Hello, pussycat, where did you come from?'

She reached down and stroked a black cat which had suddenly appeared. It politely put up with the fuss for a few moments before going over to James and insisting in the way that cats do, that he should fuss it too. 'Farm cat, probably' he said, as it purred and nuzzled around his ankles.

They drank in the view, and the coffee, in silence for a few moments.

'Did you look out of your window last night?' asked Emma. 'I did for a long time. You could almost see in colour. The moon was been so bright!'

'Yeah, I could see the farm and everything' said James. 'I left the windows and curtains open all night.'

'You are going to change those curtains aren't you James? Because they are a bit old.'

As Emma's voice went on about curtains and things, James's thoughts went back to his room. He had seen a reflection which was like a slow wave motion on his ceiling but the moon had been shining onto dry ground. It didn't make any sense.

'A soft shade of green might look nice in there if you don't mind it, James... James?'

'Oh... Yeah, I think that would be good. Shall we get some more coffee?' They wandered back to the kitchen with the cat following. Emma gave it some water and then took a coffee up to Phil.

After breakfast Phil helped James reassemble some of the flat packed furniture and move it into position while Emma insisted on sorting out the kitchen. By the time they had finished it was late morning so they decided to try the local pub for some lunch before Phil and Emma left for London. James had taken some time off work to get settled in and he was eager to get started.

They said their goodbyes at the pub and James walked back along the lane making mental notes of where to put things and what jobs needed doing first, when his mind wandered back to the ripples.

He went up to the bedroom and looked around. Everything looked normal. He crossed to a window and looked out into the glare of the early afternoon light. Nothing from the farm would have caused the effect because there wasn't a pond or anything to reflect the moonlight, and even if there were, the moon would have had to be virtually on the horizon to reflect it into his room. There were no rivers or streams close enough, in fact nothing but fields, hedges, grass and trees.

He lay on the bed and waited for his eyes to adjust to the softer light indoors. The room definitely had a warm pleasant atmosphere and he allowed himself to slip into a relaxed, almost dreamy state. Closing his eyes heightened his other senses and he heard a bee pass the open window and the sounds of the birds outside. If he allowed it he could easily fall asleep, but there was so much to do.

Reluctantly he opened his eyes again. Above him on the ceiling was the rippling reflection. It was very subtle, and in a slightly different place. He got up to examine it but it seemed to fade away almost to nothing.

As he continued to watch, it seemed to grow slightly stronger again so he stood on the bed and studied it more closely. It was getting stronger by the minute now, and James could see clearly the many pairs of hypnotic jewels of light moving in equal and opposite directions along the ripples, just like a reflection of sunlight on water.

Dust in the air was now glowing as it floated through rays of golden light which were also becoming noticeable. He stepped down onto the floor and put his hand into the light rays to see if it cast a shadow and recoiled immediately. It felt of nothing, no sensation at all. He sat on the bed and felt his hand as if to check that it was still really there.

He couldn't understand why he wasn't scared. The room felt just as warm and peaceful as it had done earlier. The light had spread out now and was more of a warm subtle ambience. Maybe it was like that yesterday when he first noticed the atmosphere in the room. James got the impression that it had been trying to get his attention, and now that it had, it was trying not to scare him.

He stood up and held out his hand, and very slowly, he reached out towards it. His body started to feel lighter as the light grew more intense around him and carried him forward, away from all that he knew and understood.

Chapter 4 - A girl and a letter

In Amber Lodge, Dunwiche, at precisely that same moment a girl appeared, lying on the floor of the grand bed-chamber. The girl was dressed in "Nonnye" clothes which obviously weren't her own, an old white tee shirt, worn out jeans and a pair of socks, all much too large for her small frame.

She stirred and muttered something incomprehensible as if waking up from a deep sleep. After a few moments of staring vacantly up at the ceiling, she pushed herself up with the palms of her hands to a half lying half sitting position and stared around.

The room was large and rectangular except for an open circular area which extended out from one corner into part of a turret. A huge carved stone fireplace stood on one of the plain walls and an ancient, faded tapestry hung opposite.

Dark, heavy oak furniture dominated the room. A massive wardrobe, blackened with age stood adjacent to a mountainous bed with an ornately carved wooden canopy. A huge, full length, arched mirror stood over near the window, canopied in the same style but with the addition of brass candle holders on each side. The thick mirrored glass had been silvered so long ago that it too, had become blackened and crazed in places. A blanket box stood on the wooden floor boards at the end of the bed, decorated with engraved panels depicting hunting scenes, fishing vessels and a blank coat of arms. All the wood had warped and split over the last few hundred years but like everything else in the room, it was cleaned and polished as if in constant use.

With some effort, the girl managed to stand up. The jeans slipped down her legs and she stepped out of them taking a couple of faltering steps to find her balance. She stared at the ancient tapestry, noticing an area where there was no pattern, just a faint discolouration as if some of the thread had lost its colour completely over the years. Then, carefully, she made her way over to the turret windows where she clung to the stone casement for support, and while holding her hand up to shield her eyes from the afternoon sun, she looked out.

To the right, was a large area of sheltered water where some fishing boats had been pulled up along the shore beside a line of black tarred huts which stood on rickety stilts. To the left was a lighthouse and the sea. Below her, the gardens of the house sloped gently down towards a high wall and a pair of wrought iron entrance gates. Beyond them, a track ran along beside a channel from the open sea through to the area of sheltered water and a wooden lifting bridge offered access to a quay side opposite.

As she raised her eyes to look further, she caught a glimpse of her reflection in the window and gave a gasp as self awareness hit her for the very first time. Remembering the mirror, she went to it immediately to see what she looked like.

Her first impression was of looking at a stranger, but it was definitely her own reflection standing before her in the giant mirror, now wearing only the tee shirt and one sock. She had a mass of dishevelled golden white hair, so long that she could pull the outstretched ends far enough to meet around her waist. Her eyes were pools of liquid blue and her skin was the pale biscuit colour of a fine porcelain doll and absolutely flawless. *I look about sixteen,* she thought. *How do I know that? I wonder who I am.*

She pulled some facial expressions and stuck her tongue out at her reflection as if to try to find an emotion but there was none, her face simply returned to a blank normality each time. All the things which map the history of someone's life on their face were missing: anger, fear, happiness, laughter, love, hate, excitement or frustration, none of these emotions had ever touched her.

The hollow and distant sound of a door being unlocked disturbed her thoughts and she listened as the sounds of occupation drifted into the house. Various muffled clanks and knocks disguised any meaningful conversation but she could make out the occasional words. '- garden needs weeding and the - - while I check the bed chambers.'

A door closed somewhere below and footsteps echoed across a stone floor, changing to a softer clump as they came up the stairs. Moments later a key turned in the lock of the bedroom door and the girl watched in wide eyed blankness as a large woman with a pink face and a flowery head scarf and apron appeared.

‘Oh hello - err - sorry’ she said, and shut the door again very quickly. After a few seconds the door opened again and the woman entered once more looking a little less flustered.

‘Well!’ she said ‘Here’s a turn up for the books and no mistake. My name is Mrs Larkin dear... And what’s yours?’

‘I do not know’ said the girl. ‘Do you know my name?’

‘Blessed if I don’t dear, but it don’t matter for now. Why don't you come down stairs and have a nice cup of tea? I’ve just put the kettle on.’

She led the way down to the kitchen and pulled a chair from under the table motioning the girl to sit while she made a large pot of tea. ‘Are you hungry?’ she said, removing the lid of a cake tin and thrusting a knife into it. ‘When did you last eat?’ She placed a large slice of cake and a steaming mug of tea in front of her.

Margaret Larkin also cut a slice of cake for herself and sat opposite the girl. ‘I suppose you woz cold last night in that room all by yourself . How did you get in there anyway?’

‘I do not know’ said the girl.

‘Yes but you must’ve got in there or you couldn’t have come out, could you?’

‘I know only of the present’ said the girl. She

stared into Mrs Larkin's eyes, reading her thoughts and intentions as if they were on public display. Mrs Larkin was testing her, she seemed excited and also quite anxious underneath the friendly smile, and her questions, although innocent enough, were asked with an underlying purpose.

'Who's Ralph Lauren then, dear?'

'I do not know.'

'Well you've got his name on your', she paused 'that under-shirt thing, whatever it is that you're wearing, is he a friend of yours?'

'I do not know. All I remember is being in the room and the blue trousers fell down, they are too big, like this shirt. Then you came.'

Mrs Larkin was suddenly tingling with excitement and although she kept calm on the outside, every nerve in her body felt as if it had been given a small jolt. The cat was purring loudly and rubbing against the girl's leg, and as she reached down, it jumped up and nuzzled against her before contentedly sitting on her lap.

'Well I never did!' exclaimed Mrs Larkin 'That cat won't go near anybody but me. Never has, but it surely likes you, sure as eggs is eggs.'

'What is its name?'

'I don't know dear, just "Cat", well that's what I calls her anyway.' Her expression changed to a frown 'I'd better take some tea out to my husband, dear, he's in the garden doin' some weeding.'

'Bert' she whispered excitedly as she reached him 'We've got a visitor, I found her locked in the master's bed-chamber and you know what that means! She could be the one we've been waiting for all these years. She don't know her name but she makes sense when she talks, *and* the cat likes her!'

'Well I never' said Bert taking his cap off and scratching his head 'd'ya want me to come in?'

'No, dear, she int properly dressed and what she *has* got on is Nonnye clothes. I'd better see to her for now. I'm going to give her the test and if she passes it then she'll probably be the one we've been keeping house for all these years. If she don't pass it, then we'll call for the parish constables.'

In the kitchen, the girl was examining the cups and saucers on the dresser. 'They are pretty.' she said as Mrs Larkin came in. 'That's all right, Dear, they are. You can look as much as you like. In fact, while you're looking at things, you might as well read this. You can read, can you, Dear?'

'I think so.'

She handed an envelope to the girl which contained a piece of note paper, the girl sat at the table and studied it carefully.

Dear Sir, Madam, Young Master or Young Miss,

If all has happened as I muste hope it will, then you are in safe handes. My trusted housekeeper Margaret will helpe you with anythyng you neede so please do not hesitate to ask.

You maye not yet be aware of who you are or whye you are here but these things maye become apparente to you over a period of time, however, there are some things that you muste do now. At Once.

There is a persone in another place who woulde like to knowe about you. Write a letter to them on the back of this paper and tell them about yourselfe .

On your owne, take the letter to the place where you first remember existyng and look for a softe golden light, it maye take you some time to finde but it will help if you can place yourselfe where you had your first thoughts.

Carrye the letter with you and walk towardes the light. Do not be scared, it will not hurt you.

Margaret will help you with the letter if neede be.

Yours sincerelye
Daniel De Lara.

After a few moments, the girl handed the letter back to Mrs Larkin to read, who stroked her chin and frowned as she read the page.

'Can you write, dear?'

'Yes. I think so.'

'Do you know the other person mentioned in the letter?'

'No. Do you?'

'No, dear. 'Tis not for me to know. I don't know how I'm supposed to help you but if I can, then I will. The first thing you're going to need is a pen.'

She went to the study and took a pen and pad from the desk. At the moment Margaret was still being careful about what she showed the girl, things so far had fallen into place but the big test was yet to come and she knew that she must not take any chances. The less the girl saw, the more easily she could be caught out if she was lying. *Why would she lie though?* Margaret thought.

'Here' she said, carefully placing the pad and pen in front of the girl 'Lean on this, the table's a bit hard to write on.' The girl immediately adjusted the pad so that it was angled towards her left side and reached over for the pen with her left hand.

'Well, well. You're left-handed! I thought you might be.'

'Am I? I did not notice.'

'How can you not notice something like that, it looks all wrong. Muddle handed they calls it.'

' 'Tis not to me, I find it to be perfectly normal and not muddling at all.'

Mrs Larkin felt more strongly than ever that this young girl must be the one, the new owner of Amber Lodge, the special person whose appearance she had been waiting for all these years. All the signs were there, her appearance in the locked bed chamber, the golden-white hair like the professor had, and the blue eyes, the left-handedness and even the fact that the cat had taken to her so well. Now, if only she could pass the ultimate test and carry out the instructions in the letter it would prove beyond doubt that her instincts were right.

The girl looked up at her. 'Where is this place?' she asked.

'The house you're in, dear, is called Amber Lodge and it's on Kingsholme in the Royal City of Dunwiche in the countrye of Englande' said Mrs Larkin.

The girl started to write on the back of the letter and then asked 'What is the date for today?'

'Why, 'tis the seventh of August, did you not know?'

The girl did not respond but continued to write her letter.

'How old do you think I appear?' she asked

'Now that *is* a question if ever I heard one" said Mrs Larkin "I s'pose you might look about fifteen? - sixteen? I don't think no more than that, dear.'

The girl carried on writing while Mrs Larkin tidied away the tea things and washed up. After a few minutes she put the pen down and Mrs Larkin took her back upstairs to the bed chamber again.

'I won't be far away if you want me, dear' she said and shut the door, using the rattle of the catch to disguise the sound of the key being turned in the lock.

Mrs Larkin waited silently for several minutes outside the door and listened. After a while all went quiet inside the room and she found her hand trembling slightly as she turned the key once more and opened the door.

The room was empty, she checked under the bed, inside the wardrobe and even the blanket box, feeling rather foolish for doing so because she knew that the girl had disappeared. The room wasn't just empty as if someone had just left, it felt empty as if no-one had ever been there.

A small shift in reality had occurred again and this time, Margaret knew all about it. She now had another job to do and there was no time to lose.

Chapter 5 - The face in the mirror

James tried to work out what had happened. The last thing he could remember was putting his hand into the golden glow and being pulled away from what seemed like everything he knew and understood. Now, here he was, standing in the bedroom again almost as if nothing had happened at all. But something *was* different. He had been wearing all his clothes earlier but now he was holding his jeans and socks, neatly folded over his arm. He couldn't remember taking them off, in fact he couldn't remember anything he had done since touching the light.

He placed his clothes on the bed and wandered across the landing to the bathroom. Wiping his face with a hot flannel always helped to freshen his thoughts. As he studied himself in the mirror a fleeting impression flashed in his mind, it wasn't so much a memory as a feeling of deja-vu and it was so quick that he could hardly grasp it. Something about looking in a mirror and a girl's face.

He went back into the bedroom and put his jeans on and sat on the bed to think. At least an hour had passed between his entering the light and the present but he didn't miss it, he wasn't upset about not knowing his movements for the last hour or more.

Why wasn't he upset though? Why wasn't he worried about something so strange? He put his head in his hands and started to try to rationalise everything but he couldn't, nothing made sense. Then he noticed a piece of paper on the floor. He picked it up and read it.

Amber Lodge,
Kingsholme,
Dunwiche,
Englande.

7th daye of August

Dear Persone Unknowne,

I am a girl. I have long hair of a golden colour and blue eyes. I do not knowe if I have a name or an age but the ladye here thinks that I look sixteene or thereabouts.

If you knowe me, I am safe and well and the ladye gave me tea and cake. Her name is Mrs Larkin and she is verye nice.

Do you knowe mye name and mye age or in fact, anything aboute me?

Yours sincerelye.

James was astounded. He had another small flash of deja-vu about the mirror, and a girl's face reflected in it as if he were seeing what she saw through her own eyes and he heard her voice think the words "I look about sixteen".

He turned the letter over and read the other side. It was as confusing as it was revealing, the change of tense from past to future in the opening sentence, the spellings and the comments about the person not knowing who they were, suggested that Daniel De Lara, whoever he was, had some knowledge of what would happen in the future. Then there was the reference to someone in another place and also to a soft golden light. From the mention of the light he knew that somehow he was involved, but to what extent he had no idea. The light or glow or ripples or whatever they were, had drawn him into something from which he didn't feel he had the right to walk away, and this girl whoever she was, needed his help.

He made a decision to try to find out something about both her and this Daniel DeLara person, and went downstairs to put some coffee on. It could percolate while he set his oldest computer up and went online by modem as there was no broadband in the house yet.

After making a bodged connection to the old phone line, he carried out a painfully slow internet search. Using the name Daniel DeLara, he found several thousand results but none of them seemed to show up anything useful. He tried Dunwiche but nothing was relevant. The computer displayed the message "Did you mean Dunwich?" He clicked on it and the search trawled in hundreds of thousands of results and those at the top of the list were right on target.

With a supply of coffee now on hand, James entered some of the most relevant websites and started to read up on Dunwich. Apparently, what was left of it was situated on the coast of East Anglia near Southwold. It had been a city with much influence owing to a Royal charter which was granted in the year 1199, then, a hundred years later, a huge storm lashed the town and it fell into decline and since then it had mostly been washed into the sea. There were some pictures of the ruins of the Greyfriars Monastery and the few houses, museum and church which were, by the look of it, all that was left of the place.

The address puzzled James, apart from the odd way it had been written, he couldn't find anything much about Kingsholme. The only references to it were as a shingle bank which had been washed away hundreds of years ago. Doubts started to enter his mind again and he started to ponder on the possibilities once more. Had he fallen asleep on the bed and dreamt it? No. He had the letter beside him on the desk. It was written in real ink from a fountain pen, and on good quality paper. No ordinary person used paper of that quality these days. He felt fine, he wasn't feeling ill or anything like that. Somewhere at the back of his mind lurked the suspicion that this could be totally genuine.

He made a decision to write back to the girl and walk into the light once more so that he could give the letter to her in person and spend a bit of time finding out what the heck was going on. The reply however, was harder to compose than he thought and he eventually gave up trying to edit everything to make it sound sensible and just typed his feelings as they came to mind.

Dear girl in the letter,

I have sent you this just in case I don't get to meet you in person. Sorry but I don't know who you are or how old you are. This whole thing is a mystery to me so I searched the internet to see if I could find anything out about Daniel De Lara but I couldn't get anything useful.

Where abouts in Dunwich do you live? I found some sites that gave a lot of info about the town but most of it is just his tory and there is no mention of Kingsholme.

Actually, thinking about it, I wonder if you know what I'm talking about because some strange thoughts have been crossing my mind since I walked into a light like the one mentioned in your letter. Have you considered that we might be on different sides of it or something weird like that?

After all, both of us must have walked into that light at some point.

I feel a bit stupid typing this but just in case you don't know, the internet I mentioned above is a sort of world wide library of information which I can access through my computer (it's like a book with a keyboard). You are probably going to laugh if you know this stuff already.

By the way, my name is James. I also have blond hair and blue eyes, I am older than you by a few years and I've just moved to the country from London. I found the light in my new house and walked into it for the first time earlier today.

I must try to find out more about it.

Regards,

James Hadleigh.

He printed it off and read it through. It was a bit random in its content and rather poorly typed but he signed it anyway and put it in an envelope before going back upstairs to try once more to enter the light.

Chapter 6 - Self discovery

As soon as Margaret was sure the girl had really gone, she hurried out to buy some clothes for her. There was a shop in one of the many alley ways behind Havenside which sold used clothing for the seamans' mission which would be quite adequate for now. Time was of the essence because the girl might reappear at any moment.

When she got back to Amber Lodge, Bert was sitting in the kitchen and he listened sullenly as Margaret told him all about the girl.

'She speaks so lovely' gushed Margaret 'Not posh and certainly not Suffolk but, well, nice and proper, like a well brought up young miss ought to. I know you'll like her when you meet her 'cos she's just got that way about her... And her eyes! She's got the most beautiful eyes you ever did see! Blue they are, blue! There's some people round here as'll find that hard to live with, 'specially with the hair 'coz, well, when was the last time you ever saw anyone with golden hair and blue eyes? They used to say the professor had the same colour hair when he was younger, till it went just silver of course.'

'Yep all right, I got the lay of it!' snapped Bert.

He was suspicious of the girl. Everything had

happened so quickly and out of the blue that he hadn't had time to get used to the idea that things might change. The conversation may well have built up into an argument if it weren't for a slight noise which echoed through the house as a belt buckle hit a bare wooden floor board. They sat quietly for a moment and listened, 'I'd better go and take them clothes up to her' said Margaret quietly.

Upstairs, the girl stepped out of the jeans once more and smiled to herself at the new familiarity of it. She was holding a letter and was eager to see what it said so she sat on the bed and sliced it open with her finger nail and started to read.

Thousands of image flashes danced across her mind as the contents of the letter revealed themselves to her. A man being puzzled and washing his face. A bright, shiny picture of a ruined building with some writing and lots of small pictures with labels under them in a kind of frame. A green mug nearby, next to a flat box with rows of buttons with letters and numbers on them.

She put the letter down and went over to the mirror to examine her face. It wasn't for vanity, it was more to do with the fact that the mirror was the only way she had as yet, to help her to understand herself.

Questions were forming in her mind, some very basic questions. The mirror helped her to work out her thoughts by reflecting her newly forming facial expressions back at her so that she could read them. She knew that she was intelligent and could make sense of the world around her. She could read, write, count and probably do many other things of which she was not yet aware. But why?.. How?

She was only able to remember as far back as her first appearance and her memories were vivid because her mind was not cluttered by years of use. People are usually conditioned from birth by the unfolding history of their own lives and they form values from their own unique experiences. But she had never been born, she was only a few hours old if age were measured by the time a person existed in the physical world.

Margaret listened at the door for a moment but there was no sound. She knocked lightly.

'Are you alright, dear? Can I come in?'

'Yes. I am well, thank you. Please come in if you wish.'

The door opened and Margaret flowed in carrying an armful of clothes.

'I thought you might like to try these on' she said while perching on the edge of the bed. 'Is everything all right? 'Coz you were very quiet and I thought, well I just thought I'd come up and see that you woz all right.'

The girl tried on the clothes which were a reasonably good fit considering that Margaret had to guess her size. Margaret brushed her hair for her and then pinned it up saying that it would be cooler in the heat of the afternoon, then she finished off the whole effect with a triangular head scarf.

'There! You look pretty as a picture!' she said as

she showed the way to the mirror with a flourish, and with a few final tweaks and touches she stood back to admire her handiwork.

'What's the matter? Don't you like them?' she said as the girl stared at her reflection.

'I have seen no others to judge them by' said the girl.

'Well, they are a bit young looking for you but they're all I that could find while you woz gone.' Margaret smiled at her encouragingly 'I think you look very pretty in them though. They'll do for now, just 'til you can get some for yourself.' She paused as it occurred to her that the girl needed more than clothes. 'You need a name, dear, I can't just keep calling you "Dear". What about Mary or Deborah or maybe, Rachel?'

'I do not really think they sound right for me. What other names are there?'

'Well - there's lots. How about Helen or Sarah, Elizabeth, Catherine, Grace, Prudence, oh and there's Constance - Any of those suit you?'

'No, not really. I think that having a name must be more than just something for people to call you, it must be something which tells people who you are. I think I will know the right name when I hear it or think it.'

'Well you're a funny one and make no mistake. Most people have to take the name they were born with and like it or lump it. You'd better just pick one for now in case anyone asks, you can change it when you've found one that you like.'

They went downstairs to the kitchen where Bert was still nursing a mug of lukewarm tea. When he saw the girl he immediately snatched his cap off his head and stood up, fiddling with it like a schoolboy who had been summoned to meet the head.

'Bert, I'd like you to meet the young miss I told you about' said Margaret removing the cap from his grasp.

'Young miss' he mumbled, hanging his head.

'Hello Mr Larkin, 'tis a pleasure to meet you.'

He looked up at her just for an instant before riveting his gaze back to the floor.

Sensing his cringing discomfort, Margaret decided he'd be better on his own while he came to terms with everything. She suggested that a walk in the sunshine might be good for the girl.

'It'll do you good to feel the sun on you. There's a nice walk along the sea wall or the beach, else you could go across the bridge and walk along Havenside to the Park. Here, take this' she said pushing a five shilling note into the girl's hand as they walked to the front door 'and buy yourself a water ice.'

As they opened the door, a wall of stifling afternoon heat met them and Margaret shrank back into the hall. 'Whooh, 'tis hot!.. And don't worry about Mr Larkin he'll come around, he just needs time. Oh, and make sure you keep your head scarf on, it'll keep the heat off your head.'

When she returned to the relative cool of the kitchen Bert was standing at the window staring out at the back garden. She slipped her arm into his.

'What's on your mind then?'

'She in't nothin' but a little-ole mauther*' muttered Bert under his breath.

'She's much more'n that and you know it, Bert' said Margaret softly. 'You saw it in her, same as I did. And you felt it. I know you felt it.'

'I in't feeling nothin'. They're all goin'ta call her a Gildenhair, either that or a witch. All the troubles'll start again, you'll see!.. That'll all come back just like before. Tell me, what good can she do? She in't no more than just a little-ole slip of a thing. Just a little-ole mauther.'

'So why did you take your cap off to her like she was the lady of the house then? She's got something special about her. I *know* you felt it too. Anyway, they never left, the troubles I mean, they just got hidden, like the dust wot gets brushed under the carpet.

* Mauther is an old Suffolk word meaning a young girl.

Chapter 7 - The name in the wind

Havenside was part of the Dunwiche Quay, it was paved with cobbles and large stone slabs, some with rusty iron mooring rings set into them. A couple of slipways sloped down into the water and groups of noisy children were having lots of fun using them to run crab races.

The girl wandered along the quayside, past the black, clapboard sheds and warehouses, enjoying the heat of the late afternoon. She looked through the entrance of a boat chandlers which proclaimed itself to have "All you ever neede for sea fishyng and repairs". Part of it was a mission shop with souvenirs of Dunwiche in the window, most of which were made of small pieces of polished drift wood in the shape of a cross with a tiny plaque held on with a single nail. Each plaque read "Leste We Forget".

In an alley just off the quayside she found a sweet shop and just had to go inside. Once her eyes had adjusted to the relative gloom inside, she looked around at all the jars of swirly and stripy, magically coloured sweets on the shelves behind the lady at the counter.

'Anything catch your eye, Young Miss?'

'I am looking for something called a water ice.'

'Well ya won't see 'em up there, I keep the water ices out the back in the freezing room' she said in a broad Suffolk accent. 'What flavour d'ya want?'

She tapped a list on the counter and the girl chose Elderflower and Sweet Nettle.

While it was being fetched for her, a rather prim looking lady with two young children, a boy and a girl, came in and stood waiting patiently to be served. The boy had one wrist attached to a leather cuff on a short chain which was tethered to his belt, but the girl was free to move. She teased him by asking him to reach things and then playfully chastising him with 'Other Hand, Josh! Will you ever learn?' He stuttered badly as he tried to retaliate, his mother held a warning finger up to her grinning daughter, scolding her for annoying her brother's demons.

'Is 'at hot enough for ya?' the shop lady asked them on her return. 'I rec'n we'll heva storm agin tonight, the wind's dropped... There y'are, Young Miss'. She placed a small glass of green tinted ice and a tiny wooden spoon on the counter for the girl to take 'There's nine pennies for you if you bring the glass back... You must be boiled to a frazzle in that scarf on a day like this!' The girl agreed and untied it. She shook her hair out and swept it all back in a tumbling wave over her shoulders.

All conversation stopped and an awkward silence took its place. The shop lady fixed her face into an uncomfortable, forced smile. The woman customer sharply drew breath and gave the girl a hostile stare while holding a protective arm out in front of the two children.

The girl, realising that the hostility was somehow aimed at her, turned and walked to the door saying a polite ‘Thank you’ as she left.

Outside too, she could feel people watching her now. They didn’t openly stare, in fact they seemed to be avoiding her rather too much, but she knew that they were looking at her hair. At first, feeling self conscious, she put her head down and walked a little faster to get away from them but soon realised that it wouldn’t make any difference. Short of hiding her hair again there was nothing she could do about it. Anyway she thought, it was *her* hair, not theirs, there was nothing wrong with it and Mrs Larkin had said it looked lovely.

She stopped walking and straightened up, pulling her shoulders back and purposefully holding her head up in defiance of them. An elderly couple glanced at her and she said a friendly hello to them. They replied with a rather forced “Good Day” and a pained expression which suggested that they didn’t like being spoken to by strange young girls.

Hen Hill park was a very pleasant area of grass and shady trees which sloped gently down to the edge of the haven and the reed beds beyond. The girl sat on a bench in a secluded spot and watched the late afternoon scene unfold in front of her.

Near the reeds, a man in a rowing boat was busy attaching nets to a series of vertical wooden stakes in the water, his boat gently rocking as he shifted his weight around. A young girl was walking aimlessly along by the water's edge and a couple of older children were playing with a dog. They suddenly stopped their game when they saw the younger girl and shouted something rude at her about the way she was dressed. She made a gesture at them with her fingers.

The mother and two children from the sweet shop walked into view and the girl watched intently as they sat down near the waters edge. The mother took out a story book and started to read out loud to them. They sat in rapt attention, sharing glances and eagerly awaiting more from their mother who was dramatising the story with much melodramatic overacting. This was a loving family scene, the stiff hostility from earlier at the shop had completely evaporated and in its place was a tableau of relaxed happiness. The boy would sometimes try to pull his hand out of the leather cuff, and each time his mother would reach out to him and give him a sympathetic touch and a smile.

Suddenly things started to fall into place. *'Tis his left hand!* she thought. *They do not want him to use his left hand!* She thought once more of their shop encounter and realised that she had held the glass in her right hand so that she could use her left hand to free her hair and sweep it back... And another thing, her hair. Every single person she had seen so far, had far darker hair than her own. She had wondered why they stared at her in such a suspicious way! She suddenly realised that, like the younger girl by the water's edge, she was an outsider, someone to be feared.

The sky was slowly turning to a murky bluish grey colour. The sun, although still reasonably high, had dimmed to an ominous dirty yellow and the wind had dropped even more. The man on the boat having placed his nets, was now preparing to leave and one by one, people started to drift away from the park.

A small whisper of wind rustled the leaves of the trees making a "ffffFFFFFFFfffff" sound. The girl raised her head and listened to it with interest. Another tiny whisper of wind made the leaves of the bushes nearby rustle with a "shshshSHSHshshsh". Their heavily laden branches started to sway, slowly marking out figure of eights in the otherwise still air. She watched them and saw not only a pattern, but the resistive forces behind their movements. Other branches started to move in sympathy with the first ones, widening out the movement and absorbing the energy like the ripples on a pond.

Something stirred in the very deepest recesses of her subconscious. It was as if the pattern in the swaying branches had somehow unlocked a secret code and set a primal sequence into silent operation.

An understanding of it slowly began to rise and filter through to her conscious thoughts. One branch would cause another to sway and they would move in perfect harmony until yet another caught the movement and the whole process would continue to evolve. She could imagine all these sine wave movements reaching out as a kind of subsonic music which extended to the trees, the moon and the tides, the sun and the planets. Everything in nature was vibrating in one huge symphony.

The leaves rustled and made a sound once more.

“fffffFFFFFFFFffffffffffhhhhh”

‘Tell me’ the girl whispered back softly.

“FFFFffffffffHHHHHHHHHhhh”

‘Thank you.’ she said quietly.

The last whispers of the wind died away and, as the heat and humidity increased under the dull glow of the sun, she sat alone in the eerie stillness watching the colours slowly fade and blend into the grey half light.

Chapter 8 - Boxes and secrets

Evening was drawing in as Margaret spotted the girl walking back over the bridge and onto Havenside. Bert had gone home already because of the impending bad weather. She would join him later but, for now, there were things she had to do. She now knew that this young girl was the one she had been instructed to keep the house ready for all those years ago. All her earlier doubts had gone.

She followed the girl's progress along the quay and noticed that there was a difference in the way she carried herself. Gone was the blandness from earlier in the afternoon. She now held her head up in a confident, almost proud way. Her gait had changed too. When she first left the house, she had reminded Margaret of a young fawn, rather unsteady on its long legs but now she had a gentle and elegant swaying walk which counter-balanced the movement of her long hair perfectly.

'You've been gone a long time' she said brightly as the girl walked into the kitchen a few moments later. 'Did you have a good walk, dear?'

'Yes thank you. I found my name. It is Faye. I just listened to the wind and it whispered my name in the leaves... Why do people stare at my hair?'

She just threw the question in as if it was just an afterthought but the forceful, child-like innocence of her stare demanded an answer.

Margaret gave her a kind and sympathetic smile, the time had come to drop the veneer of dispassionate brightness. 'Sit down and we'll talk over a nice cup of tea, there's a lot of things you'll need to know.'

She poured tea for them both and then settled herself at the table.

'Some things I can tell you myself but most of what you need to know will come from things that were left for you. I don't know what they are 'cos I was given instructions to keep them secret until I was sure that the right person would see them. That person is you. This is your house now and it is my job to look after you as long as you have need of me.'

She paused to take a small sip of tea.

'You want to know why people stare at you? Well, you're different, different to all of us. The first thing people will notice is your hair. That's because there aren't many, if any people left now with hair as light as yours, not since the Great Day of Judgement. That was a bad time. The whole world was leading up to a great and terrible war, they teach about it in the schools and the churches.

The fact is, you look like someone from before that time. Your hair and your eyes are a different colour to almost anybody else's and that makes people nervous. They'll think you are brash and defiant. Some will think you're a witch and others will think you've got demons whispering in your ear.

The Judgement took millions to their doom one way or another. Not just here but everywhere, and when it was over, the people that was left behind had to make the best of things. They turned to the church for answers and the churches made sure that they gave them what they wanted to hear. Now, most people live in fear what God will do next.

We live in troubled times and it doesn't take much for people to start making up stories and panicking, especially with all the Nonnies being kept up at the priory.'

A silent, yellow flicker of lightning interrupted the dim remains of the evening light. The cat, who had been comfortably dozing on her blanket in the corner, got up, stretched and walked slowly out of the kitchen with an air which suggested she was entirely unafraid.

Margaret stood up and turned on the light. 'That's the last we'll see of her 'til after the storm. They're not stupid - cats.'

She motioned Faye to follow her to the study. 'I still don't like storms, even though I know as how I shouldn't be afraid of them. Lots of people cover all their mirrors and cutlery and hide in the basement or under the stairs but I won't do it now. I tried to watch one once but I really did get frightened then. So these days, I just sit quietly with Bert and wait to see 'em through, telling myself it is just electric like the professor said and there aren't really any storm demons - silly me.'

The study was generously proportioned. The old

leather chairs and panelled walls lined with books and papers gave it an air of learned coziness. Margaret led the way past the central octagonal table to an old trunk in the far corner.

'You'll need this' she said as she handed Faye a small sealed wooden box. Faye broke the paper seal and found inside, three numbered keys and some instructions.

'I've kept this box at my house all these years, hidden under the floor boards so as it couldn't be found.'

Faye read the instructions. 'It says that we have to turn the three keys together for the first time or the contents will be destroyed.'

They knelt down together and worked out where to insert each key. When they were sure that they had the correct combination, Faye counted down and they turned them in unison.

The lid raised slightly, and a hissing sound emanated from the trunk as fresh air from the room rushed to replace the vacuum within. Margaret wanted to leave at that point but Faye insisted that she should stay to find out what treasures the trunk contained, after all the years of patient wondering.

Gingerly, they raised the lid.

At first sight, the contents looked a bit disappointing, just some more books and assorted junk. Faye picked up a coloured cardboard folder and examined it, she thought it was a book at first but it held a thin black plastic disk with a small hole in the middle. The picture on the front of the folder showed some military gentlemen and a crowd of other people in bright garish colours standing behind a mass of flowers which spelled out the words "The Beatles". The spellings on the smaller print reminded Faye of James's letter and the odd way he spelt everything without many y's or e's. They had even spelt the word Beetles wrongly, she thought.

Next, she picked up a small flat plastic box with the words "Hewlett Packard" printed on it. The front of the box had a window below which were small numbered buttons and also some with mathematical symbols. She picked it up and pressed the buttons but nothing happened.

Margaret stood watching her, feeling as if she was intruding on what should have been a private moment. Faye sat cross legged on the floor, her small frame leaning towards the trunk, her hands touching and exploring the objects inside.

Another distant flicker jolted Margaret into action.

'I had better get off home soon, Bert will be wondering what's happened to me. Here, you'd better take these.'

She took a bunch of keys from her pocket and held them out.

'There is one more thing I must show you before I go. 'Tis the door to the turret room. You might never find it if you don't know of it.'

She showed Faye a section of book shelves near the window at the base of the turret and moved a piece of decorative trim under which was a key hole.

Once the key was turned, the section of book shelves smoothly slid back to reveal a stone staircase inside the wall.

'I don't go up there much, only to clean sometimes' said Margaret. 'The professor used to spend hours up there.' She looked out at the sky again 'I had better make my way home, you can come if you like, it doesn't seem right to leave you here all on your own.'

Faye politely declined the offer and saw Margaret to the door, promising to lock up behind her and to stay in a safe place should the storm come.

She returned to the trunk in the study and selected a letter and two books, she then closed the lid and secured it with one of the three keys. Grabbing the key box, she headed for the shelves which revealed the hidden stairs to the turret room, and after carefully closing them behind her, she climbed the stairs. Sixty four steps later, she pushed open a trap door and walked up the final few steps into a most amazing space.

Apart from the stone floor, the turret room was almost entirely glass. Eight metal frame pieces held the huge curved glass panes. They swept up and curved inwards to meet at a central crown some fifteen feet above the floor. They then continued to rise up to form a spire, topped with a weather vane which was connected to an indicator dial back down inside the room. The indicator was rigged to sound a bell of a different pitch for each compass point.

A comfy leather chair and a small round table

with a reading lamp on it sat on an old threadbare rug in the centre, and a desk with candlesticks and some carefully laid out scientific instruments stood to one side near a brass telescope on a wheeled stand. To Faye, it felt like being on top of the world.

She sat in the chair. It felt settled and old. She imagined Daniel DeLara sitting there reading, making his notes and watching the weather. This, she thought, was like the secret inner sanctum of the house, which was strange because it was actually completely open to view from across the water. She felt as if she were alone on top of a high rock, completely exposed to the forces of nature, but protected from them by the gleaming metalwork and glass shield which surrounded her.

Night had now fallen. The flickers of lightning on the horizon were becoming more frequent and were occasionally followed by a long low rumble. Faye felt a tingle of excitement run up her spine. The thought of a storm didn't worry her at all. In fact, she quite hoped the storm would come. There was something exciting in the atmosphere which she couldn't quite define, a kind of charge.

She opened and read the letter. This one was much more personal than the first, and it made her feel for the first time, as if she had really found her home. Daniel DeLara's words were so kind, it was as if he knew that she would be alone in the world. She clung to the thought of him. He was the only link to a past which she did not yet understand. She decided that her full name would be Faye DeLara, she would be the Granddaughter of Daniel DeLara and James would be her cousin, or so she would tell people. She thought about how he would feel when she wrote and told him of her day. To her, it seemed quite normal that he could be living on the other side of the light.

The books from the trunk were both about history. One of them had a cardboard cover, it was printed on cheap paper and all the spellings were the same as the ones James had used in his letter. She briefly flipped through it and looked at pictures of something called "The First World War". They were quite frightening but nowhere near as frightening as those of "The Second World War" a few pages on, where an illustration of a mushroom shaped cloud was shown rising above the burnt remains of a city.

This, she thought, *must be from where James comes from.* At the end of the book there were some pictures of impossibly tall buildings called Skyscrapers and a section on a possible future scenario where everybody would be happy as they travelled in brightly coloured motor carriages (the book called them "Cars").

The other book had an embossed leather cover and the pages were made of fine paper. It showed a history that she felt more familiar with along with several pictures of great historic land marks. This book was the book that she would take to James later so that he could read for himself about where she lived instead of relying on his "Net" whatever that was.

A bright flash made her jump up and rush to the handrail. Thunder boomed and rolled around giving her a huge thrill. She loved the sight and sound of it. A second flash raced across the sky, lighting up the clouds from within. The town was silent. Another flash, further away this time, cast all the church towers in silhouette against the clouds on the horizon. The lanterns along Havenside flicked off and then faded back to half power. Seconds later, all electricity failed. The darkness was almost complete, broken only by the glimmer of candle or gas light in a few windows somewhere across the water.

Another huge flash. Faye pulled back, dazzled. It was followed by a heavy thud and a long, ground shaking boom. She had been looking over towards Havenside, and just for a split second, the whole area had been lit up as bright as day. The image burned in her eyes, and as it faded, she realised that there was something unusual about it. A figure, had been caught and frozen in the flash. It had been running across the open ground near the inn, a large fat ugly shape of a man.

The darkness played tricks with her eyes and she saw him as a huge beast man, constantly evolving into new and horrible forms until the image faded into nothing more than blobs of green light. Slightly shaken, and feeling more than a little spooked, she assured herself that she was safe. Nobody could reach her in the turret, but just to be sure, she grabbed a heavy candlestick and kept glancing behind her every few seconds.

The storm raged on and jagged lightning forked all over the town. She soon forgot her fright and watched it in awe. Rain lashed the turret and the wind whipped against it maliciously from all directions, causing the indicator to spin wildly above her head, playing manic arpeggios as it did so.

Later, as the storm started to move away and the wind died down, a mist rose to fill the damp night air. The air was still warm and carried with it a fresh night time smell from the land and from the sea. Faye lit the candles and sat down to write a letter to James, stopping occasionally to watch and to listen to the night.

It had been a good first day of her existence, she thought, as later on, she undressed, picked up the letter and the history book and walked into the light.

Chapter 9 - Late night phone calls

It was well past midnight and James felt wonderfully elated having just stepped back into his room. His mind was full of feelings which completely overwhelmed anything he had ever felt before. He eagerly ripped open the envelope and started to read.

Somehow, although he had no actual memory of the time between his passing through the light and returning, he could relate to things which had happened to Faye as if he had felt them himself. A kind of empathy was starting to develop between them, an understanding of each other without the need or the means to actually meet. He had heard of twins who lived far apart and would know if the other twin were in pain or trouble. They would feel a pain in the same place or maybe have an overriding desire to phone their twin to make sure that everything was all right.

A sudden pang of emotion swelled within him. He fought it down and in his usual way tried to dismiss it, but it wouldn't go away. For the first time ever, he felt as if he had someone in his life who was so much more than just close to him. The thought nagged at him until he had to allow it to work itself through.

His adoptive Mum and Dad were great and he loved them dearly, he couldn't have asked for a better childhood although he didn't know it at the time. A few years ago he had quietly tried to find out where his "Real" parents were but all his enquiries had drawn a complete blank. Any documents he saw only revealed things he already knew such as his history from when he'd been found as a baby in a basket with a note, and that his birth mother had never been traced.

When he was in his early teens, the troubled young James would sometimes wonder what it must be like to have natural parents and a family which he could truly be a part of and call his own. That line of thought had been painful though, and after several months of heated and upsetting arguments with his parents, he had eventually come to realise that it would never resolve anything for him. He was an adopted child, and he could either deal with it and get on with his life or wallow in self-pity and blame it for every failure which befell him.

He had no idea where he came from or who he really was. In fact, after a while he came to realise that he could even take pride in being a bit of a mystery and that it could protect him from being hurt by taunts at school. It had worked really well for him and the hurt had eventually faded as he grew older.

He looked round at the room. The house was open, just as he had left it earlier in the day. Luckily there were no lights on to advertise the fact. He got dressed and then walked around checking in each room, shutting windows and generally making sure that everything was in order. The answer phone in the hall was flashing, he pressed the button and listened to the messages -

"Beep - You have - three - new - messages. Message one."

'Hi James, it's Emma, just letting you know we got back safely after getting lost trying to find the A11. Give me a call when you can, I s'pose you're up a ladder or something. Bye.'

"Beep - message two."

'Hi James, It's eight fifteen and I haven't heard from you yet, Hope you're O.K. Bye.'

"Beep - message three."

'Er James, it's only me again. I'm sure everything is O.K. but I haven't heard from you yet and it's now eleven at night. You know what I'm like... Give me a call when you can. Bye.'

"There are - no - more - new - messages."

He picked up the phone and dialed. Emma would worry until she heard from him. It was her nature. 'James!' croaked a sleepy voice 'For God's sake it's one o'clock in the morning and some of us have work tomorrow! Where have you been?'

'I know, I'm sorry, but I've had an amazing day - I found this - well, it doesn't matter now but, well, I think I've met someone who... Look, I don't know why I'm telling you all this but I can't help it. Maybe I shouldn't but it's so fantastic that I don't know how to describe it and -'

'James! slow down. I haven't got a clue what you're talking about and it's bloody late and you should have phoned earlier or waited 'til morning.'

She hung up.

James steadied his thoughts from the race they had been in, and started to calm down. Of course! What was he thinking? He must get a grip on himself and rationalise everything that had happened. He went and and poured himself a whisky, just a small one, and downed it in one gulp. Then he poured another. The phone rang and he snatched up the receiver guessing who it might be.

'James, I'm sorry I snapped at you just now, but you know how I get, and it's gone one o' clock and I was asleep.'

'That's O.K. I wasn't thinking at all, I just returned your messages without thinking of the time.'

'What was all that crap you were coming out with? I couldn't make sense of it and now it's keeping me awake.'

'I don't really know how to tell you, or even if I should, but I think something strange and rather wonderful has happened. I suppose I'd better explain somehow, now that I've started to blurt it out, but it might take a while and you don't sound awake enough to take it in right now. I think I need to work it out in my head and then try or you might think I'm a weirdo or something.'

'You *are* a weirdo but I'm used to that, everyone is. Just give me an idea so that I can get back to sleep.'

'O.K. but - yeah O.K. I think I've found someone, sort of like a - someone close. She's amazing and I want to try to meet her.'

'What? That doesn't make sense.'

'No. I feel as if she's more like a long lost sister or something. I feel close to her, it's as if we share something.'

'And you've never met her.'

'No. Not yet, but I want to, as soon as possible.'

'She didn't contact you on Insta or Facebook did she?'

'No! I don't take unknown friend requests, and if I did, I wouldn't get taken in by a few obvious posts. Look, everything is O.K. and I shouldn't have phoned you like that. I'm just full of energy and bouncing off the walls but I will calm down and let you know more. I owe it to you now that I've started to tell you. Is that all right?'

'Yes. That's all right' said Emma in a long suffering tone 'I'm used to your oddball ways by now. Good night. Get some sleep!'

James replaced the receiver, picked up his whisky and went through to the living room, absent-mindedly picking up the TV remote as he flopped onto a sofa. An old re-run of "Will and Grace" clicked into view. He watched them sorting out their time-frozen life issues on the screen, being surprised at the same old things, saying the same old punchlines, and all to a manic piano accompaniment.

He couldn't settle though. For once, his own life

seemed to be moving faster than theirs. His mind wandered back to the events of the day, and the feelings which dominated his whole being. He muted the sound and went to fetch the book which Faye had sent him.

He placed the book on the table and thought about the letter. The thunderstorm was obviously why he felt so elated, he had loved them for as long as he could remember.

His Mum had warned him as a child, to stay away from trees and open spaces but he had told her that storms were his friends and that one day, he would see inside the lightning. His Dad had told him very firmly not to tempt fate, but, if he really wanted to watch storms more closely he should sit in the car because it would act as a Faraday cage and he would be safe from a lightning strike. Later on he realised that his father had probably hoped he'd be scared enough on his own in the car, not to be so silly in future.

The silent TV had moved on and was now showing a summary of the news. James turned the sound back on and poured another whisky. The news reader looked tired underneath her professional glossy expression as she read the headlines from the autocue. He wondered why he'd noticed her tiredness and looked again at her eyes. A distinct impression of hurt and unease came from her as if she were coping with an unseen problem while doing her best to be professional in front of the camera.

As the news droned on to lesser stories, James

found himself drifting a bit, maybe he was over tired and the whisky had just helped to ease him out of his mind race, but suddenly, the the local news was on.

He made a conscious effort to watch it, as if defying the onset of sleep but it was no good. He hadn't got the energy to move any more and finally drifted into a deep sleep as the local news reader was giving a more detailed description of the missing Isla Williams.

Chapter 10 - A mysterious book

Late next morning, James, still on the sofa, woke as the jangling of the front doorbell filtered through to his consciousness. The postman had a parcel for him which wouldn't fit through the letter box and he had used this as an excuse to introduce himself to the new occupant of The Grange.

He told James that he was pleased to see the house being used after so long, although it didn't show all the usual signs of neglect due to Mike in the village who looked after it. There had been a rumour that it was owned by somebody rich who had never actually lived there but Mike always told people he didn't know anything about it. There was a pause for a moment as if he were hoping that James would tell him something more, but nothing was forthcoming.

James found his chat with the postman quite amusing. He was being checked out by the locals who obviously thought he was going to be someone important. Questions had been slipped in quite subtly by the postman but James was ready for local curiosity and fended them off with vague half answers.

They had heard that he came from London...

Had they seen him on TV?... Did he work in the city?... Of course he would be keeping Mike on, wouldn't he? It made sense, Mike was a good bloke... So, did he play any musical instruments?

James allowed himself a little fun with that question, he mentioned "Keyboards" and let slip a couple of famous band names in the same sentence without actually telling any untruths. The wheels of gossip would soon turn and fill in all the gaps, giving him a valid reason for having moved into such a big place on his own.

Local gossip though, was a bit of a double-edged sword, it was a good thing if somebody noticed that milk was collecting on a doorstep or that a light was still on through the day, but gossip could easily get out of control and *that* was the source of potential problems. He made a mental "Note to self" about locking the house, turning all lights out and making everything look normal before going through the light in future.

After a shower, a shave and some lunch of whatever was available from the fridge, he made himself busy by starting to pull the ivy away from the fountain. Later on in the afternoon, the people from the installation company arrived to set up the new extra fast broadband system so that he could work from home. After they had gone, he made a pot of tea and headed for the garden with the book which Faye had sent through to him.

He settled on the bench under the arbour and poured some tea. The cat appeared and jumped up beside him, nuzzling into his hand and pulling at his jeans with sharp claws.

'Hey, puss-cat. Careful with the claws if you don't mind' he said to it affectionately as he picked up the book. The cat ignored him and settled itself beside him while he read. The book was entitled "A Historye Of The Countrye of Englande"

James opened it carefully and examined the first few pages. Apart from a musty smell, it seemed to be in new condition. The writing style was very wearing on the concentration because of all the extra "E's" and "Y's" and he soon found himself skipping bits of it and then having to re-read.

The book had a whole section on "Dunwiche" which had received a royal charter from King John in the year 1199 and started to grow in prosperity and power. He skipped on to the next paragraph, this was interesting but it wasn't what he was looking for.

On New Years Eve 1287, a huge storm washed away some of the town. Many people were killed and there were several cliff slides.

This was more like it, the website he had found mentioned this too. He read on about the flooded areas, smashed ships in the Haven and how a group of merchants had tried to capitalise on the situation for their own gain. The chapter eventually described how law and order had been restored and the town had been rebuilt. With the sea breaches in Kingsholme repaired, and further help from the King, Dunwich managed to survive and prosper.

He surveyed the garden once more in order to give his eyes a rest from the text. So far, the history in Faye's reality was similar, or even the same as the story on the website he'd seen. He turned his attention back to the book, and looked through names and dates, looking for events and turning points for the town.

He soon found one. In January 1328 another huge storm struck the town and swept even more of it away. The sea had swept shingle and sand into the gap between Kingsholme and the town, effectively blocking off the port entrance and another whole section of the shore line had been lost. He read on about fighting between local towns and yet more rebuilding of Dunwiche, until he found the first fundamental difference between the book and the website.

The book described how the people of Dunwich had tried to remove the blockage from their port, and that the mariners had employed many men to dump rock and drive wooden piles into the beaches on the seaward side of Kingsholme to break up the power of the sea. Dunwich became known as "The Venice of Englande" due to the many waterways which were created to manage the shore line and keep the tides from causing such damage again. This was never mentioned on the website, in fact the website gave the impression that people allowed the town to drift into decline.

James poured more tea and sat back to think while watching the early evening sky. He mused about the fact that he had so easily defined his and

Faye's existences as being in two different realities, but try as he might, he couldn't think of a better way to understand the situation.

The phone rang. He jumped up and ran into the house to answer it.

'So, who's this young babe then?'

'She's not some young "Babe"!'

'So you say.' said Emma. 'You don't have to tell me if you don't want to but you have to admit, it does sound a bit iffy.'

'Look, I think it might be a good idea for me to tell you a bit about what I was saying last night, but not over the phone. Can you come up at the week-end?'

'I'm not sure, maybe... If not, I can make it the one after, are you sure you want me to tell me? I was so tired and grotty last night.'

'Yes, I want you to come. Please don't tell Phil about it though, he might take the piss or some-thing. You know what he's like. I just want to tell you at first.'

'O.K. I'll come if I can.'

'Great!.. Bye, Emms.'

He put the phone back down on its rest and went back outside to clear up, letting his mind drift about and freely explore wherever it wanted to go. Suddenly, he saw a flash of a girl standing by some water, a girl dressed in a grey school uniform. He quickly made the connection to the Anglia News reports of the missing girl, but surely, it was Faye who had seen her because the flash came from her thoughts.

He was starting to understand the nature of the flashes now. They had a very different feeling to normal flashes of memory because they weren't his own. He always felt as if he was seeing these things through Faye's eyes, and not only that, they conveyed her feelings and mood as well.

Puzzled, and not wanting to wait for the next news bulletin, he went into the library and searched online for some information. The Suffolk Police website had a clear head and shoulders image of her which he printed off and studied for a while. In his memory flash the girl had been ambling along by some water near other people who, James felt, were also familiar. He closed his eyes and tried to clarify the images in his mind but it didn't work, the flash had been too vague.

He sat in silence for a while, thinking yet again about the events of the weekend. So many things ran through his mind, the discovery of the wave-like reflections, or light as he called it now, the strange feeling of detachment when he entered it and the equally strange feeling of having seen through the eyes of someone else and experienced their feelings. He looked towards the hall and the stairs. Up there, was a pathway to another reality which seemed to have split off from his own at some point, and had created another route through history.

Chapter 11 - To and fro

As Margaret expected, Faye had disappeared again, this time however, the evidence of her existence remained. A knife and plate were out on the draining board in the kitchen, and upstairs, her clothes were draped over the bed with the cat regally stretched out in the middle of them.

On the previous evening at home during the storm, Margaret had lit a fire and burned three files full of of legal documents and, in accordance with the instructions of Daniel DeLara, she made absolutely sure that no trace of any of them remained. The file she kept was written so that it related to a junior female.

Now, she sat at the desk in the study of Amber Lodge with the only remaining set of documents. She checked carefully through each page and wrote the name "Faye DeLara" in every blank space. When it was done, she telephoned the solicitor and the bank manager on their own private lines at home.

Both men were now in their mid to late sixties but had known Daniel DeLara well, and both had helped him to construct the legal handover of Amber Lodge. They duly arrived at eleven o'clock the next morning, wearing their formal sombre black frock coats. Margaret showed them into the morning room and served them with tea as they read over the documents. Conversation was limited to pleasantries and comments on essential matters until the job was finished. Afterwards, all three shook hands warmly and a feeling of great relief swept over them all as they realised that a small but very important task had finally been completed and put to rest.

Over the next few days James and Faye passed through the light many times, and on each occasion, they learned more about each other and the nature of their co-existence. Faye quickly developed a stronger, more defined personality and with it, a sharp and wicked sense of humour. This showed in the notes they wrote to each other. Sometimes, Faye would test James by cheekily writing *Do not open until ye've reade mye thoughts* on the front of the note.

James would then have to write an embarrassing reply and Faye, on receiving it, would squeal with delight and have a fit of the giggles.

Many of the notes though, were about more serious things, such as the question of the missing girl, Faye remembered seeing her by the water and replied that she would keep a look out for her in future. She needed time to organise herself, and although it was fun to keep sending notes through to each other, there were far more serious things to be done.

They arranged that Faye would have a day to buy clothes for herself because the only ones she had were those that Margaret had given her. James in return, would use the Saturday to meet Emma. The rest of the time they would divide up as the need arose.

As for James, he didn't realise at first that the experience was changing him, he had a brighter outlook on life and looked forward to the new things that each day would bring. He also found himself able to see things in other people which he had never noticed before. Tiny, fleeting expressions seemed to speak to him almost as if they were spoken words, and it occurred to him for the first time in his life, just how much people could hide as they spoke.

With practice, the history book became easier to read and he soon found himself accepting the spellings without question. While on his own side of the light, he worked hard on the house and garden, explored some of the local area and managed to make acquaintance with some of his neighbours in the pub.

He had now come to form the distinct feeling that, somehow, while Faye existed, he ceased to exist in a physical sense, and that the same was true for her. He found whole thing a little uncomfortable because it clashed with his common sense approach to life and the world around him but it was a feeling based on his strange experiences so far with the light.

Until recently he'd been pretty sure that there was no such thing as luck, ghosts, fairies, parallel worlds, space aliens or the undefined "Energy" that all the mystical weirdos kept going on about. He tried to keep an open mind though, and he usually accepted things as unproven until they were proved to be true or false. He still wanted to find out more of the nature of the light and maybe, to travel all the way through it to the other side.

At first, he'd tried to find a reasonable explanation for it such as spores from a fungal growth which made him hallucinate, maybe from old paint or the wallpaper paste or something. Maybe a gas which collected in that area and knocked him out when he stood by the wall.

But it didn't explain the book or the notes and letters, they were physical proof that he'd been somewhere else, or at least that he had not been here.

Chapter 12 - Dunwiche market

Wednesday was market day in Dunwiche, it had been since it was changed from being held on Mondays in 1672. It was always considered a social event though, as much as it was a chance to trade. Faye walked through Havenside and then along past the houses on St Leonard's Street before turning right over one of the many narrow footbridges and into Duck Street.

The dazzling light of the morning sun reflected off the sea and gave the sky a silvery sheen which in turn, made the houses and the cobbles look clean and fresh as if they had just been washed. As the street opened out and crossed Cock Lane, she stopped to look in the window of "Owen and Daughter" an interesting looking hotchpotch of a shop. It was adjacent to a tumbledown yard with several outhouses, a fishing boat and a tough looking amphibious lorry and trailer.

The shop itself was in two parts, one selling men's waterproof clothing, fishing and hunting equipment while the other, separated by a heavy curtain, sold ladies clothing, jewellery and fancy oddments.

A man came through from a back room and

greeted her as she entered, he had a cheerful and engaging lilt to his voice, Faye immediately liked him.

'Hello, Young Miss, if you want anything just give me a call, mind you, my daughter's in so she would be better be able to help.'

'RHIANNON! COME DOWN, WILL YOU NOW? WE GOT A LADY CUSTOMER.'

A girl appeared at the foot of the stairs, she looked about the same age as Faye but she had a mane of jet black hair, dark but twinkly eyes and spoke with the same rhythmical lilt as her father. The two girls immediately liked each other.

After spending some time searching through the packed rails and shelves of clothes, Faye found a beautiful black bodice, embellished with lace and heavy embroidery. Rhiannon found some more of slightly different designs and colours and helped Faye to lace herself into them.

'You like black and the dark colours a bit much don' you?' said Rhiannon 'Mind, they suit you, I s'pose you've got to be careful about colours... This pewter colour and the dark red looks lovely against your skin.'

Faye said she would take one in every colour, and seeing the look on Rhiannon's face, felt she ought to explain her seemingly extravagant purchases so she made up a story of losing all her luggage on "the long journey" to come and live in Dunwiche.

'Oh' said Rhiannon grinning widely as they went back to look through the rails once more 'and I thought you just had more money than sense... but I'm very happy to sell to you.'

After much more searching Faye tried on a pair of flat suede boots which came right up to her knees, Rhiannon said that she had some and they were really comfortable. She also chose some long gloves and four skirts of different designs, adding at the last minute, a knitted bag with a shoulder strap. The two of them, loaded with armfuls of clothes made their way to the counter.

'I've seen someone like you before, Young Miss' said Mr Owen as he added up the total. 'When I was a child back in the Principality of Wales, only she was about forty-ish though, I would think. People called her a witch because of her wild mop of golden hair.'

He paused and gave her a meaningful look. 'You're always welcome here if you want to call. You know, when we came here it was hard to get to know people, us being outsiders, so you're welcome anytime.'

Faye thanked him politely and shared a grin with her new found friend, Rhiannon who offered to keep all her purchases behind the counter until she returned later from the market.

When she reached the market square, it was buzzing with activity. People were talking and laughing. Seagulls were trying to steal food from the trays of fish and boxes of produce behind the stalls and the stall holders were trying to shout their wares over the general din. People were generally a little wary of her and kept their eyes down as they passed, but the stall holders were polite and spoke to her cheerily even though she could see they were a little uneasy about her looks.

She found a stall selling lace from Nottingham. The quality was very good and she couldn't resist some fashionable gloves. Further on, she found another stall selling Lavenham wool and came away with a shawl, perfect for summer evenings.

After she'd seen the market she wandered down a side alley, away from the noise and bustle of the stalls for a while, and stopped at the window of a small but expensive looking shop, admiring the dresses which were on display. They were beautifully made and Faye immediately fell in love with them.

A monk passed and bowed his head slightly to her, she nodded back to him and then turned towards the little door of the shop and entered.

Inside, clusters of candles in wrought iron sconces cast a soft yellow glow over all the satin and the deep rich jewel colours of the silks and velvets. She wanted to try everything on there and then.

'You'll need to be measured first' Miss Madgwick, the proprietor told her 'then we can look through and see what suits you.'

As Faye was being measured, Miss Madgwick chatted away about nothing in particular, it made the customers feel more welcome and also relieved some of the loneliness of her day. This young, potential customer was well spoken and therefore obviously well-educated. Because of that, she thought, she was very possibly wealthy, even if she was a gildenhair.

Miss Madgwick considered herself to be a good judge of character so she risked a slightly more personal question.

'Do you know the monks from Greyfriars? I saw one of them acknowledge you as you came in. They're good people as far as I can see. They do a lot for the poor and needy, not like those "True Path" people! Now, I go to church of course, like we all do but -'

'Do you?' cut in Faye 'I have never been to a church.'

'Oh. Sorry, Young Miss! It is just that most folk are church-goers, and if they don't go they're made to feel so guilty about it. I must admit that some of my customers would notice if I didn't attend, and I don't want to lose them.'

With the measuring done, Faye selected and tried on some clothes while Miss Madgwick suggested ideas on how to complete the outfits.

'Of course, you will need to find some fine shoes' she said, looking down critically at what Faye was wearing. A shadow passed over her face as she recommended "A & C Leadpenny", the shoe shop on King Street. It happened completely unconsciously but Faye picked up on it.

'Oh 'tis nothing much really' she said reassuringly 'they're just a bit of an odd couple, husband and wife you see. He's a bit "oily" and full of flattery, a sort of weaselly type. And as for his wife, she doesn't say much to anybody, well not unless she thinks they're important and then she's as oily as he is. They have the only fine shoe shop in Dunwich, unless you want something for more everyday wear. 'Tis all I meant'

Faye was sure that it wasn't quite all, but pressed no further as the clothes that she had chosen were placed to one side.

'I will adjust these for you this afternoon and have them delivered before closing. Where are they to be delivered to?'

'Amber Lodge - 'tis over the bridge on Kingsholme. Thank you.'

'Oh yes, I know it... Hasn't it been empty for years?'

'Yes. My grandfather left it to me.'

Another fleeting expression clouded Miss Madgwicks' face at the mention of Amber Lodge. She leaned forward and took hold of Faye's hand.

'Maybe I shouldn't say this about another business, but you should be careful! They may be a bit "Off" with you, the Leadpennys. I don't agree with their views at all. They're high up members at the "True Path" and they have some funny ideas about people. I can see that you have a resemblance of your grandfather in you and what with the fact that you live in that house ... 'Tis the history of the place. I'm sorry, Young Miss, I don't mean to cause offence. I liked your grandfather, God bless his soul. You are so nice and I just don't want for you to be treated wrongly for who you are.'

Faye assured her that she would be careful and went back out into the sunlight and the fresh sea air feeling determined to find out who these people were and why they may not like her. It had been a very unpleasant feeling when she first removed the head scarf and found people staring, but she was starting to get used to it.

In a way, there was something quite satisfying about watching the reaction of people when they met her, because she would look them in the eye instead of trying to hide from their gaze, and in her mind, it became their problem, not hers.

Somewhere behind all these thoughts, she knew it was really just a way of dealing with the hurt that she felt, and her newly forming character was also seeing it as an injustice. She fully intended to make people justify themselves if they did show any signs of prejudice to her face.

Chapter 13 - Tobias

As she reached the market square again, Faye caught the smell of freshly baked bread wafting on the air, she headed over towards its source suddenly feeling hungry.

The bakery was an old and well established mixture of charity and business, an old red brick building with several domed, fiery ovens facing out into a courtyard. It was run by the monks from Greyfriars. No one was ever refused food and water, but those who could pay more, were asked to cover the cost of their purchases and to also make a small donation to the funds.

She sat at a table and looked around at the people seated nearby. Most of them were busy chatting or reading the Dunwiche Herald. A well dressed, superior looking man sitting at the next table looked back disdainfully at her for a moment. He was tall and thin and his voice was high and reedy when he spoke to the monk who was waiting on his table.

'I assume you will not be attending "That!" ' he hissed, waving his copy of the Herald towards Faye.

The monk said nothing and departed with an empty plate as the man reached for his walking cane and stood up. He looked down once more at Faye disapprovingly before turning on his heel.

One of the monks came over and poured some water from a pitcher.

'Young miss.' he said in a quiet calm voice 'All are welcome here. Do you wish to partake of food?'

Faye nodded and looked up into his eyes, he seemed embarrassed for her. She chose from a menu which was scratched out on the wall in chalk.

As she watched him rejoin the hustle and bustle to fetch her order, Faye noticed a rather handsome young monk who was taking a break from working at the bread oven. He was downing a large glass of water and wiping beads of sweat from his brow. As he turned round, they made eye contact for a moment, he flushed bright red and averted his eyes immediately.

Eventually, the older monk brought her food, it was delicious. A large fresh bread roll, still warm from the oven and oozing with butter and tender pieces of rabbit.

The young monk at the ovens stole an occasional glance at the girl when he thought he could get away with it. Something about her had caught his attention. He could see that she clearly stood out as a stranger amongst the local people and was not quite like anyone he'd ever seen before. She didn't even look like a Nonnye.

He wondered if maybe she knew something about where they came from, after all, she did share some similarities with some of them. He had been troubled for some time now by things which the Nonnyes in his care had been saying to him. They asked him about things he'd never heard of and they spoke of things and places which didn't exist. Most of the other brothers just thought they were deluded or still had muddled minds but recently, he had come to the conclusion that there was more to it. He would have to speak to her.

Realising that he was also quite attracted to her he muttered a prayer under his breath for forgiveness. If anyone realised it, he would have to report to Father Prior, and the others would tease him because he was so shy.

He started to huff and puff a bit to make himself look as if the heat was getting to him and then, hopefully he could convince Friar Gregory to let him go. The girl seemed to take ages and he started to worry about overacting, but eventually she left some money on the table and stood up, so he made his move.

'Friar Gregory... May I please be excused for a short while?'

'Oh - and why would that be?' the friar said sternly but with a twinkle in his eye. 'You don't normally suffer at the ovens.'

'I am suffering today. Please, just for a few minutes rest from the heat.'

'Could it be that you have seen temptation in the form of a young female perhaps? I saw your glances.'

'No!' He hung his head 'Rather yes, but not for

any temptation, Friar. I have a good reason… Please?'

'Tobias my boy, I was just making jest with you, off you go, I'm sure your reasons are honourable but mark my words, you'd better account well for it later.'

Tobias quickly pulled off his apron and made for the back door. He would have to get back round to the market square and hope to catch sight of the girl before she disappeared into a side street or somewhere else.

He skirted the front of the bakery and looked around, there was no sign of her so he dodged round an awning and ran between the stalls, frustrated at the many groups of people who were milling about everywhere, impeding his progress. When he was nearly at the south western corner of the market, he saw her hair shining in the sunlight. She was heading up by St Peter's towards the High Street.

He slowed to a more acceptable pace and walked along at a respectful distance, hoping that he would be able to talk to her without too many people being near. She walked along the High Street and turned into Kings Street, Tobias stopped to watch from the blacksmiths nearby, he was starting to panic and hoped desperately that she would keep moving.

She turned towards the door of the shoe shop. He had to move now, or give up the whole idea.

'Excuse me.'

As he said the words, time seemed to slow down, his heart started thumping and he could hear blood pounding in his ears. She was slowly turning her head back towards him, and as she did so, he could feel his legs turning to jelly and his face starting to flush. She directed her beautiful gaze at him and he froze completely under the spell of a pair of intensely clear ice blue eyes. He tried to speak but nothing came out but a kind of "Erh" noise.

She wasn't just looking at him, she was looking right into him. He was sure that she could see all his faults and weaknesses and he started to feel silly and inadequate. He was hot and sweaty from the ovens and his robe was covered in flour and soot.

Suddenly she broke the spell with a smile, he unfroze and at last, managed to speak.

'I - I'm sorry to bother you, young miss, but I think you may be able to help us.'

'Me? How?'

'I cannot speak of it now, but may I meet with you again this evening? I have free time after evening prayers. Is half past seven suitable? I have to go now... Please, it is important.'

'Where should I meet you?'

'Do you know Maison Dieu Lane?'

'I could find it.'

'There's a place where you can walk down to the waters edge and sit on a bench.'

'I will see you there.'

'Thank you. Thank you very much indeed.'

He excused himself and ran back to the bakery, relieved that he had managed to pluck up the courage to speak to her. The only thing he had to do now, was to tell Friar Gregory and seek permission.

Faye watched him as he ran off, he seemed to know that she could see into his soul and that was something that other people usually didn't notice at all. He was sensitive and kind and strong and... Why did she now have a fluttering feeling in her tummy?

Chapter 14 - A & C Leadpenny

Faye turned to peruse the shoes in the window, aware that she was being watched from within. A man and a woman were standing tautly, watching her from the back of the shop. She could feel tension radiating from them.

As she entered, the man burst into life and approached, hands waving as he weaved towards her. His wife stood like a perching raven behind a tall desk at the back of the shop and forced a mask of a smile.

'Ah... Young Miss! Now... Do we know our name?'

'What a strange question' she said, looking him in the eye, deciding that he wouldn't be aware at all if she looked deeper. 'My name is Miss De Lara.'

His face flickered at the formality of her reply but he snapped out of it and beamed at her in what he thought was an engaging way.

'Now, let me guess... The young miss is in need of some school shoes for the coming cold season - and Father and Mother will be along soon to assist?'

'No actually, I like the look of the sandals in the window, the ones in the corner at the back.' said Faye, pointing to a pair of very high wooden soled sandals, heavily embellished with dark glass jewels and metal tracery work.

'Ah those! They are, maybe, a little expensive for the young miss, they have come all the way from London.'

'May I try a pair, please?' she said, wishing that he would just call her young miss instead of 'The young miss' in that patronising tone.

His smile faded slightly and he inquired again, whether any parents would be following soon. When Faye replied that she had no parents but was well able to pay by herself, he glanced inquiringly at his wife, beamed once more with renewed vigour and played "guess the shoe size" before sending his wife to fetch a pair down from the shelves.

Faye found all this play acting very interesting because the raven was obviously the driving force in their relationship, but he kept certain areas of power for himself. He was the man, the proud owner of the shop, and his wife did his bidding, or so it seemed.

She brought a brown cardboard box over a few minutes later and smiled a smile of pure hatred at Faye who pretended not to notice.

'That will be all, my dear' said Leadpenny as she shot him a hostile glare from behind her still smiling face before returning to her desk.

He ushered Faye over to a seat by the window and placed a carpeted footrest before her, then, before she was aware of what was happening, he grabbed her ankle and lifted her foot onto the foot rest. She felt trapped because although his grip wasn't tight, it was rock solid.

He smiled up at her while he unfastened the buckle of her shoe and removed it, using small flourishing movements which also involved a little too much touching of her foot. She felt quite repulsed and tried to pull away as soon as his grip weakened. He let go and smiled again as if completely unaware of her discomfort while reaching for one of the new sandals, placing it on the footrest and motioning for her to try it on.

She slid her foot in, hoping he wouldn't make a grab for her again. He didn't, instead he reached down, took hold of the strap and buckled it around her ankle for her.

'Would the young miss like to try the other one?'

'Yes please' she said coldly, moving her other foot away from him and undoing the buckle herself.

He prepared the other sandal with the same flourish as before and waited for her to slide her foot into it. Once again he reached for the strap and secured it. This time however, as he finished, he caressed his hand over her foot while beaming up at her as if he was doing her a special service as a valued customer.

Faye recoiled and brushed away the feel of his hand before standing up and walking a few steps. She wanted them so much but didn't want to do business with the horrid little man. Inevitably though, the shoes won.

'I will take them' she said.

'Ah good! A wise choice the young miss makes.'

She took them off herself, being careful to keep

him at bay. He picked them up and placed them back in the box.

“Is there anything more I can assist the young miss with?” He inquired, beaming at her and rubbing his hands. Faye didn’t want to spend more time than she could help in the shop but the temptation was too great. She justified it by telling herself that if she bought more now, she wouldn’t have to go there again for a long time. She chose another pair of shoes and a pair of long pointed boots which were no where near as crippling as they looked.

Leadpenny beamed and lead her to the back of the shop for his wife to take payment. The raven sneered down at her.

‘The total is seventy five pounds, nine shillings and ninepence please - if you have that much money of course.’

Faye reached into her pocket and pulled out a one hundred pound note, which she purposely held up with her left hand.

‘Do you have change?’ she asked, allowing herself a little smile of triumph.

Mrs Leadpenny appeared to grow in stature, and with nostrils flaring, she tapped the wooden desk with a talon like finger nail. Faye, suddenly feeling out of her depth, obediently placed the note on the desk and watched as the tables were turned even further on her. The raven took a cotton glove from a drawer, put it on, and picked up the note as if it were diseased. She then put it in the till and counted out the change, placing it on the edge of the desk without looking at Faye once.

'And where shall they be delivered to?'

'I will take them with me, thank you' she said, picking up the boxes before they could be placed out of reach.

Mr Leadpenny, the weasel, was totally oblivious to the whole battle and ushered Faye out of the shop with more flourishes and one final wave before shutting the door.

Faye walked without thinking of where she was heading, tears were prickling from behind her eyes and she wanted to hide herself away. Images were fighting for space in her mind, complex images of hate, greed, lust and prejudice. Mr Leadpenny and his horrid hands, he genuinely hated what she was, but he also wanted to touch her. His mind was devious and guilt ridden, a dangerous combination which scared her. She didn't get a chance to see more of Mrs Leadpenny, and for the moment, didn't want to.

Chapter 15 - Gravestones

Eventually Faye found herself at the south gate of the city wall which was still known as the Palesdyke. A long time back in history it had merely been a dyke with a line of pointed wooden posts or "Palings" but later on, a high stone wall had been constructed along with the gilden and middle gates.

The gatehouse was made of stone, with battlements and slits for firing arrows. The wooden floors had fallen away hundreds of years ago.

Faye walked right up to it and looked beyond. Tall hedges and trees lined the road for several hundred yards, until it continued on its way across the heather and gorse of Dunwiche Heath towards Minsmere. She walked underneath the high arch in the stonework and out along the road until she reached a break in the hedge and a pair of wrought iron gates, behind which, flowers had been planted to spell out the words "Leste We Forget."

The gates were unlocked and as she went in, a blanket of silence slowly enveloped her as the outside world was screened off.

Row upon row of gravestones and memorials stretched before her, many of the rows were interrupted by long-deserted buildings which themselves, had memorial plaques on their walls. Every single gravestone and plaque had the same date inscribed on them. She walked on into the heart of the cemetery, reading inscriptions and staring at the buildings.

In the very centre was an open area with a raised stone table which had fresh flowers on it, she walked over and read the inscription on a wall behind it.

In this place,
we keepe the memorye of those
who vanyshed on the
Greate Daye Of Judgement.
A warnyng to those who woulde
tempte the wrath of Godde.

An engraving in the wall showed a giant, robed man with long, billowing hair, blowing a tiny image of a town away with his breath, while lightning bolts shot from his hands and made holes in the ground below, which people were falling through. She supposed the giant man must be called Godde, and wondered how such a fantasy picture could relate to the reality with which she was surrounded.

Something bad had happened here though, something huge and frightening and terrible. A silence of respect from every living thing hung in the air. Birds didn't sing, only the sound of the wind in the trees disturbed the quiet.

Still feeling hurt, she sat for a while to think. Margaret had said that these were troubled times and that some people saw her as if she were a ghost from before the Judgement. She thought about the Leadpennys and their treatment of her, and the handsome monk who asked her for help, but how could she help? And with what?

A small change in the wind moved the leaves, and for just one split-second, it looked as if they shimmered into fragments and then re-formed themselves. A woman with a dog came walking along the outer edge of the ruins. She had a coat on, which was odd because it was such a hot day and as Faye watched, she faded from view. It was puzzling more than anything. The woman was real, at least for a few moments and presumably, was now in some other place, still happily walking her dog.

Faye wasn't bothered by being alone in a cemetery. After all, dead people couldn't do you any harm, it was the living that needed to be watched. It dawned on her however, that if other people had seen similar strange apparitions, it may answer the question of why they looked at her with anything from fascination to fear. She stood up and gathered her boxes and bags, it was time to leave.

Margaret was in the dining room cleaning the silver cutlery when a heavily laden Faye walked through the front door. She put everything down in the hall and went through to her, picking up a cloth as she did so.

'So what did you buy, then?' asked Margaret as they stood and buffed knives together. She listened to a detailed account of the day's events, adding the occasional comment in the appropriate places. Faye didn't mention the cemetery, she had a feeling that the time wasn't right, and that if she waited, the answers would probably come to her when they were ready.

'Leadpenny's a lecherous old bugger!' said Margaret. 'Now don't you take any nonsense from him in future, not that you'll need to have that much to do with him for a good while. Anyway, let's finish up here and then you can show me what you bought before Bert gets back from his work.'

Faye blushed 'I did not mean to buy as much as I did.'

'Oh, that's pretty!' said Margaret as Faye held up a dress. 'I can see you looking pretty as a picture in that... What's in the small box?'

Faye opened the smallest of the boxes and held up a black velvet and lace bustier with satin ribbons, just as the door opened. Bert walked in and stared, first at the bustier, then at Margaret, and then he made a tutting noise.

'She's been clothes shopping, Bert. What do you think?' said Margaret, taking hold of the tiny bustier and posing teasingly with it herself.

'Load of frivolous nonsense, that's nothing but a bit of froth, wouldn't keep a flea warm. Load of frivolity in my opinion.'

Still muttering under his breath, he went outside again and disappeared into the garden shed. Margaret put her arm round Faye and gave her an encouraging hug.

'He don't mean it really, 'tis just his way. He was brought up with nothing and he don't like what he sees as waste - clothes are just for keeping you decent, or warm - well that's the way he sees it anyway. Mind you, he's right, 'tis a very expensive bit of nothing in particular.'

They gathered everything up and carried it all upstairs for Faye to arrange and hang. Margaret cast her eye around the room with a sense of satisfaction, it had the feel of use about it now, a sense of being owned. As they laid out all the clothes on the bed, she noticed something.

'You in't slept in your bed' she said with some surprise. 'Not even the once, and that's not a good thing. You need to dream my girl otherwise you'll suffer and get ill. Dreaming is what we all need to do, it refreshes your soul and makes you shine.'

'I feel fine and well, and not at all tired' Faye said watching the concern showing more on Margaret's face.

'Well... You mustn't let your Mr James do all your dreaming for you. You have to dream your own dreams, 'tis not something to be scared of, 'tis nice!.. Well, most of the time.'

'And when it is not?'

'Still far better than having dark thoughts and demons entering your head when you're awake! In dreams, you can face your demons and let them out, and if they get too frightening you'll always wake up and realise as how it was just a dream.'

'How must I do it?'

'You just fall asleep and it happens, you don't need to learn, and lots of times you don't even remember a dream, it just works its wonders while you sleep and you wake up feeling fresh and ready for the day.'

Chapter 16 - Maison Dieu Lane

It was about half past six when Faye left the house to meet Tobias, she wanted to be there early as she had a feeling that he may lose his nerve if he had to wait for her.

The humid early evening air carried the scent of the sea while the sun cast a bright shimmering haze over the waters of the haven. This was the time when people would take a stroll, perhaps with family or a loved one. Groups of people were talking or just gazing out over the water.

With plenty of time to spare, she slowed to an ambling pace through the park. The water here was calm because, although tidal, the energy from the open sea had been absorbed by the channel and the many gullies and inlets on the other side of the Haven. She sat by a tree near the waters edge for a while, just staring out and allowing her thoughts to wander until the delicate chime from the chapel of St. Francis announced that it was seven o'clock.

As she got up, she noticed a small, bright object on the ground. There was something about it that seemed out of place so she picked it up. It was a small box, transparent but not made of glass, with a bright green label which had "Tic Tac" printed in large letters on it. *James would know what this is,* she thought as she slipped the box into her bag.

Maison Dieu Lane followed the shoreline of the haven from Cock Hill to the northern end of the Palesdyke. Faye could see why Tobias had chosen it for a meeting, it was quiet and just a little off the beaten track. She soon found the place he had described, a short path through the bushes to the waters edge and a bench in a small clearing. She sat and waited.

Long before she heard him, a sensation like a small tingle down her spine told Faye that Tobias was near so she stood up and looked for him, pulling her shawl up over her bare arms to spare his blushes. This time he looked fresh and clean, he was wearing a newer robe and sandals and seemed to be much less nervous than he had been earlier, though he still blushed a little when Faye greeted him.

'I thought you may not choose to come' he said, 'much has happened since our meeting earlier. I was seen as I returned to my work and Father Prior himself requested to know about my absence but Friar Gregory -' he paused for breath '- had already heard my story and had intervened on my behalf so here I am.'

'Then shall we sit?' said Faye, smiling 'And you can catch your breath and tell *me* your story as well.'

She listened intently while Tobias told her all about the work of the monks with the "Nonnye" people. They had started to appear in very small numbers just after the Great Judgement. At first they had been welcomed as returnees who had managed to find a way back but it was clear that something was very wrong. They seemed to be damaged by their journey and unable to communicate or co-ordinate properly.

These appearances were happening everywhere, but most of the activity locally was centered around Dunwiche, which had also seen the most damage on that fateful day. As the years went by, people began to lose interest in them and the word "Nonnye" started to be used as a derogatory term.

Rumours started to build around them, some said that they had been punished by God for their sins and had escaped from hell, others claimed that they were set free as they had paid for their sins in full. The situation had divided the various faiths, and after calls from some of the more zealous preachers from several churches for them to be imprisoned or worse, the split had become permanent, spawning the birth of "The True Path To Salvation".

Throughout all these troubles, the local monks at Greyfriars had stood firmly by their own values and continued to offer help and comfort to all people whatever race, creed or colour. They took more and more of them in, doing everything they could to help them, hoping to find out who they were and where they came from.

Tobias, after being involved with several of them, had noticed some unusual but consistent patterns in the things they said and did. This had made him curious to the point where he had started some research of his own. While the others had dismissed the strange requests and behavior as just the workings of deranged minds, he had made notes and found recurring words and phrases common to most of them. Such words as iPad, Tescos, Web, Texting, Chips, and many more.

‘There are more of them appearing now, more than ever before, and they are becoming more strange' he continued. 'They look so different and say things which we don’t understand. We have a whole room full of objects which they have brought with them, sometimes they cling to them and hug them like a child does with a toy.’

‘Things like this?’ said Faye, reaching into her bag and producing the box.

‘Yes!.. I’ve seen one like this before but slightly different, an orange one, they usually carry some form of sweet. Where did you find it?’

‘By the water’s edge in Hen Hill park.’

Tobias suddenly looked alert and bright ‘We found a girl near there on Sunday. She was taken back and given a meal - which she did not like at all I may add - before the policemen came to take details of the event. Would you like to see the priory? Father Prior gave his permission for you to be allowed to visit for yourself as long as it does not disrupt the prayers and work of others.’

‘Yes, I would very much like to. That reminds me - why *did* you choose to ask me?’

‘Err - it is rather - difficult to explain’ he said, flushing bright red once more ‘It was really a feeling from inside, an unplanned thing. I looked at you while you were at the bakery and knew that I had to act. You are different from -'

Faye felt her cheeks suddenly burning and she cut him off.

'Yes, I know! Different from all of you! I keep hearing this from everyone and they all try to be so careful not to offend me!'

She calmed herself down 'I'm sorry, 'tis just that I've heard it so many times now, please forgive me and continue.'

Tobias composed himself once more. 'I suppose my reasoning was such that, if you wish to find a sailor, you should look for a man with a boat. And if you wish to find a coal merchant, you should look for a man covered in coal dust... When I saw you at the table -'

'Yes?' she said, waiting to see if he would actually give her a valid reason.

'I saw someone who had the same golden/white hair as a man who once lived here in Dunwiche. People still speak of him as a mystery and even though he has been gone for many years they still speak in hushed tones of his strange powers and his ungodly experiments. In an entirely odd way, I wished I could have met him as he must have had great knowledge.'

Chapter 17 - Greyfriars

Faye and Tobias walked in silence over the Bridge, past the end of St James street and up the hill towards Greyfriars. When they reached the main gates Tobias opened a small side door and they entered the grounds. Sheep were grazing in front of the priory house and several monks were going about their business with quiet diligence.

The priory house was an impressive building with an imposing crenelated facade facing out over the town and towards the sea. Tobias led Faye round to the back, past the refectory hall, the library and the chapel, towards a separate building they called the infirmary which was shielded from casual view by some carefully planted trees. They stopped outside and he warned her to be aware of her surroundings at all times, just in case one of the inmates tried to do anything they shouldn't.

They entered and Tobias drew back a curtain, leading the way down a stone corridor to the first of several stout looking oak doors. It opened into a room where a group of people were sitting at tables making the small wooden crosses which Faye had seen for sale in the shop on Havenside.

'We try to give them a purpose. These people are

able to learn to make simple objects which we sell to help pay for their care.'

Further down the corridor the air became more stale and carried the smell of dozens of people mixed with disinfectant and the occasional nastier odour.

'These are some of the more helpless ones. There are some who are even worse than this but we keep them separate for their own good. We cannot give them anything which they can hurt each other with, it seems cruel but they are a danger to themselves.'

'Where is the girl?' said Faye looking slightly uncomfortable.

'Come with me, she is in a much more settled state than the people here, and may regain much of her speech in time.'

They passed through a stout door and into another corridor. Tobias showed Faye into a small office and had a quiet word with the duty assistant, a large jovial man with a deep booming voice, before joining her. After a few moments the door opened and a the duty assistant ushered a frightened looking girl into the room. He motioned for her to sit and then took up a position by the door.

'This is the young miss they found on Sunday' said Tobias in a gentle voice. 'She is quiet most of the time but she does not like our food.'

The duty assistant gave a loud laugh and the girl looked worried. Faye looked at her with concern. 'Will she understand me?' She asked the duty assistant.

'If she does young miss, she won't show it, the

most we get from her is gibberish but she seems quite happy in her way.'

Faye sat in front of the girl and gained her attention.

'Hello' she said.

'Hellolo lo' the girl replied through a lop sided grin.

'Hello' Faye said once more.

'Hello lo lo LO LO LO - LO!'

'Do you know your name?'

'HELLO!'

Faye reached into her bag and found the little box.

'Would you like a sweet?' The girl made a grab for it.

'What is this?'

She held out the box to the girl. The duty assistant was about to exclaim out loud but Tobias held a finger up to silence him, the girl seemed to recognise the box and held out her hand eagerly for it.

'What is it?' asked Faye.

'Tac Tac TACK!'

Faye faced the girl squarely and looked deeply into her eyes for a few moments.

'She is just like us' she said 'but her soul is in such a great turmoil. She knows something of what has happened to herself but she cannot yet tell us of it. 'Tis as if her mind has been shaken up and muddled.'

Faye reached into her bag once more and unfolded some pieces of A4 paper.

'Who is this?'

The girls expression changed to a frown as she concentrated on the picture of herself which James had printed from the Suffolk Police website.

'It is you!'

'You.'

'No. You!'

'Me.'

She looked up at Faye, suddenly tired from the effort of trying to speak, her eyes told Faye that she was very frightened but that deep inside she understood that she was being helped. The two monks now stood together, both of them were astounded at the appearance of the picture.

After the duty assistant had taken the girl away, Faye asked Tobias if she could see the objects which the inmates had brought with them. He led her downstairs to some cold dark vaulted cellars with lines of shelves placed between the stone columns, they were full of all sorts of objects, all dated and catalogued.

She wandered around, looking at things at random. A black metal hat with A.R.P. painted on it was dated 1943 and had a brief description of where it was found, and by whom. Next to it was a frightening looking rubber mask with glass eye pieces and a long corrugated tube connected to a box. On another shelf, a packet with "Smiths Crisps" printed on it was dated 1967, and further along the same shelf, was a printed cardboard sleeve with a disk inside similar to the one in her trunk at home, but this one had a picture of a man sitting at a table with a black box with wires attached, and the words "Walter Carlos - Switched On Bach".

They moved on until they reached the newest shelf. There were only a few items on it so far, among them a small thin white box with a black screen, and a smooth, shiny block with “Samsung” printed on it. The block had a lid which flipped up to reveal some tiny buttons. Faye picked it up.

‘I have seen a device with tiny buttons like this before’ she said ‘I think it may be for doing sums. Do you know what it is for, Tobias?’

‘I confess I do not.’

‘And this?’ she said, holding up an old iPod.

‘This we think, is a small device to control a larger device’ said Tobias in a low voice ‘but it is all so very small, maybe for a child’s hand?

Faye turned and gave Tobias an expectant stare. ‘I know it is asking a great favour but, may I take this? I know somebody who may be able to tell me more about it.’

‘As long as you are quick to return it, there will be questions if anyone finds it missing, but hopefully nobody will come down here for a while.’

Faye slid the iPod into her bag and they went back to the stairs.

A deep, guttural voice stopped them in their tracks.

‘Oi!’ it boomed.

The sound shook the air and Faye gave Tobias a worried glance, he looked worried too and turned to her and whispered.

'I hoped he would not hear us. We call him "Mr Oi" because that is mostly what he shouts, I had better see what he wants. Would you like to wait here?'

'I would rather come with you.'

She followed him back through the cellars until they reached a heavily studded oak door secured with heavy bolts. Tobias looked through the bars and checked that all was well before inviting her to see. She stood on tiptoe and peered into the gloom.

'OI!' shouted a shape at the back of the cell.

'OI!'

As her eyes adjusted to the gloom, Faye could make out the form of a man, he wasn't that tall, but he made up for his lack of height with his build. His tattooed arms and legs were thick as tree trunks and his bald head grew wider from its dome down to his fat neck which bulged over his dirty shirt collar.

He stared back at her as if she was no more than a piece of dirt and as their eyes met she felt a chill start to creep through her bones.

A feeling of being in the presence of evil swept over her and a darkness started to close in all around. The colour drained from her face and her legs felt weak and wobbly, she turned away and tried to take a breath but it was too late, a rushing sound like water filled her ears and stars spangled behind her eyes as slowly, she slumped to the floor.

Tobias rushed to her aid and held her as she came round, she leaned her head forward and threw up.

'There, there' he said holding her gently 'We will find some water. Can you walk?'

'I think so.' she said, trying to control her wobbly limbs.

'Are you ill? What happened?'

'I don't know, everything went black.'

A low chuckle followed them as they made their way to the stairs and back out into the fresh air. He found her a seat at the edge of the lawn and went to find some water. By the time he returned, she had recovered slightly but still looked pale and rather drawn.

He waited patiently while she sipped from the glass. 'You get used to the situation with these people after a while but he is different. Maybe I should have stopped you from seeing him.'

'Don't try to blame yourself for my curiosity, Tobias, it was I who wanted to see, and in a strange way, 'tis a good thing that I did.'

She drank some more water and continued. 'I think you should be very careful down there. What I felt was -' She took a quavering breath and looked up at him, dark rings around her eyes lending gravity to her words. 'That vile creature down there that you grace with such an innocent name, is evil, and he knows everything that goes on around him.'

Tobias had the distinct feeling that Faye was hiding a deeper worry and it stirred up some hidden feelings within him, the kind of feelings which gripped the pit of his stomach and then gave it a subtle twist. He wished they had stayed hidden.

Faye would not be drawn further on what she had said, only repeating her warning that Mr Oi wasn't what he seemed and that nobody should discuss anything within his hearing.

They sat for some time together in silence, just staring into the distance while the sun slowly reached down towards the horizon, creating as it did so, a beautiful blend of pastel shades and ever-deepening evening colours across the sky. Eventually Faye decided it was time to make her way home. Tobias walked through the shadowy streets with her to make sure that all was well. It was dark by the time they reached Amber Lodge. She stood and watched his shapeless silhouette as it made its way back over the bridge, giving the dark area where he stood a final wave before finally shutting the front door.

As the latch clunked home, an empty silence descended over the house and settled over everything like a layer of invisible dust. She shivered at the thought of what she had seen and went to the study to write a letter to James, comforted by the pale yellow glow of the desk lamp. She was to spend her first night asleep in her own bed.

Chapter 18 - Dreams

Faye sank gently down into the ample mattress and lay for a while, staring at the billowing curtains in the turret window. The bed smelt of fresh linen and also lavender from a small bag hidden amongst the mountain of pillows. There would be no storm tonight. The stars were a myriad of bright silver pinpoints against the black sky and the air was fresher and somewhat cooler than usual. Faye found herself trapped into thinking about what she had seen in the eyes of the man the monks had so naively named Mr Oi. She was sure she could still taste the sick in her mouth even though she had eaten mint and then cleaned her teeth thoroughly later on.

Her mind kept circling around and around, going over and over the intense hatred and evil cruelty which had seemed to radiate from him. She wished so much that she had waited at the steps for Tobias instead of being so curious. Why was she so stupid?

She looked round the room yet again, just to reassure herself that she was safe and alone. The front door was bolted, the kitchen and scullery doors, the french windows were secure as were all the lockable internal doors. She had even placed marbles on the stairs, just in case an intruder tried to climb them. The only open windows were in her own bed chamber and they were not big enough for him to climb through even if he could find a way to scale the walls of the turret.

The circuit of thought started again. She had to break the cycle or she would drive herself mad and never get to discover sleep, so she tried to steer her mind elsewhere.

At first, she had found her short existence to be very easy, everything had been so clear in her mind and she had enjoyed so many simple pleasures, like walking in the warmth of the sun, the sound of the sea, and the thunderstorm. People had been interesting to watch in a detached way. They seemed distant as if she were watching them through a pane of glass. Things were different however, when it came to actually talking with them because they had views and opinions of their own which cast doubts over the clarity of her own thoughts.

She had the almost unique ability to view everything from a different perspective, it was just as if she could somehow look down on a situation and see it for what it really was, instead of what it appeared to be, and she, like James, had the distinct feeling that she ceased to exist while he existed.

Her thoughts became random and the more she tried to hold on to them, the more elusive they became until she eventually gave in and unknowingly drifted off to sleep.

Vague impressions started to drift into her

mind. Tobias appeared and her dream-self smiled as he turned and stared directly at her. He was both handsome and shy, a combination which she found very attractive. A soft warmth swept over her as she faced him and she immersed herself in it until the image started to change.

She now saw him plucking up the courage to speak to her and she realised that she was being horrible to him, taunting, teasing and having fun at his expense. She felt as if a weak poison had entered her blood, her smile faded and tear ran down her cheek. She turned and ran away over a hill which wasn't there a moment before.

Rhiannon came into view and they smiled at each other for a moment before her image started to drift and slowly evolve into a shoe covered in sparkling jewels, she was drawn to pretty things like a moth to a flame. The shoe faded and Margaret appeared, reprimanding her for her expensive indulgences. She felt guilty and wanted to hug her and apologise for it.

Suddenly she was entering an old boarded-up house which vanished and left her in a void. She could feel an impression welling up from the depths of the dark regions of her mind. It appeared at first as a black wisp of smoke which grew and writhed around in its own agony, thrashing and twisting wildly as it tried to take on a form. A sensation of cold fire started to burn in her blood, It gripped her muscles and made her clench and grind her teeth. The evolving form started to tower over her and peck viciously towards her before finally turning into an image of Mrs. Leadpenny as a raven, with her husband peeping out from behind her black form.

Faye trembled with fear. The whole scene started to become very intense and her fear was growing into hate. She found herself wanting to kill the raven and strangle the leering grin from the face of the pathetic little man who was still hiding behind it.

The huge bird sneered down at her for a moment before flying off, holding the weaselly form of Mr Leadpenny in its talons. He turned and leered sickeningly once more as they flew away, Faye thrust all her hate at them and watched, sobbing as they burst into flames and perished.

Suddenly, and still sobbing heartily, she was in her bed. She was so hot from the flames that the sheets were stuck to her body and the pillows were damp from her tears. She took a moment to regain some control over her sobs and tried to take stock of the situation.

The alarm clock was ticking loudly in the darkness and the fiery void had vanished. She reached over and switched on the bedside lamp for a moment to look at the time, it was half past three in the morning, several hours had passed and she could not place exactly where they had gone but as she lay back in the bed, everything slowly started to fall into place and she realised that she must have been asleep.

What a strange experience sleep was, she

thought. It was a bit like walking into the light because you couldn't remember the exact point of entry and didn't have any conscious memories of having been there. The dream was now a fading memory; she couldn't quite grasp the details of it any more. Margaret had been right, she had faced her fears in a safe place.

She got up and poured a glass of water from the decanter on the bedside table before going over to the turret window. The night air wafted in through the open windows, ruffling the curtains and playing with her hair until she felt calm and quite recovered. Outside, the sea made its usual muffled pounding noise but that was the only sound. All the lights were off in the town, everything was pitch black except for the stars, the distant lights of a vessel out at sea and the occasional flash of torchlight as the night-watch made their rounds.

The cat jumped up onto her lap and Faye sat stroking her for a while, staring out at the night sky.

''Tis so beautiful, Cat' she said 'The stars are so pretty, they are like bright jewels on a cloak of black velvet.' The cat nuzzled into her arm, purring loudly and kneading her with sharp claws until she gently detached them from her night clothes. 'You need a name, Cat. 'Tis time, I think.'

The cat lay across her arm and looked impassively back at her 'I will call you, Starlight. Do you like it?.. Then it is done. Your name shall be Starlight from now onwards, my beautiful.'

The cat just continued to lay and graciously accept more fuss while Faye let her mind wander into thinking about how it would be light in a couple of hours and how people would say that the sun had risen, rather than how the planet had turned. Surely people must know the - - well most of them anyway - to fit their own personal philosophies - maybe, that was why - ideas - not -

Her dream-self watched from the turret room as a dark storm grew around her, no flashes or thunder, just the threat of it. Clouds swirled, as did the room, until a sudden bright flash lit a close up of the face of a brutal-looking fat man skulking in the shadows on Havenside. The face of Mr. Oi faded through a series of grotesque distortions and she snapped awake.

It was light outside, the bridge was raised and the customs men were overseeing the passage of a fishing boat through to the haven. Hurriedly, she washed and dressed leaving the bed unmade and ran down to the study to add more to her letter before having breakfast and then entering the light.

Chapter 19 - A pub lunch with Emma

James was now desperately wishing that he hadn't mentioned anything to Emma on the phone. Of course Emma would be fine about it all and would listen to him without poking fun but he felt sure that she would have a hard time believing it. At least Phil wouldn't be there while he told her.

Damn! Why did he have to open his mouth? A sinking premonition swept over him and he looked at the phone just as it started to ring, he knew it was Emma.

She had inadvertently let slip to Phil that she was coming at the weekend and had felt awkward about it so she had invited him, would it be O.K? Luckily however, he had to catch up on some work and couldn't travel up with her in the morning so they would still have some time to talk.

It wasn't O.K. but how could James tell her after giving both of them an open invitation to visit any time? He'd arranged to meet her in the pub for lunch as he didn't want an awkward silence until the subject was raised. Anyway, she seemed to have stopped going on about some imaginary "Babe" now, which was a relief.

The fact that Faye had actually met with the girl from the news reports was incredible and James was fascinated by the idea. Somehow the girl must have passed through a hole in the very fabric of reality itself and ended up in Faye's world, but how did it happen? All the news reports had since moved on to show the girl's last known movements but there was nothing unusual that James could see in them. She had left school with friends and taken her normal route towards home. CCTV had captured them walking along a main road and a witness had even told them off for being noisy.

He busied himself by clearing up all the discarded coffee mugs before Emma saw them and did it for him. Then at midday he walked down to the pub and ordered a half of Abbot Ale while he waited for her.

The bar hummed with muted conversation and the clatter of cutlery. James sat and watched as the barmaid juggled pint-pulling with taking money, handling change and keeping at least three conversations going at once. When Emma finally arrived, they ordered lunch and settled themselves down in a quiet corner.

'I'm sorry about Phil' said Emma, obliquely making the first move towards the subject of Faye.

'That's O.K. I did say that you both have an open invitation to visit me so I can't complain. Anyway, it's nice to have the company. It's just that he's a bit of a piss-taker sometimes. I don't mind usually, but this is different, if you know what I mean.'

'Not really. What's so hard about telling us you've found a girl friend? Do you really like her or something - like - *really* like her?'

James' heart sank. Emma was still presuming a lot and wouldn't let it rest until she got everything out of him.

'O.K. Hold it.' he said firmly 'I can't tell you anything if you're going to keep pushing me all the time. All I will end up doing is saying no and trying to backtrack on everything. If you want to know, I'll tell you in my way. God! it's hard enough.'

'I'm sorry, I'll shut up then' said Emma indignantly, ' but I still don't see why it's so hard.'

They sat for a few moments in a silence which begged to be broken while James worked out how to start. He'd had it all worked out in his mind for days but of course, as soon as it came to the crunch, nothing went to plan.

'Do you think I'm sane?'

'What? Yes! Well - apart from being the usual nutcase we all know and love - as sane as the next person. Why?'

'Because you might not think so in a few minutes. I'm going to tell you some strange things and I need you to listen and hopefully believe me because it's all true.'

He told her about the light and the feeling of seeing into another persons life through their own eyes, about the letters and the flashes of the things that she had seen. His face became more and more animated as he poured out his feelings for Faye, feelings of having someone who was so close to him that they felt closer than a sister, or even a twin. Emma listened intently, her eyes searching his face for anything to help her to understand.

'You don't believe me, do you.'

'I believe - that you believe it.' she said carefully 'It's a bit hard to swallow, you might have to let me think about it for a while.'

'Do you still think I'm sane?'

Her hesitation told him all he needed to know. His heart sank as he saw her expression, it was the same one that people had on talk shows when the partner admitted to having an outrageous secret or habit. It was a look of concealed shock and dismay, masked with concern and a desperate bid to try to remain composed while trying to understand.

'So you - become her, then - when you go through this light thing?'

'No! Not at all. Oh God no! She's a completely different person. I only catch glimpses of things as if I'm seeing through her eyes. She lives in a place called Dunwich on the east coast, only it's a different Dunwich in another England in another place where they spell everything differently. Look, I can show you the book she sent through to me, and the letters. Please believe me!'

Emma's expression relaxed a little and James knew from it, that he had managed to at least buy some more time. The waitress, a Saturday girl, brought the food and smiled sweetly as she placed it in front of them while repeating her usual rehearsed phrases in a singsongy voice, such as “Would you like any dressings at all?” and "Enjoy your meal”. It broke the atmosphere nicely and they soon joined the rest of the bar in lunchtime small talk.

Later on, back at the house, Emma examined some of the less personal letters as if they were evidence in a court case. She took the book from him and sat in silence with it for ages, mostly reading from near the back where the accounts of recent history were very different to anything she knew.

‘What do you think, then?’ asked James.

‘I don't know... It's incredible’ she answered, shaking her head in disbelief. ‘I actually want to believe you but it's just impossible! But you've got the evidence to prove that it's not. I just don't know.’

‘Thanks for at least trying anyway.’

‘Do you think I would be able to see this light of yours?’

James looked uncomfortable, if either of them had been there when he first discovered what it was, he would have probably shown them both, but now, it was as if she had asked to see a personal and very private possession.

‘You don't have to’ she said, sensing his unease.

‘No, it's O.K. I just feel a bit “you know” about it.’

They went upstairs, Emma commenting that Phil was bound to arrive and get the wrong idea. They laughed uneasily at the thought and became overly serious as they entered James’s bedroom to compensate. He showed her the wall.

‘It happens here, I don't even look for it any

more, I just know it's here.'

'I can't see anything' said Emma, squinting at the wallpaper.

'Nor can I now, but I know it's here.'

'What happens if you want to decorate or something? Can you touch the wall or would you just fall through it?'

'No, I can touch any part of the room including the whole of the wall, it's just a case of focusing my mind to feel for the nothingness when I want to go through.'

She didn't ask him to try, something inside her was scared of seeing the actual proof and it was much safer to only believe in something rather than being confronted with a truth that she may not be able to handle. The book was quite proof enough for now.

'Will you tell Phil?' She asked.

'I don't know. Don't tell anyone else will you?'

'No. I promise.' She took his hand 'This is too important to you, I can see that. Anyway, I need time to get my head round it.

Chapter 20 - Inside the light

Phil arrived just after four thirty with a bottle of wine and the three of them went out to the garden and enjoyed it in the warmth of the afternoon sun. It was a luxurious and civilised way to spend an afternoon as Phil pointed out while leaning back and stretching idly.

Late afternoon drifted into early evening while they sat and talked. James though, felt detached. He knew that Emma was feeling the strain of what he had told her, he could see it on her face. It was unfair of him to load her with so much and then expect her to keep it a secret, but what else could he do? She would need someone to talk to, someone to share and offload the weight of it all, but who?

He looked at Phil. Women always said that he was such a "Typical bloke". He loved gadgets and sport. Things for Phil were either black or white, anything else was "Girlie". It was all bluff of course, people usually only saw the surface but underneath it all was an intelligent and articulate man, the sort of person who would fight to the end for what he believed in. A true man of honour. It would be difficult to broach the subject because of his habit of ridiculing pseudo-sciences and anything which couldn't be backed with hard scientific facts. He would place this in the same category as Religion, Astrology, Feng Shui and Crystal Healing.

Thoughts about the light itself also kept surfacing, James had a nagging feeling that he should go to it before he revealed any more. Eventually, he made an excuse and left the two of them in the garden for a while with the remains of the wine.

Once upstairs, he quietly locked the bedroom door behind him and undressed as usual before facing the light. This time, instead of passing straight through, he would explore the boundaries of it and hopefully find some answers. He hadn't thought about it until Emma had asked, but the light was actually invisible now, it seemed almost pointless to call it "The Light" because it no longer was, it didn't need to be seen because he now knew exactly how to feel for it with his mind.

He held out his hand and allowed the strange feeling of nothingness to close over his fingers and creep along towards his forearm. It was a little easier this time as he knew what to expect so he edged very slowly forwards until he felt the void fully envelop him.

It felt as if the ground were falling away from under his feet, as if somehow, he was becoming weightless as he walked over the edge of a cliff into an endless space. He stopped and turned to look back at the room; his naked body was standing before him as if waiting for him to call it to follow or maybe to fade out of existence until he returned.

As his soul moved a little further away from the images of earthly reality, they started to become more vague. Up, down, left, right, past and future, time and distance, in fact the whole feeling of being James was becoming a misty blur and the last thing he noticed before turning away, was the seconds hand of his bedside clock jumping forward.

Ahead, if it could be described as such, was the most beautiful sight he had ever seen. There was no detail to it, nothing on which to focus but an all enveloping light which seemed to radiate all colours and hues at once, even the darkest black was as blindingly intense as the brightest white.

The soul was still near enough to reality to keep a sense of perspective and it lingered for a while, sensing what else was around it. Then, as it started to journey back, space, time and physicality slowly began to return along with the feeling of being James.

As he stepped out and looked around the room, he noticed that the sun had moved quite a long way, the shadows were longer and the temperature had fallen by several degrees. Everything he was seeing and hearing at that moment surely should not have happened yet. He'd only been gone for a matter of minutes, if that but the the clock had moved over an hour forward. It dawned on him that he must now be out of step with his own time.

He sat on the bed deep in thought, studying all the things which were so familiar to him, they all looked the same as ever but somehow also seemed strangely detached. His questions about the light had indeed been answered but at a cost.

He could never return to the blissful ignorance of normal life and the beliefs and assumptions which went with it. He also had a strong gut feeling of having passed through that place before. Faye would have it too because he now could see that they shared the same soul.

He could remember the point when reality started to blur and the feeling of "Self" faded into a blend of images and experiences which he knew were not all his own. Wispy images now floated through his mind like the distant wash of someone else's memories.

A noise from outside jolted him out of his train of thought and prompted him into action. He threw his clothes back on and tidied himself up before going out to rejoin his friends.

'You were a long time' said Emma as he walked towards them.

'Yeah, sorry about that, I should have come back out sooner but I got bogged down in some stuff.'

He tried to join in the conversation again and pretend that everything was normal but he couldn't after what he had just seen. Emma, to a lesser extent was having the same kind of problem, he could see the tension showing on her face as she tried to make idle chat with Phil.

'I'm sorry' he said, not realising that he'd said it aloud.

'What for?' she asked.

'Oh - just what we were talking about earlier.'

'You look like you've got the troubles of the world on your shoulders, mate. Are you O.K.?' said Phil.

'Yes. Yes I'm fine.'

'You don't look it, it's not bad news is it?'

'No, honestly'. It was crunch time. 'It's not bad news but things have been happening to me recently' he broke off mid sentence. 'I'll be back in a minute.'

He stood up and went to fetch the book, realising that giving Phil the proof first was the only way to get through to him, otherwise he wouldn't listen to any of it.

'What do you make of this?' He handed it over and motioned Emma not to say anything.

'Why are you asking?' said Phil

'I just want to know what you make of it. It isn't a trick or anything.'

'You seen this, Emma?'

'Yes' she said looking inquiringly at James, unsure how much to say.

James held a finger up to his lips and watched as Phil examined the cover and then opened it at random. His face dropped its usual light-hearted expression and changed to one of study and interest while he turned the pages back and forth.

'How old do you think it is?' said James.

'Pretty old - no - look at the date, it's only 1990'

He started to examine everything again much more carefully and after several minutes, shut the book and looked at James in defeat.

'O.K. what is it? I give up.'

'Tell me what you think first.'

Phil looked frustrated for a moment before answering, he thought it might have been made for a film, but he couldn't work out why anyone would bother to go to the trouble to make up all the internal detail unless it was on camera as part of the plot.

'O.K. I give up.. So, what is it then?'

'A history book as far as I know.'

'Bollocks! Come on, where did you get it?'

'From someone in another England.'

Phil looked at him as if he had suddenly turned into the worlds' biggest idiot and then turned to Emma.

'Did he tell you the same or is this some wind-up?'

'Count me out of this' she said looking very uncomfortable indeed as she stood up and took her glass into the house, leaving the two men alone.

'It's not a wind-up, Phil.'

'Yeah well -'

'I can only tell you what I know. I don't just believe it, I actually *know* it's true, I brought it back myself. There's more than this to show you... God! I *knew* you would be like this!'

'Well, I never thought you of all people would fall for something like this.'

'It's not a case of falling for it, I *know* it's real.'

Phil didn't grace him with an answer as he stood up and walked off to find Emma. James knew that

Phil would try to talk her round to his way of thinking and he realised that the best way to handle the situation was to let him blow off some steam.

Muffled sounds of a heated discussion wafted from the house as Phil mouthed off about James and then tried to use scientific arguments to convince Emma that James was deluded. Emma seemed to be challenging him for some time before their voices subdued and they eventually came back out to the garden and sat rather awkwardly with James.

'I'm sorry, mate' said Phil after a while 'I shouldn't have caused all this bad feeling, it's just - showing me something like that - and you of all people!'

'Yeah, I know. I guessed how you would react but I didn't really have too many options. I told Emma earlier and she gave me the benefit of the doubt.'

'You know what, mate? I spend my life trying to get people to take notice of science and all most of them want to do is find some bloody crackpot theory to believe in. I thought all my friends were the same as me but -'

'I didn't make this up you know. I wouldn't believe it myself unless I saw some tangible evidence which, incidentally, is why I showed you the book.'

'Yeah well... Enough said.'

'Well if it means anything, I still give you the benefit of the the doubt' said Emma 'I don't think anyone could fake what you showed me.'

'Thanks Emma. I think we should get off this

subject now and make the best of what's left of the evening.'

Chapter 21 - Power and deceit

High Elder Iain FitzJohn walked up the gravel drive with a measured, unhurried air, the slow deliberate crunch of each step gave enough notice of his arrival to allow those he was visiting to peep from behind curtains and panic just a little before welcoming him eagerly to their humble abode.

He smiled to himself as the tell-tale signs of his impending visit followed a predictable course. He knocked the door and listened to the muffled noises from within as small details were fussed over before the front door was finally opened with a flourish.

'Arthur! I do hope I haven't inconvenienced you too much by calling unannounced and so soon after work' his thin reedy voice offered magnanimously.

'Not at all, High Elder, not at all!' gushed Arthur Leadpenny.

'Good man! I need to speak with you about a small problem which has recently appeared. Can we sit down?'

Leadpenny took his coat and instructed his wife to go and make tea while they discussed church business. She smiled at the high elder and dutifully went to the kitchen while the men entered what Leadpenny proudly called, "The Leounge".

'A small problem, Iain?'

'At the moment, yes. I think you may have seen it for yourself. It is a problem which takes the form of a young girl, a "Gildenhair" who has suddenly manifested herself. She flaunts herself in public as if she has no shame at all.'

'Why, yes we have. She came to the shop. All by herself she was, we were suspicious but - what can you do? She had money and she accounted for herself very well, we could hardly refuse her, could we?' Leadpenny said weakly.

'No, I suppose not.' The High Elder paused for a moment 'Is she a Nonnye do you think?'

'I think not. As I say, she accounted for herself very well and knew her mind. She had plenty of money as well, offered my treasured wife a one hundred pound note in payment!'

'Did she indeed? Hmm. She could have stolen it but if as you say, she speaks well, it is possible that she has her own means. We will have to find out. I actually saw her sitting at a table in the market the other day, she was quite shameless and defiant in her demeanour and nobody did anything about it, one can only wonder at how she has the nerve.'

'I quite agree, she acted in the same manner when she came to the shop. My dear Catherine was most put out, and we have also noticed that she is left handed.'

Silence followed while the two men pondered the situation.

'What should we do, High Elder?'

'I don't know yet, but I will pray about it and ask our Lord God for guidance.'

The tea arrived and High Elder Iain FitzJohn politely suffered a report of the progress of the junior Leadpennys from their proud father while Mrs Leadpenny sat dutifully and listened. Eventually the conversation turned once more to the matter in hand.

'So tell me, Catherine, what did you make of the girl?'

'She was obscene!' Mrs. Leadpenny's face soured as the words of hate spat from her mouth 'that "Gildenhair!" I wouldn't be surprised if she was possessed by the devil himself. She stares you hard in the eye like a wild cat and holds her head up in a proud, hoighty manner as if she thinks she's so much better than all of us - and she's clever - like a spiteful imp. She knew when I was on to her and -'

FitzJohn held his hand up to stop her 'Possessed you say?'

'Oh yes! Her eyes have the look of the very devil in them.'

The High Elder considered for a moment. 'We must warn of her presence in church so that she may be avoided, meanwhile, I want you to find out more about her, if she has friends, where she sleeps and that sort of thing. Let me know your findings, we can't let our people see us doing nothing. There are those in society who would protect her, the monks in particular, they welcome all types.'

As he stood up, Mrs. Leadpenny collected the tea things and took them away leaving them men alone.

'I hope that I am up to the task, Iain.'

'You will be' FitzJohn narrowed his eyes. 'Remember your rather "Special" position, Arthur. You hold a position of trust with the higher brethren. You have the Elucidatum to guide you and I am sure you will find some answers in it. This is perhaps, a chance for you to pay back the church for some of the many gifts it has bestowed upon you and your family.'

As the quiet menace behind the words sunk in, Arthur Leadpenny reluctantly agreed, although he wasn't quite sure where to start. Iain FitzJohn excused himself from the room, saying that he needed to discuss arrangements for a forthcoming event with Catherine and made his way to the kitchen. She was sitting at the table idly twiddling a teaspoon, when she saw him, she gave him a wry grin.

'Good meeting?'

'I think he will need some comfort.'

Her face soured 'Well he won't get it from me!'

FitzJohn paused for a moment in thought.

'There may be a chance in this for you to help your own situation, if you know what I mean. Let him hang himself with his own rope, so to speak. I'm sure you will find a way to steer him in the right direction if you want to, Catherine.'

A noise stopped further conversation and the atmosphere changed back to the formal politeness of before.

'Yes, and roses were specially requested... Ah, hello Arthur, we were just discussing fine details.

I think it will look fine, Catherine. I'd better leave you to discuss our other problem now, I will pray in earnest about it this evening and if the Lord God instructs me, I shall carry out his word - *Totally!'*

Arthur Leadpenny watched him leave with a feeling of awe and relief, the High Elder was such a Godly man, so steadfast and unbending in his faith. Surely God would speak to him that night and he would announce his revelation tomorrow in church before the Minister, the Elders and all the congregation.

His thoughts turned towards the task he had been given, guilt washed over him as he thought about the girl, she was so young and -. No, he mustn't think like that, he must be strong, He had no doubt that the Gildenhair was a sign of trouble. He must pray for forgiveness of his sinful thoughts.

He fetched the family copy of the Elucidatum Divinicus, the holy book which, in hand with the Bible, was the foundation on which their particular faith was built. His finger ran down the index until it found the desired page and with trembling hands, he turned to it and read eagerly from the text.

> -- and it shall come to passe within the time of storm and turmoille, that a messenger of Satan will appeare unto the true people of Godde and will cause them muche disharmonye. Three demons will possesse it and thou shall know it bye the three signes.

Arthur wished that the book would be more precise, it seldom was, though. The source from which the holy texts were taken was shrouded in mystery and its authenticity was never questioned. It all had something to do with faith and humility.

He sat down to consider the facts as he saw them. Three signs. He flicked over the pages to the section on signs of demon possession and read through.

> **Rolling of the eyes and fittyng:** A more common forme of demonic possessione whiche is soothed bye the handes of the prieste. Feele pittye for the victime and makeste thou them comfortable for they are trulye in turmoille until the demon is caste oute.
>
> **Involuntarye blasphemye and cursyng:** There is little to be done but to praye for the victime of this demon, the more which is done to caste oute the demon, the more the demon will resiste and fight.

Arthur had seen sufferers of these conditions before and he believed like the others in his church, that they were caused by demonic possession. He turned over and read some more.

> **Mockerye of the image of Godde:** Signes of possessione which are of the most grave concerne as they are onlye outwarde signes of a muche deeper and subtle possessione - -

There it was in print. Arthur's prejudices filled in the detail around the vague suggestions as he read on, and produced some damning evidence.

The brazenly displayed golden-white hair was the most obvious sign. How dare she openly suggest such Godly purity? The same with her unearthly blue eyes, that defiant penetrating stare as if she considered herself to be the equal of any man, and as for using her left hand, it was a sure sign of evil spirits working inside her head.

And yet -

Guilty thoughts once more strayed across his mind.

Chapter 22 - The True Path

Later that night, James lay in bed unable to sleep, he felt annoyed at Phil for being so pig headed about everything. The "Enough said" comment had really got to him because he usually associated it with people who would not face up to a problem. Not people like Phil.

He thought how strange it was that a part of human nature could make people focus on small issues rather than the really big ones. He had just stepped outside of reality and gained a whole new understanding of, well ,everything! And yet, he was so bothered by an insignificant comment by a friend.

It was no good, he just couldn't sleep, and after mulling over the same thoughts for yet another hour, he decided to go through the light and allow Faye some time to use more wisely.

◆ ◆ ◆

Faye slipped on her nightgown before heading down to the kitchen for a glass of hot milk. Bert had left a copy of the Herald on the table and she sat and read it while waiting for her milk to warm on the range. The front page headline read “Another Bodye

Founde" and this was followed by an editorial about the inefficiency of the policemen involved in this latest find. On the second page was a small write up about the Nonnye girl who was found in Hen Hill Park. She read it through before climbing back up the stairs and towards the turret room.

Placing her milk on the table, she sat down under the hazy moonlight and scudding sky. Staring out over the roofs and spires of the sleeping city for some time. Thinking about their shared experience of the void and sifting through her own newly acquired images and memories of James.

She, like James, found the whole experience in the void too enormous to cope with and her mind kept wandering to other small matters as if it were trying to protect her from the sheer enormity of what they had seen and learned.

A soft "Ding" from above informed her that the wind direction had changed. Her perfect pitch told her that it was an E note, so the wind was now coming from the south east. Silent flashes of wildfire lit the sky on the horizon and she felt a slight upturn in the temperature. The E struck again several times as the weather vane swung to and fro across the compass point before settling as the wind steadied. Faye finished off her milk and sat back in the chair and drifted off to sleep.

Next morning she awoke as the bright silver disk of sun rose above a sea of thick fog and flooded into the tower room, she went to the handrail and looked out with awe. Her tower room was completely isolated, standing like an island on top of a swirling cloudy world punctuated only by church towers and the occasional tall chimney.

The clock on the table read five thirty, James would not need to rise until at least eight o' clock and Faye had a childlike eagerness to go out and see what it was like to walk in the fog below.

She dressed and found her long hooded coat and boots before creeping out of the front door, it shut with a loud hollow clunk in the stillness.

Every noise seemed to be amplified in the dull white shroud of fog and she felt the need to be stealthy and light on her feet. The bridge was a little bit tricky to find but once there, she crossed it quickly, not wishing to meet anyone as she did so.

The bell of Saint Leonard's started its low solitary toll, calling the faithful to an early morning service and she shrank back into the shadows as footsteps approached. Grey shapes passed within five or six feet of her and she waited until they were swallowed up by the fog before moving on. She followed the sound of the bell until she could hear people being greeted at the door of the church. They all seemed to be expected and as she quietly edged a little closer, she could see more grey shapes shaking hands and being ushered inside.

As the bell stopped its chime, others started and she spent a few minutes identifying them by their tones. The sound of an organ heralded the start of the service. She was most curious and pushed the old door gently so that she could slip inside and see what mysteries went on.

The inside of the building was quite dark and musty, with carved and painted effigies of men in robes set into niches in the walls. All the ordinary townspeople were standing and facing the front while others, dressed in robes, walked slowly around the church holding a cross before them, taking their places in some raised seats before a kind of offering table.

The man who wore the most decorated robes held out his arms and welcomed them all. Everybody knelt down and started to recite something which she couldn't quite understand.

A man who was standing at the back of the church suddenly turned and saw her. He held out a book for her so that she could join in but she fled and hid herself in the fog. He followed and called to her, inviting her to come back but she was a little scared of what she had seen.

She pulled her hood back and made her way towards home, keeping close to the walls of buildings so that she could be sure that she was heading in the right direction. Suddenly three grey shapes loomed in front of her and before she could sidestep, she came face to face with the mother and two children she had once met in the sweet shop. The mother froze with fright.

'I beg your pardon' said Faye politely.

'I - we must pass. Please let us pass' said the woman, making the sign of the cross and pulling the children closer to her. 'Please! We did not mean to stand in your way, I am most sorry. Please do not curse us young miss.'

'Why would I curse you?' said Faye, puzzled.

'Please! We must pass, my husband, he will expect us at prayer. Sorry, I didn't mean to -'

'I am confused. Why do you think that I would want to do you harm?'

The woman hesitated and relaxed her tight grip on the children a little. Faye knelt down to them and spoke in a kindly way, asking their names and their ages. They answered shyly and with young wide eyes looking up for approval from their mother. Faye decided to be direct and risk a question.

'Why does Joshua wear this Strap on his wrist?'

'Because the devil wants him for his own, my husband instructs that his left hand be strapped to save him from being a sinister.'

'And you? What do you think of such a thing?'

'He is my husband, 'tis my duty. His wish is my wish. We want Joshua to be healed and be rid of the demon which tries to ensnare him.'

She suddenly flushed, realising what she had just implied and tried to take back her words but Faye ignored her stammering and held out her hand.

'We should introduce ourselves. My name is Faye.'

The woman pulled away but said weakly 'My name is Ann... We must go. Please!'

Faye stepped aside to allow them to pass but followed under the cover of the fog. Their voices drifted back to her as the children asked who the lady was and why mummy was upset. She replied by imploring them not to tell their father and begging them to pretend not to know the lady if they saw her again. Faye felt pity for them.

They entered an austere-looking building on Scotts Lane. It didn't look like a church because it had no tower and was not named after a saint. Faye pulled her hood up, making sure that her hair was completely covered and waited as before, until everyone had been ushered inside. Then, when she was sure that all was quiet, she gently pushed open the door and peered inside.

A wooden paneled lobby with doors at each side separated the entrance from the main hall. She tip-toed over and hid behind the heavy velvet door curtain so that she could hear and see what was going on without being seen.

The inside was packed full of people, all the men wore grey or black suits and sat in the main body of the hall while the women and children sat separately in a gallery above. At the front of the hall was a tall wooden dais with three gilded chairs on it. The central chair was taller than those at each side and had a gilt cross and crown embellishing it's leather back.

After a few moments a small side door opened. Three men solemnly walked onto the dais and faced the assembly. Faye was shocked to see that one of them was Arthur Leadpenny. He addressed the congregation with an oily, well practiced ease. He welcomed them to prayer and pointed out particular members for various deeds or efforts before turning his attention to the man in the immaculate dark suit who occupied the highest chair.

'And now, if you will excuse me Minister, I will hand our morning prayer meeting over to High Elder FitzJohn for what I believe to be a very important announcement.'

'Thank you, Elder Leadpenny - Minister.' he turned and faced the congregation, suddenly a towering figure before the upturned heads of the men.

'I have a grave and important announcement to make this morning. As you all know, following the true path to our Lord God is never easy, it is a path full of temptation and turmoil but we have triumphed before the face of evil on many occasions.'

There was a general murmur of agreement at this and Faye wondered what the evil was which they had such a problem with.

'Sometimes the path has been hard to follow - BUT my friends, we must NEVER give in. To give in is to allow sin to win. Recently, I have seen something which I hoped I would never see again.' He paused in his melodrama while everyone murmured once more and leaned forwards in anticipation. 'As you all know, the Devil's work is all around us and sightings of his army of ghosts are becoming more frequent as are those of the Nonnyes who become flesh and are left here for us all to deal with. However, it now appears that we now have a genuine *Gildenhair* once more in our midst!'

The atmosphere in the hall became agitated, all the women in the gallery were exclaiming and looking fearfully at one another while the men below shook their heads and murmured in a woeful manner. The High Elder held out his arms as if to embrace them all.

'Settle down - Settle down, everyone, please! This gildenhair takes the form of a young girl, I have seen her myself, but Elder Leadpenny has actually spoken with her so I will now ask him to share with us all.'

Leadpenny stood once more, swelled with the importance of his task and recounted his version of Faye's visit to the shop. He made it clear to all, that she was clever, devious and wicked and that she used her left hand openly in public. Then as his finale he quoted the Elucidatum and pointed out the three damning signs he had found of her demonic possession.

'Has anybody else seen the girl?' he asked 'We must establish who she is and where she comes from, so any information would be of help at this time.'

Several men and some uniformed youths stood and swore a pledge to help in the hunt the for the gildenhair and bring her to justice before their Lord God.

A woman in the gallery stood and asked permission to speak. She asked if the gildenhair was a witch or if she could cause harm. The minister took the floor and answered that there were no reports as yet and that the girl may not actually know that she carried demons.

'We must assume for the time being, that she is the innocent victim of the evil which lives within her and that her apparent brazenness is due to her ignorance of her condition. We must not act in haste. She should be saved if it is still possible to do so, in fact, let us start now by praying for her.'

Faye was stunned, *'Tis me they are speaking of!* she thought as she slid from her hiding place behind the curtain and went back out into the street. The fog was lifting and she could see underneath it in places so she ran back towards home as fast as she could, suddenly fearful for her safety and also hoping that she wouldn't be too late for James.

Chapter 23 - A small shift in reality

It was almost nine o' clock when James stepped into his room and he wasted no time in making an appearance. Outside his locked door was a cold cup of coffee which he downed as he descended the stairs.

'Where have you been?' said Emma rather reproachfully. James mumbled an apology as he made a hot, fresh cup.

'Things are happening too fast' he said, grabbing some toast and sitting down next to Phil.

They all sat through breakfast in a guarded silence until James couldn't stand it any longer. He apologised once more and tried to explain something of what had happened over night, hoping that they would ease up on him a little when Phil cut in.

'Look, mate, I don't really want to hear it. Talk to Emma, she believes you.'

James took him at his word and beckoned to Emma to follow him out to the garden, she quietly listened as he told her of what had happened since the night before.

'I'll have to go back through at some point today' he said, 'While I'm standing here talking with you, there may be people looking for her or trying to find out about her and - anything! Things don't stop there just because I happen to be here and quite honestly I'm worried about the situation.'

'Those people can't hurt her though, surely.'

'They could if they wanted to, they have a different way of life to us, different laws, even the churches have their own police!'

'My God! Don't you worry that something might happen to you?'

'No, not really, something could just as easily happen to me while I'm here. I'm more worried about what goes on while Faye isn't around. I never really understood before last night just how much things actually change around us all the time.'

'Well you've certainly changed. A couple of weeks ago or so, the only thing you had on your mind was moving in.'

'God! Is it only that long? It feels more like a couple of months'

The rest of the morning didn't go well and the subject was carefully avoided, Phil could not accept any of what James had said and had decided to return home early because, as he put it, things were getting weird. Emma stayed for a while and kept James company while he prepared for his next trip through the light, only leaving him a few minutes before he was ready.

As her car reached the end of the lane she pulled over and sat for a while agitatedly drumming her fingers on the steering wheel. It was no good, she couldn't leave him like this, she had to turn the car round and head back to find him if only to apologise for Phil and make sure things were still O.K. between them. If she were being completely honest with herself, she also wanted to see if he had actually gone.

The moment the car swung into the drive, she instinctively knew that something was different. Maybe it was her imagination playing tricks but the leaves all seemed to shimmer in the wind for a moment as if to warn her that her presence was somehow an intrusion. Nevertheless, she locked the car and walked up to the front door giving it a loud knock and calling to James as if to assert her right to be there. There was no reply. A feeling of emptiness radiated back at her and she started to feel a bit creeped out.

She walked round to the back of the house and peered through the glass at the scene she had so recently left, everything was in the same place, she imagined herself sitting on the chair and talking to James just before leaving but it just didn't seem real now. Bits of their conversation kept coming back to her, the things that James had said about how much things changed all the time. *Perhaps,* she thought, *perhaps this is is not the same house I left. What if all that he said was true and I've passed through into another version of here? No, I'm just being stupid now!*

James kept the spare key hidden in a knot in a tree in the garden, against all advice, just in case he ever accidentally locked himself out. She took it and, feeling a bit like a criminal, let herself in just as the phone rang. Phil's voice loudly cut through the silence.

'Hi, mate, it's only me. Sorry about the way I was earlier. Now I'm driving down the A14 like everyone else it all seems a bit daft. Maybe the "Good ole country air" got to me. Anyway, I'll give Emma a call later and square things up with her. Speak to you soon. Bye.'

That was it, Phil would phone her later and say the same thing and as far as he was concerned it would all be fixed. She felt better at hearing his voice though, somehow it broke the spell and made everything seem a bit more normal.

After looking around the ground floor, she went upstairs and tried the door to James's bedroom but it was locked from the inside so she hammered on it, calling him to see if he was there but of course, there was no answer. At last, the realisation that he had gone - really gone - started to sink in.

Chapter 24 - Rose petal scent

As soon as she could, Faye called on Rhiannon. This was partly because she would be most likely to hear any word or rumour about the True Path, and partly because she needed a friend to cheer her up.

Rhiannon was preparing to make a new batch of rose petal scent to sell in the shop. Faye was happy to give her a hand and the two girls, armed with baskets, set off to collect rose petals together. Rhiannon eagerly told Faye all about the fact that wearing perfume and make-up made the boys go silly and they would do anything for you if you asked them.

‘ 'Tis like magic!’ she said ‘They get this funny smile on their faces and keep looking at you like puppies do, then you know you have them under your spell. Daft they are!’

Faye wasn't sure it was all so easy. That same look had been on Mr. Leadpenny’s face and she didn't like it on him. Just for the sake of it though, she agreed and willingly joined in with the rose petal harvest.

They chatted as they worked and found out many things about each other, like the fact that Rhiannon also felt that she was an outsider, being from Wales. She was a bit of a rebel at heart and secretly enjoyed getting her own back on the "Hoighty" people whom she felt looked down on them.

'We buy lots of things from the traders on the market boat and then resell them through the shop to those who think they are too grand to buy from the boat themselves. They come in with their noses up in the air and say things like "Is this bracelet from where you come from?" Well, 'course I lie and say it is so they buy it even though it came all the way from Constantinople or somewhere. Mind you, I only do it to people that I really don' like because they've said something nasty about me or my Dad. Why don' you come with me when the boat comes in next time? They sell kohl and loads of other good stuff, it would suit you - make you look all mysterious and knowing.'

Through all the chatter, Faye learned about boys. She hadn't met one of her own age yet, but she could tell that Rhiannon found them exciting because she kept bringing them into the conversation at the slightest excuse. Her real concern though, was of what she had heard about herself that morning and she now had the perfect excuse to bring up the subject.

'What do think of the True Path people? I do not like what I have seen of them as yet.'

'Oh Lord! Them! Sorry to blaspheme but I'm sure I'm going to Hell anyway. I hate 'em! They're the worst. No one else likes 'em much 'cos they think they've got all the answers and everybody else is damned. They think they know the only way to be saved and every one else'll fall into the pit. They keep on saying that they can see signs of when it will come, and then when it does not, they claim credit for saving everyone by their actions alone.'

'Is that why they don't like me - because they see me as a sign or an omen?'

'Probably, why? What makes you ask?'

While they worked together, Faye told Rhiannon in great detail, of all the things she had overheard in the meeting house that morning and also about her meeting with the woman called Ann.

'If they've called you a gildenhair, 'tis bad, 'tis a great insult to you as if you are a ghost or a devil. You *must* have seen a ghost at some time, I used to see them all the time when I was younger but now I only see 'em occasionally, mostly at dusk or before a storm. I speak to 'em but they seldom hear, mostly they just walk on and fade away into nothing.'

Faye realised that the woman in the cemetery was probably what Rhiannon would call a ghost, someone who faded in and out of another reality without knowing it.

'Anyway' continued Rhiannon 'they will probably claim that you are a witch or a manifestation or something. 'Tis why they'll say you've got demons 'n' things in you and that you are a sign of bad things to come.' She suddenly became more serious for a moment. 'It would be prudent for you to be careful around 'em and make sure that your friends are true indeed.'

'Do you think others would see me as a threat

like they do?'

'Some might 'cos that sort of talk gets people frightened. It's your hair that startles 'em. You might as well mark yourself with the sign of the Reaper.' She gave Faye a mischievous look 'I suppose that I envy it because if it were mine, I would wave it in front of them and taunt them with it... We are good together, you and I, we are like good and evil all mixed up and juxtapositioned.'

They had by now, collected enough rose petals and were starting to make their way back to prepare them.

'What if I *were* a witch?' said Faye playfully.

'Oh that would be so great a thing!'

'Maybe I am.'

'And maybe you're not!' Rhiannon ran ahead shouting in mock fear 'She be a witch! She be a witch and a New Day of Judgement is coming to claim us all, 'specially the True Path!'

They both broke into a fit of giggles and ran down the lane towards the shop as fast as they could, panting by the time they reached the yard. The afternoon sun beat mercilessly through the haze and both girls were glad to draw some cold water and sit in the relative cool of the kitchen. Rhiannon then showed Faye the process of carefully removing the white petal bases before layering the petals in a jar with salt.

When they had finished, she filled the jar with clear alcoholic spirit, replaced the cork seal and placed the jar in a dark corner of one of the outhouses.

‘There, it will be ready to press and tap off in about three months.’

‘Three months! I thought it was done!’

‘Oh no, there's more to do yet. Mind you, I've got some I made before, you can have some if you like 'cos I got plenty to spare.

The afternoon heat was becoming oppressive and the sky was now turning an all too familiar ominous steely grey. Mr Owen pulled the amphibian truck into the yard just as the two girls emerged from the outhouse and he greeted them with a wave as he climbed down from the cab.

‘We'll have yet more storms tonight, I've just been helping tow some of the boats out of the water, the fishermen say it is looking really bad. There were church constables asking questions about the body they found. Getting in our way they were. One of them asked about you.’ He looked straight at Faye and continued ‘He said that there were reports of a girl like you being seen around and had any of us seen you? Well of course I said no and asked him right back why he wanted to know but he wouldn't say. Funny really, I don' think it was normal police business.’

‘The True Path are after her, Dad. She snuck into their prayers this morning and heard ’em calling her a witch and a gildenhair and saying she has demons.’

‘Did they now?’ he looked thoughtfully at them both ‘Rhiannon, will you give us a moment please, I have something that is best said in private.'

Rhiannon said that she would look for a bottle in which to decant some perfume and slipped away without questioning her father. He gave Faye a probing, almost knowing stare for a few moments as if he was searching for words.

'Do you remember when you first came into our shop and bought all the clothes - and I told you I'd met someone like you before? Well, some of the people from my home village used to say *she* was a witch. I used to visit her when I could sneak out without being noticed. Got on well with her I did. She never judged them back, nor anyone else, she just stayed silent and watched.'

Faye said said nothing and waited for him to continue. 'I could swear she used to be able to disappear! Sometimes, when I called on her house and she wasn't there - well - I don't know - I just got the feeling - Do you know what I'm trying to say?'

Again Faye said nothing but he didn't seem to take it as rudeness, it just made him go on as if she had confirmed a suspicion.

'She told me once that words got in the way of the truth of things and that I should take time to listen to nature and see what was really happening. You're like her aren't you, a wise one. Don't worry, I had that feeling when you first came in the shop, that is what made me say that you'd always be welcome. I won't ever tell anyone.'

Faye gave Mr Owen a look which, without a word being spoken, told him all he needed to know and sealed a silent pledge that they should never discuss it again.

Rhiannon called to them from the house just as the first drops of rain pattered softly onto the ground. She had bottled some scent for Faye and wanted her to smell it.

'I've just put some Whimsye leaves in with it, see 'em on the bottom? 'Tis a bit naughty but I think it would suit you especially well' she said with a discreet smile.

Rhiannon was a good antidote to all Faye's rising problems and worries, she chatted on and on about nothing in particular while the rain drops softly fell outside. She showed Faye how to darken her eyes with kohl and how to braid her hair in a traditional Celtic style. Mr Owen left them to it until distant thunder rumbled somewhere out at sea.

'Excuse me, girls' he said, knocking before putting his head round the door 'Tis getting more gloomy and overcast and I think it is time to stop now.'

'Can Faye stay here with us Dad? She could have supper.'

'I think it would be better if I left for home before the storm comes,' said Faye ' 'tis a very kind offer though.'

Rhiannon was about to protest but Mr Owen quietened her with a raised finger and suggested that they should all walk together but Faye declined. She had a slightly apprehensive feeling about something she couldn't quite place, it was nothing to do with Rhiannon or her father, it was something in the air.

Chapter 25 - The void

The streets of Dunwiche were almost deserted. The leaves had stopped their playful rustling and the grass along the roadside was now motionless.

Faye acknowledged several people as she walked towards home but only one of them noticed, his feet made a wet crunchy noise as he walked by. She turned and watched a lady in brightly coloured clothing glide by silently and then fade out of existence. A few steps further down the lane, a man with a shiny black thing held up to his ear was speaking and gesturing wildly to nobody. A shiver ran down her spine and the apprehensive feeling turned itself up by a degree.

A lone, shambling old woman looked up as she passed and muttered distractedly towards Faye. 'Dripping down the walls it is, that 'lectric stuff... Just keeps on seeping out... What's a poor old lady to do 'bout that? No one'll listen to me though, oh no. Mad, that's what I am. Mad! Mad old Esther, that's what they all say... Esther's mad!'

Her voice ranted on as Faye turned the corner onto the quayside and made her way to the bridge and home. The almost becalmed water in the channel looked black and very deep as she crossed. Once inside the house, she dried herself and changed. Starlight had disappeared and she guessed that she wouldn't see her again until the storm was long gone, then she would suddenly appear and demand food.

She put the scent bottle down on the table and then stood in front of the mirror, her eyes were still made up with kohl and she quite liked the look. Rhiannon, although seemingly full of mindless chat, had a keen eye for detail and a good understanding of the power of perception. She had said that it would make Faye look mysterious and knowing and it certainly did.

'Tis strange she thought *that this scent is a parallel to my very self, as is the kohl against the very lightness of my hair and skin, and how all these details when added together, make such a powerful image.*

She stared deeply into her reflection and thought.

I walk in places that others cannot and I am seen as a ghost, a witch or an omen by many. 'Tis as if they suspect something but cannot see the truth and dare not ask it so they weave me into their own theories and beliefs. I must stay true to myself and be proud of who I am. I must stand up to those who would do me harm and if there is a purpose to my existence, I must do my best to find it and to carry it out.

The moment of self enlightenment passed without even the smallest breath of wind acknowledging its existence.

Faye sat in the window for a while, staring out

over the town and the haven. A number of fishing boats had been hauled out of the water and stood in a line along the south shore near the boatyards. All of them were covered with tarpaulins while others, still at their moorings, moved around slowly, one at a time, as if a great unseen creature was passing silently underneath them.

She still had a sense of unease, it wasn't the stormy atmosphere because she actually found peace in the eerie stillness. No, this was something else. Something unusual was happening, something vast, she couldn't put a name to it.

Everything looked grey and drained of colour. The sea was dark and calm except for the dull white foamy tops of some distant waves where a sudden squall had whipped them into a momentary frenzy. The storm was still out at sea and now looked as if it may pass without incident after all. With that in mind, she decided to inform James of the latest events. This time, instead of writing to him, she would try to carry her thoughts directly to him.

She undressed and laid her clothes out neatly on the bed. Then just as James had done, she entered the light, moving forward slowly and carefully to the point where everything started to become hazy. Then she turned to look back towards the room in order to keep her bearings. She allowed herself to drift further away, little by little, until she could sense the emerging presence of James.

It was only here that the two of them could make any form of connection, moving towards the void in the centre of the crossing where their remaining strands of being could touch and intertwine. Here, the soul was a part of both of them, and both of them could share the moment as one entity, softly dancing in each other's existence before Faye cast off from the last strands of her physical being and let James continue on the journey to the other side.

◆ ◆ ◆

As he stepped into his room, James felt the full force of the experience hit him at once. He sat on his bed and cried until the tears ran down his cheeks and dripped off his chin, then he laughed, and laughed, and then he cried once more. Once he had recovered from the initial burst of emotion, he grabbed a pair of underpants and pulled them on before going downstairs and finding himself confronting Emma.

'What are you doing here still?' he said, trying to cover himself with his hands and pushing his knees together 'I thought you'd gone hours and hours ago!'

'Sorry' said Emma looking uncomfortable and embarrassed, 'I got to the main road and stopped, I don't know why, but I suddenly decided to come back and I've been waiting ever since... I heard you laughing and stuff.' she looked at the floor uncomfortably.

Now it was his turn to feel uncomfortable, 'I've had some pretty amazing experiences, things are happening around me so fast.'

'Things to do with - you know?'

'Yes... Look, hang on and I'll go and put some clothes on.'

He returned a few minutes later fully dressed, and sat down with her and listened as she tried to explain why she had suddenly changed her plans.

'I had to know I suppose. It all sounded so crazy but you seemed to really believe it. Phil put doubts in my mind though and I nearly got swayed by him but I'm glad I didn't.'

'So now you believe that it's all true?'

'Yes, absolutely.' She studied him for a moment, 'James, you look different, you've changed.'

'You said that earlier.'

'I know but, there's something about you that wasn't there before. It's hard to explain. Can I ask you a question? It might sound a bit stupid though.'

'Yes, of course.'

'It's just that, when I came back to the house, it felt sort of spooky and I had shivers running up my spine. I knew you'd gone before I even knocked the door and it felt really odd. I remember you saying that things change much more than we realise or something like that. Do you think I'm being really silly and starting to imagine things because of what you told me?'

'No. I just think you're starting to notice things more. It's the same sort of feeling as you get when you think someone is behind you but there isn't anyone there. Small details change around us all the time but we never actually see it happen.'

'That makes me feel really scared.'

'Don't be... Look, maybe I've spooked you a little bit and it made you jumpy. Just try to forget about it and carry on as normal. Mrs Larkin always says that she doesn't want to know about things like that, though I think she actually has a good idea about them.'

'Who's Mrs Larkin?'

James was taken completely by surprise at the way the words came out, he had never met Mrs Larkin but now he felt as if he already knew her. He had to compose himself quickly before he could answer.

'She's just someone from the other side. Look, when I came back just now I -' He stopped himself just in time. He hadn't yet had time to realise the full implications of being at one in the void with Faye as yet. Her strength of mind and clarity of thought was embedding itself into his very being.

'What I'm trying to say is that Faye and myself are linked by ever closening ties and we are responsible for each other now in everything that we do.' He faked a yawn and stretched his arms out above his head. 'I need a coffee to wake me up. Do you want one? All this reality travelling takes its toll.'

'You know what?' said Emma 'The time is getting on and you look tired. We both need a break from all this madness and I think I ought to hit the road. I've got work tomorrow and I should really get back before dark.'

'O.K. Thanks for coming back and waiting for me. I'm glad you did even if you *did* catch me by surprise.'

She gave him a sheepish grin and a hug before going out to the car. James watched and waved after her as she drove once more into the lane, before turning away and going back inside.

This is it, he thought. *This time I have to try to get through the void myself, I feel useless here.* He skipped the coffee and went straight upstairs.

In a box room which he'd used as a dumping ground for all the things he didn't have a home for, he found a suit which he had last worn for his Granddad's funeral. After a bit of rummaging, he matched it with a pair of dark grey socks and some plain black leather lace-up shoes. *It's no good going through looking like a Nonnye,* he thought as he tried them on and added a few details to make himself more likely to blend in. His hair was a little on the short side but he thought that he should be able to get away with it.

Once he had dressed he went and stood nervously in front of the wall of his bedroom, hoping that his idea would work.

Edging forward slowly, he allowed the nothingness to enclose him completely, all the time making sure he still kept inside his body, this being the one important thing that both of them had not done before. As he moved further into the void and his own reality faded away, James lost consciousness.

Chapter 26 - The other side

The next thing he knew as he came round, was that he was stepping forward into a room. As he took control of himself once more, it started to sink in that he had actually done it! He had travelled to a different reality. He really was in Faye's bedroom in Amber Lodge, a house in an ancient walled city which, in his own reality, had long ago been washed away and lay in ruins under the North Sea.

He looked around. Faye just accepted this room as her bedroom and so his perception of it so far, had only been of the kind of indifference anyone would have to their own bedroom. He hadn't really thought about it much, but if he had, he probably would have assumed that it was like any ordinary girl's bedroom, full of posters, clothes and mess. This was different though, and to see it with his own eyes for the first time was quite a strange experience.

The room smelt of wax polish, roses and lavender. Some of Faye's clothes were still neatly laid out on the bed and they too, were quite different to what he would have expected,. They were more like stage costumes or museum exhibits and yet he knew that she wore them as everyday clothing.

On the table was the small glass bottle of rose

scent. He opened it and breathed in. At first it smelled of roses but with a slightly musty air before subtly releasing a much deeper fragrance which made him feel a little light headed. *Wow* he thought as he replaced the stopper.

Faye was everywhere in the room, her presence was all around him and yet she was still so impossibly far away. He suddenly felt desperately alone.

Evening sunlight broke through for a moment and flooded the whole of the turret window in a soft primrose yellow light, making patterns on the floor and shafts of gold in the air. It lifted his mood once more with its beauty and reminding him of the first time he'd noticed the afternoon warmth of his own room. Reflections from the waters of the haven were rippling slowly over the stonework. He recognised them, he had seen them before in his own bedroom.

Suddenly fired with a burst of renewed energy, he went to the window and looked eagerly out over the haven and the town, gasping in amazement at the scene before him.

He recognised Havenside just over the water but there were none of the usual sea-side trappings of his own world. No chip shops, candyfloss stalls and amusements. Instead it looked rather quaint and old. Further along, a pitched clapboard pub, the "Lion and Lamb", stood at the end of a line of flint cottages. It was closed as was the custom on Sundays and James suddenly realised that he had the perfect opportunity to explore without having to meet too many people.

He made his way down to the front door, stopping several times on the way to look into various rooms. Outside, the air was oppressive and humid, a marked difference to the thin, delicate atmosphere inside the house. He walked down to the front gates and turned to look at Amber Lodge and its setting. The turret room shone brilliantly in the evening sunlight and cast golden reflections down into the shadows beneath. Its location was certainly impressive, facing the town from across the water with the haven beach on the left, and to the right, only the customs house and lighthouse before his gaze reached the open sea.

After a studying it for a moment, James turned and opened the gate onto the track by the sea wall. He wasn't sure what direction to take and decided to stay on the track, at first walking towards the sea.

As he rounded the lighthouse, he could see northwards along the coast where a huge machine was parked beside a mound of boulders. It looked as if it were for repairing sea defences. He turned and walked back past Amber Lodge to the sheltered beach of the deserted haven. Wild, coarse grass and stubby wind-blown bushes clung to the crumbly earth above the shingle and sand. He stood and stared at the stark beauty of it before finally going to the bridge and plucking up the courage to cross it.

The sun had disappeared and a vague, shapeless shadow closed in over the quayside. He hurried over the bridge, suddenly feeling vulnerable and unprotected. As he reached the other side, feelings of mild panic nagged at him and he looked back at Amber Lodge just to reassure himself that it was still there.

Everywhere was so quiet, the silence seemed to impose itself on him, to envelope him in its lonely grip. Only the muted sound of lapping water and the distant cry of the gulls broke its complete hold. This was England, but it wasn't an England that he knew. It wasn't *his* England. Who was Prime Minister? Who was Queen?... Or King?

He shook himself and regained some control. After all, he was here for a purpose. He would start by making himself familiar with his surroundings, then if he met anyone, he would be less likely to panic and say something stupid.

Once more, he chose to walk by the sea, judging that it was safer than risking a walk through a built up area. Turning left along where Havenside became Dam Street, he walked beside the channel to the start of the clifftop.

Some flint fishermen's cottages stood in a neat line close to the shore. Their gardens were full of neatly tended lines of vegetables and each one had a boat on a rusty launch rig, winched well above the high tide level. Ahead, the crumbly cliffs were a sandy yellow in colour and looked as if they could slide onto the beach at the least excuse, but they were shored up and protected by some very substantial sea defences.

As the path climbed with the cliffs, James felt more and more as if he were far from home and he noticed an ever increasing number of differences.

Where the path reached its highest point, he sat for a while and looked out over Dunwiche.

There were no recognisable modern styles of building, no housing estates or any of the usual rows of Victorian houses to be seen anywhere. A dense cluster of chimneys and steep roofs were gathered around the largest of the many church towers which, he presumed, must be the Cathedral of St Felix.

He swept his gaze further towards the outskirts to where there were only a few rambling thatched dwellings, some farms and some derelict buildings. Beyond, a wild and lonely countryside of gorse and heather met with the horizon.

The clifftop path just went on and on, following the curve of the coastline into the distance so James decided to turn back. The sky was getting gloomier and he could remember Faye's feelings of apprehension from earlier in the afternoon. He was getting used to it now and could separate her thoughts from his own quite easily.

As he reached Havenside once more, Faye's familiarity with it helped to settle his mind. He felt as if he already knew it as he walked on past the warehouses, past cottages and the Lion and Lamb before making his way carefully into town.

By the time he had reached Duck Street it was even more obvious just how different everything was. There were no pavements anywhere and most roads were either cobbled or laid with stone slabs. Some of the side roads and lanes were just bare earth with quaint, gnarled little cottages and tumbledown yards spread out along them. Most dwellings had door knockers in the shape of a crucifix and some had religious items displayed in the windows too.

Everywhere was so quiet. He hadn't seen or heard a car and even the market square in the centre of town was deserted. He felt as if he were walking around a gigantic film set or even actually inside the film itself.

He turned a corner and walked straight in front of a man on a bike.

'Woah, I nearly gotcha there, suh!'

'Er - yes' said James, stunned for a moment. The man looked just as if he had come to life from an old black and white photo. He wore a cloth cap above a shabby suit with bicycle clips and a belt made of a piece of string, and he was towing a small wooden box on wheels behind his bike.

'Ass gornabee a rough ole noight tunoight, enut?' he said in a broad Suffolk accent.

James had to struggle to think what the man had said so he half-guessed.

'Yes, I think we may see some rain.'

'Ass gorna be a bad storm, my ole beauty. Yew wanna git indoors if yew can... I thought yew was a forner but you're English, intya, Suh?'

'Yes, I am.' James felt pinned by the man's alert curiosity and tried to keep conversation to a minimum but the man persisted.

'Where yew from then? Yew int local.'

'I've been away for a long while.'

'Oh yes? Where abeauts?'

'Er… London' he said.

A forced, toothy grin crept across the man's face which completely failed to mask the fact that he suddenly felt inferior in the presence of someone from London, a gentleman of a different class.

'Well, you're a very clever young man int ya… I gotta git gorn.'

With that he climbed on his bike and pedalled off, wheels squeaking as he went until the silence closed in once more.

James wondered for a moment, whether Emma would be home yet. The thought was surreal and distant, he couldn't imagine her as if she were only a couple of hours away. It seemed more as if she was on another planet.

He turned in the direction of Amber Lodge once more, relieved that he'd survived his first encounter in this strange place.

There was however, a kind of homeliness about Dunwiche, a settled feeling as if none of the stresses and strains of his own modern life were relevant to it. Maybe it was due to Faye's memories but every hour he stayed, the more James felt at home and although he didn't make a conscious decision to stay overnight, things just happened that way.

Chapter 27 - Young Masters of Christ

That same evening, Joshua Leadpenny entered as usual by the side door of the church hall for the weekly meeting of "The Young Masters Of Christ". He was a little early on purpose this week because of the letter in his jacket pocket. As he expected, Luke Bavent was already there, preparing the evenings agenda. Luke was the captain of the Young Masters and at twenty one, would soon leave to become a full member of the adult church and wear the red sash.

Joshua had only recently turned seventeen and was immensely proud of the "Eye of the Lord" lapel badge his father had given him for his birthday. It was the first step on his way to a position of responsibility and authority within the church and he fully intended to bid for the position of captain as soon as he was able.

Luke was his hero. Luke was a wonderful leader. Luke was everything he wanted to be. He had already started to model himself after Luke. The slicked back hair and the neatly trimmed moustache - well actually just a few straggly hairs at the moment but there was no harm in trying. He approached the top table.

'Excuse me, Captain. May I have a word with you please?' He deepened his voice and copied the smooth well rounded intonation of his idol 'I have an important letter for you.'

Bavent took his time to look up. 'Ah, Leadpenny. You got a cough or something?'

'No Captain.'

'Good. Nice to see you here bright and early. Now, what's this all about a letter eh?'

'It is about the gildenhair, 'tis a letter for you and a speech from my Father on behalf of the High Elder himself to be read out to the Young Masters.'

'Well don't just stand there telling me about it lad, hand it over and let me have a look at it.'

Joshua gave it to him and stood to attention while Bavent turned away from him and unfolded it. After glancing over its contents for a few moments, he turned back towards Leadpenny Junior and looked him up and down.

'So, Joshua. You want to become more active in the Young Masters?'

'Oh yes! I feel it is my calling.'

'Well we need keen and enthusiastic leaders in the church. Your father seems to think that you are already well on your way to becoming one.'

Joshua blushed. He may have been a little enthusiastic at home in some of his descriptions of previous meetings but he hadn't actually lied, not really *lied*. It could easily have been true, everybody did it a bit. Bavent saved him from further embarrassment by ignoring his redness and changing subject.

'This gildenhair is to become our business. Your father surmises that we would be well placed to find out about her as she is young and more likely to speak to people of her own age. He suggests that we form a plan of action. As you are apparently such a blossoming future leader I will place you in charge of reading the speech out during the meeting.'

'Thank you, Captain.' Joshua glowed with pride and leaned forward, lowering his voice. 'Actually, I may be able to dig a bit deeper than some of the others, most of them do not have the contacts I have.'

Bavent said nothing as he watched Leadpenny take his place at table two. He had no place for a self serving creep of a boy who used his fathers' position to further his own ends. However, there was no harm in letting him try, he might actually come up with something.

Boys were filing into the hall and taking their places. The younger ones would leave after prayers and go into the main hall for supervised games and lemonade while the older boys held their meeting and drank ale. Most of the meetings were used to plan social activities for the coming month and to act as a training ground for later when they joined the adult church as full members. Luke Bavent called the meeting to order.

'Gentlemen. Gentlemen... We have a full agenda this evening and if we are to finish in time for prayers with the littleys, we must make progress.'

'Not forgetting the sing-song, after!' shouted a

wag from the back.

'I assure you the ale will keep, Master Butt.'

A general roar of approval carried round the room and the grinning Robert Butt cowered as his friends stood and beat him about the head with their caps.

'Now to the first item on the list. We must decide where to send the young ladies of the church for their annual outing. Any *sensible* suggestions? The minister is concerned that we take this subject more seriously this year.'

'We could send them to Framlingham, they enjoyed it last year' said a boy on table three.

'Yes, and with a one way ticket' said a much younger boy on table twenty-six to a cheer from the other lower tables.

'And then who would cook and clean for you in years to come?' asked Bavent 'We must treat our young ladies with respect and kindness. You will understand such things in a year or two Young Master Oxenfoot.'

As the evening progressed, several events for the coming month were organised. The boys boxing club semi-final would be moved a week earlier. The junior bible study group would be split into two groups to accommodate the new members, and the girls would be sent by railway to the priory at Castle Acre for a day of reading, painting, needlework and whatever else girls did on such outings. Prayers were said and then, when the all young ones had been shepherded out, Bavent rapped the table with his mug.

'Order! Order, gentlemen, please. We now have a separate item to discuss. I have received a letter from Elder Leadpenny on behalf of none other than the High Elder himself. You will all respectfully listen as it is read out to you by Master Leadpenny... Here, Leadpenny... Come over and stand by me, they will hear you all the better for it.'

Leadpenny swelled with pride and walked carefully up to the top table, making sure he didn't trip over a chair leg or the platform itself until he was standing safely next to Bavent. He took a moment to view the room from the place he hoped would one day be his own and cleared his throat.

'This letter is to us all from - *My Father.*'

He paused for a moment, noting with satisfaction the impressed looks on the faces of the boys but failing to see the disdain on the faces at the top table and also from some of the committee.

' "Deare Younge Masters, all. As you will alreadye knowe from our service last Sunday, it has come to the attentione of the elders of the church that a yellow haired girl has been seen recently in Dunwiche. I have decided on behalfe of High Elder FitzJohn, to initiate a searche to find who she is and from whence she came, as her appearance in Dunwiche is something of a mysterye.

The girl is to be treated with extreme cautione as she is knowne to have demons and could cause harm, especiallye as she may not knowe that she is possessed.

We, the Elders, feel that the Young Masters Of Christ would be a valuable source of helpe in finding this girl as she is yet young, and will more likelye seek the companye of those her owne age. I trust that you will report anything, no matter how small and inconsequential it may seeme, to your Captaine." '

Leadpenny junior lowered the letter and looked around once more at the quiet hall. Just for a few moments, everyone had listened to his words. He could feel the power of the moment, *his* moment, and he quietly bathed in the glory of it until Bavent spoke.

'Well, one and all. You have heard the words of the elders. Bring your news of this girl to me and earn points for your teams... And now... Ale!'

A cheer went round the hall and chairs scraped as the monitors got up to serve the ale. Bavent made a quick signal for the committee members and team leaders to follow him to a side room. Once they were all inside, he signalled for the door to be shut.

'Gentlemen, I will not keep you long. I think it would be a good idea for us to form groups and question people on the streets. It will save time and will serve to produce a quick result. The groups should be of only two or three so as not to appear intimidating to the public at large. I have here, some copies of a photograph of the gildenhair. It was taken by chance and is of poor quality but it may serve to expedite matters. Here, pass them round, Leadpenny. Each of you should select a partner from your team, maybe two. In the mean time, let us return to the hall before our ale becomes stale.'

The team leaders filed out leaving Bavent and the committee along with Joshua Leadpenny, Will Percival and Peter Chrispney. Bavent allowed them to stay but ignored them, speaking only to his fellow committee members who had gathered round him.

'Well, I don't know about you fellows but I think this situation offers us a chance to prove ourselves for once and for all before we leave this "Kindergarten". I am all for a more direct approach, never mind all this "Being careful" stuff. The girl is a gildenhair for goodness' sake, and if eggs are to be broken while we carry out God's will, then it is for the greater good of mankind.

A general murmur of agreement ran round the group and Bavent continued 'Did you see the number of people in church? How many do you think there were? About six hundred? Do you think that *none* of them have seen the gildenhair?.. No... Somebody has!'

'My Father and mother have' said Leadpenny, cutting in.

'We *know* that, Leadpenny' said Bavent without turning round. 'Anyway, I think we should also question some of our own church people. You know the ones, the newer members and the lower orders, that sort of thing. Carry a clipboard and look official, push people a little. After all, someone knows something and some pressure may yield a better result.

'Now. Let us pray together... Leadpenny. Get out.'

Chapter 28 - Faraday cage

Amber Lodge reminded James of the Grange because, although it was so different in style, it was obvious that the same person had lived there. The drawing room boasted a grand piano which he played for an hour or so, doodling out some Adele and Coldplay before hunger overtook him.

The kitchen also had a familiar layout. It had a rectangular table with a well worn top where food preparation had been done over many years, a cooking range and a wooden dresser.

Purring came from under the table and he bent down, putting out his hand and drawing a “Tze Tze” noise through his teeth to the cat who immediately rubbed herself round his ankles and purred more loudly. ‘My God!’ he said ‘So you can travel here too. I’m glad I didn’t name you otherwise you would be confused. So *you’re* Starlight! I’m going to have trouble explaining to Emma and Phil why you’re called that!’

Starlight looked up at him as if she thought he was a bit slow on the uptake and then sedately made her way to her milk saucer, looking back to make sure he got the hint.

‘Milk’s supposed to be bad for cats’ he scolded

gently as he opened the larder door. A chill met him inside, the stone walls were painted white and lined with well stocked shelves, In the corner was a shallow stone sink, it was filled with freezing cold water and had a covered milk jug standing in it. He poured tiny amount into some water in the the saucer and left her to lap at it.

Feeling hungry, he removed a fly net from over a shoulder of ham and tried a piece, it was delicious so he made a sandwich with it and also poured himself a glass of the cold, rich, creamy milk, wondering if it had come straight from the churn.

The library was his next stop and he struggled to turn on the lights until he realised what the hissing sound was. They were gas lamps, the switch had to be held in the on position until they had all been ignited safely.

He put the food down on the table and searched the shelves to see if there were any books which would be useful to him. Among the extensive collection of novels and reference books, he could only find one familiar name. The complete works of William Shakespeare were sitting on the shelf between Sanforde and Sumner. Eventually he came across some unfamiliar versions of the Bible, a copy of the Elucidatum Divinicus and several books on the occult together with some handwritten notes.

After reading for a long time under the pale lemon glow of the gas lamps, his tired eyes nagged at him to take a break. He went to get another glass of milk and decided on the way back, to have a look at the turret room. He thought how strange it was that, because Faye knew where the keys and the panel were, he did too.

He moved the piece of wooden trim, turned the key and watched the panel slide open to reveal the stairway. At the top, he stood for a moment in anticipation before pushing open the trapdoor and walking up into the room.

Just as Faye had done, he sat in the chair and switched on the tiny table lamp. He was fascinated by the construction of the room and spent some time studying it before excitedly coming to the conclusion that it was much more special than first sight would indicate.

The brass frame was not bolted to the stone floor as he would have expected, instead, it was insulated from it and continued down to an unknown anchor point far below. The handrails were made of rubber and were attached to a separate frame which was fixed to the floor. *This whole thing is one gigantic Faraday cage* James thought as he examined it further. *I'm completely insulated from everything inside this. Totally safe, even from a direct lightning strike.*

As if on cue, lightning flickered off the coast and reminded him of what the old man had said about it being a rough night. He could feel the air changing and he thought once more of Faye's unease before she entered the light.

Everything felt so different here. The weather was more moody and brooding. Things he touched seemed to have more substance to them as if somehow, they were more real, more intense, slightly charged.

Another flicker followed by a low rumble prompted him to switch off the lamp and stand at the rail. Outside, all was still. The lanterns on Havenside reflected dimly in the water but apart from that, Dunwich was almost totally enveloped in blackness.

His eyes had only just got used to the dark when a huge, white flash and simultaneous deafening bang knocked his senses into disarray for a moment. *Bloody Hell, that was actually frightening!* His first instinct was to run but he fought it knowing that he was already in the safest place. Heart still racing, he sat down to recover from the shock.

Wind whipped around making whistling noises as it rushed to fill the vacuum caused by the lightning, rattling the weathervane around and making the bells above his head play wild arpeggios as it spun. A sudden gust blew directly through a vent and carried with it a faint aroma. It was so slight that all but the most gentle breathing made it vanish; it smelt vaguely metallic.

Faye's worries from earlier came again into his mind and he let them play out like a film. She had noticed the same smell, but she hadn't been the only one. The mutterings of the shabby woman in the street "*Dripping all down my walls it is, that 'lectric stuff. You know what I mean.*" She had raised her voice as Faye ran past "*You brung this on us.*" The rest was lost as Faye had run out of earshot and she had at the time assumed that it was just another insult. But now, like pieces of a puzzle it was starting to make a kind of sense to James.

A flash over the sea brought him back to the rail as thunder rumbled loudly. Another flash from the same general direction lit the clouds, allowing him a glimpse of the steamy turmoil. *What was that in the sea?*

He looked hard into the blackness hoping to see in the light of the next flash. When it came he saw an area off the coast which didn't reflect the lightning. He thought that maybe it could be a sand bank.

The lightning was much more frequent now, casting stark electric colours and bizarre shadows all over the town. He found himself enjoying the spectacle even when another huge flash crackled and banged overhead, much too close for comfort. Again there was the same faint smell as the wind rushed around, then a moment later all the lanterns went out on Havenside.

He looked out to sea once more and was surprised to find that the sand bank was much smaller than it had been only a few minutes before. In the next flash it was smaller still, and seemed to be receding at an incredible rate, then suddenly it was gone.

A chill of fear ran through him as another black hole grew and then shrank to nothing within just a few seconds. *That's no sandbank* he thought as he peered seawards through the storm - *Oh my God! there's nothing there!*

Rain lashed the turret room as he groped for the chair, his mind racing, piecing together more and more of the fragments of the puzzle. So many vague and seemingly unrelated pieces of the puzzle were starting to link together. The complexity of it all was mind boggling as the shared knowledge and experiences of Faye and himself came together to form one enormous conclusion.

It's going to happen again!

Chapter 29 - The prediction engine

Next morning still in the armchair, James awoke and stretched. He must have fallen asleep for at least a short while after the storm had subsided. Now he felt stiff and tired.

He looked out at the early morning sunlight and heaved a sigh. The sheer effort of thinking deeply for so long had taken its toll and it was all he could do to flump downstairs and find a bathroom.

Mrs Larkin was more than surprised to find him there when she turned up to work but after realising who he was, she fussed about making him a generous breakfast insisting that he should eat it in the dining room like a proper gentleman.

He selected some kippered herring from a silver tureen and helped himself to toast while she stood attentively nearby. It felt a little uncomfortable sitting on his own at one end of the table being watched while he ate but Mrs Larkin would not hear of anything less. There was a class division between them and he was learning quickly that form always came before comfort. She did however, suggest that he might like to just happen by the kitchen a little later for a piece of cake; they could talk more comfortably there.

Still in a dark mood, James spent some time in the morning room after breakfast, reading through Daniel DeLara's notes to see if anything had been written down about holes appearing in the sea. He found nothing, Daniel had been very methodical though, and had catalogued virtually everything he saw as even remotely unusual. He seemed worried that his name was not his real one and had, on several pages, tried to suggest reasons for it. He was also worried about his age and wanted to make sure that Amber Lodge would be kept as it was in case he should return in a new life.

James let those last few words sink in.

Had Daniel made a final decision to cross reality, with the idea that he could come back as a different person? In that case, was it possible that he, James was that person? What about Faye? Where did she fit in? She didn't have a past beyond a couple of weeks, and the circumstances surrounding James's own birth had been a complete mystery. Maybe Daniel had managed it but had unwittingly caused a side effect and the existence of both Faye and himself were the result of it.

Certainly time and reality were not what people assumed and Daniel had realised this years ago. He had been through the light many times and had written about aspects of it which James and Faye had not yet discovered. He had also noticed that the unusual weather patterns were a symptom of something much bigger and although he didn't know what it was, he knew it was something to do with his reality and possibly others, being slightly unstable.

In need of a break, James stood up and looked for a diversion. The morning room was decorated in shades of blue and gold and as he walked around the ample sofas, he realised how similar they were in style to the ones in The Grange. In fact, the whole layout of the room was similar except for a rather tall cabinet which mostly filled the wall space between the two windows. It was locked and none of the house keys would fit it. He tried to jiggle the doors open, after all, it was only a piece of furniture. Normally a cabinet lock had a simple purpose, to keep the doors secure against casual nosiness but this was something else. It wouldn't budge.

With his curiosity aroused, he knelt down and peered underneath, hoping to find a dropped key but expecting to find nothing but the floor. It was dusty and dark but he could just make out a shape right at the back near the skirting board. He worked his hand underneath until he could feel it and carefully pulled it towards him. It was a heavy duty electrical plug with a fat, woven cable attached. It wasn't like the funny little plugs on the vacuum cleaner and some of the lamps, they were all marked "40 Voltaire". This plug handled much more power.

He knelt down once more and waited for his eyes to adjust to the gloom under the cabinet. There was a black shape in the skirting board which he correctly assumed must be a socket so he fiddled the plug around until it slid home.

Above him there was a clunk, followed by a low-level electrical hum as the doors of the cabinet slowly swung open, revealing a mass of knobs and switches behind a sprawling mess of cables.

After dusting himself down, James stared in amazement at the sight before him. The inside of the wooden cabinet held several rows of black metal panels. Tiny lights were flashing on them, some at random, some in sequence. A plaque inside the door pronounced the machine to be a "Predictione engine".

A yellowing note book sat in the corner of the cabinet near the power switch. James picked it up and read from the final pages.

L.F.O. 1 = Time of daye.

L.F.O. 2 = Temp of daye.

n ~ offset = 30% nom.

Input 1 =Year temp.

Input 2 = 11 year temp.

S & H . 1 = Randomme variationes in year temp.

S & H. 2 = Randomme variationes in 11 year temp.

The list went on and on, declaring the intended

use of each module in the cabinet, right down to electromagnetic activity. Previous pages were dedicated to earlier experiments, some with lines crossing out errors and diagrams showing the positions of various knobs and noting precise readings from meters. He looked more carefully at the machine before him and recognised layout as being similar to the early Moog modular music synthesiser like the one he'd found on top of the piano in The Grange.

This was a field he understood and he examined everything once more in detail to verify that he was right. He found a switch marked "Chart" which, when flicked on, caused a loud clunk from a side table across the room as the top of it jumped and shook the ornaments. He cleared it and lifted the top to reveal a loaded roll of graph paper and several graph pens poised at the ready. The roll of graph paper was yellow with age but still serviceable and was marked out in voltages from minus, to plus twelve "Voltaire".

One more look through the note book convinced him that he had found a kind of analogue computer where, instead of binary data, it used voltages to generate answers to anything the operator could dream up. The rows of modules in the cabinet generated or modified these voltages which could be used to represent elements of the problem being addressed such as time of day, temperature and many more subtle additions. The results were marked out by the pen on the graph paper.

Judging by the detail of the last settings in the

book, Daniel DeLara had obviously been planning to run the machine for something important. James adjusted the initial settings for temperature, humidity and as many other factors as he could find, to those of the current day and time, checking carefully that they were as accurate as possible before attempting to run the machine. A small button on the sequencer shone red. He pressed it and a long row of tiny lamps started to chase from left to right, along the front panel. The dried out pens started to scratch away at the graph paper and James quickly pressed the stop button.

Some bottles of coloured inks stood in a recess beside the graph paper. The lids were sealed tight with age and dribbles of dried ink. James managed to open one and found to his surprise that the ink was still usable once they had been shaken up. He prised the others open and filled the tiny reservoirs above each pen before pressing the red button once more. After a few scratchy moments, the pens started to settle down and start to mark out long, slow curves and jagged scribbles as the paper wound slowly underneath them.

James shut the lid of the table and left the machine running to see what it came up with over time.

Chapter 30 - James and Rhiannon

A dark feeling of foreboding started to creep over James and the house started to feel gloomy. He needed to get some fresh air and ease his brooding mind so he decided to go for a walk.

He kept going over the conclusions he had drawn from the night before but he couldn't see any way to do anything practical with them. All he could do at the moment was to watch and see how events would unfold.

Obviously he could go back through the light and never return but that was not an option. It would mean that Faye would never exist again. He could stay and guess when the rift was about to happen, go through and wait for a week or so, then allow Faye to return, but to what? Dunwiche may have been completely destroyed. There was no guarantee that it would behave the same way as the last rift. No... One of them would have to stay through the rift and take the consequences for both.

As he walked on towards the centre of town, he saw a familiar figure, familiar at least to Faye. Rhiannon was slouching on a bench outside a tavern with two boys who were hanging around her like flies round a honey pot. She was teasing and goading them while keeping them transfixed by subtly wiggling her outstretched legs. *Minx!* he thought, and was just about to shout to her when he realised his situation.

'Excuse me' he said when he reached the group 'By any chance, are you a friend of Miss Faye DeLara?'

'Who wants to know' she said eying him with suspicion while the boys backed off a little.

'I am her cousin James, you must be Rhiannon.'

'Damn!' she said turning to the nearest boy 'and you needn't look a' me like that, Joshua Leadpenny.'

'My Father says people will go to Hell for saying things like that' he retorted.

'Your father'll go to Hell just for being your father' she said pulling a snooty face at him before turning her attention to James as both boys slunk away 'You said too much, he'll go tell his precious dad now.'

'I'm sorry, I didn't know' James said awkwardly.

She looked up and gave him a care-worn smile, he saw into her soul and immediately understood why Faye thought so much of her.

'You got to be careful these days just how much you say in public, there's people looking for Faye. When you said my name they found out that I know her. Now they'll know her name too. 'Twas alright until then.'

'I'm sorry, I haven't got used to being in Dunwiche yet. It's been quite an experience.'

She stared at him still with suspicion 'How do I

know you're tellin' the truth? You could be anybody.'

'Well, I know you put Whimsey leaves in her scent' said James carefully 'and you said that it was a bit naughty but it that suited her. Will that do as proof?'

'How on this earth did you know about that?' she said incredulously. 'Only Faye could have told you, 'cos we were alone.'

'Precisely' said James.

'I was hoping to see Faye today' she said, relaxing and brightening up. 'The market boat is due to visit soon and I promised her we'd go... Come on, I'll show you round.'

As they walked, she chatted to him about Faye and her worries about the True Path. It was all very valuable to James and he was pleased that she could offer such vast detail, even if it was biased by teenage bluntness and enthusiasm. He was surprised at her sudden and complete trust in him. It was as if, just by being seen as a cousin of Faye, he had been made a member of a secret club and could be trusted completely.

All the time she talked, Rhiannon never let her guard down. She was constantly looking around and would change the subject if anyone came near. Most of the people they passed were talking in soft worried tones about the storm being the worst they had ever seen. Rhiannon made a grim joke about the True Path falling into the pits of Hell, he looked into her eyes and saw that she was scared, deeply scared.

'Do you really think that another Day of Judgement will come?' he ventured.

'I dunno... Don' care really, I'll be going to Hell in it anyway.'

'Why do you keep saying that?'

' 'Cos it's true. I'm Damned you see... I know I'm going.'

'I promise you that you're not.'

'Reverend says I am.'

'And I say you're not... Leadpenny is though' he winked.

She laughed and slipped her hand into his in an unconscious and purely innocent search for comfort and reassurance. He turned and faced her.

'I promise that you really are not going to hell. Will you be brave and listen carefully to me for a moment? I have some really important things to tell you.'

They sat down together on a patch of grass by the roadside, Rhiannon suddenly looking very young, all her usual bravado and show had gone. She was a frightened girl in a world which used religious belief and ritual to hide its fears and control its people.

'Do you remember when you made the rose petal scent the other day?' She nodded. 'And Faye said "What if I were a witch?" Well in a way, she is.'

'Never!' Rhiannon's jaw dropped with astonishment.

'She wanted to tell you about herself but you didn't get the hint. The thing is, she - *We* - can both do things which other people can't. It's sort of like magic.'

'So it's true what people are saying about her then?'

'Well, not exactly. Magic is just a word that people use when they can't explain something. She's not really a witch but it's an easy name for people to call her because they can see that something is different about her. People on their own aren't stupid. They can tell if something seems different or out of place, even if they can't say for sure what it is. But put them in a group and they develop a kind of shared belief about something and that's where the danger lies. The belief can become bigger than the people who own it.'

'What? Like the True Path you mean?'

'Yes, but not just them, they are just the most extreme. Everyone can be affected.'

'So you're saying - me as well?'

'Maybe a little. You're sensible enough to see through a lot of the stories and that's why people tell you you're going to Hell and rubbish like that. But you won't, because there isn't one. It's just another made up story. Hell does not exist outside the minds of the people who believe in it.'

She shook her head, trying hard to take in what he was saying. 'You don' talk like anyone round here, you're so much like Faye.'

'You have no idea' he said with feeling.

James told her a little about where he came from and also about his links to Faye so that she would understand why they would never all meet together.

Then he gently explained about the possibility of another "Day of Judgement" although he explained it as kind of rift in reality rather than an act of an angry God. Her eyes were wide with fear as he tried to reassure her and say that it didn't necessarily mean that they were all going to die.

When he had finished, a different and wiser Rhiannon sat with him. She poked at the grass with a stick.

'How long do think we will have?'

'I don't know, but I think it will happen fairly soon. These thunder storms are not like the ones I know at home, they are really vicious and the lightning is almost surreal.'

He didn't say any more, realising that he could frighten her again if he mentioned the dark holes in the sea and other strange things he had seen and read about. She had taken everything very well so far but he was worried about saying too much at one time. She needed time to digest it before anything else was said and he was relieved when she changed the subject.

'That boy I was with earlier, he's the son of one of the elders in the True Path. His dad will know by now that I know Faye and that you were asking about her. He's a sneaky little snot.'

'What about the other boy?'

'Oh, Will, you mean? He's just a boy… He's one of Josh's little henchmen, that's all.'

James told her to be careful around them, adding that anyone who had henchmen was building a power base, even if that person was still only a boy. Surprisingly, she took him seriously and in turn, warned him to guard his tongue and stay vigilant.

They parted with a promise to keep in touch and share what they knew. James couldn't believe the way that Rhiannon just accepted and trusted him. At home, he would have probably been seen as a pervert or something for approaching a young girl he didn't know in the street.

Chapter 31 - Greyfriars again

Later that afternoon, Tobias was working in the gardens when a stranger arrived at Greyfriars asking for him. He laid down his tools and quickly wiped his hands on his robe as he made his way to the edge of the vegetable plot.

'How may I be of assistance to you?' He asked as he approached the stranger, clasping his hands together in a benevolent manner.

'I think we may be able to help each other with some rather delicate matters.'

Tobias unclasped his hands and let his expression slip a little. That kind of greeting usually meant that something shady was about to be offered.

'I am not interested, sir, in any private "Services" you may have to offer, no matter how pretty they may be.'

'I'm not selling anything' said the stranger. 'I need your help and I know you need mine; It concerns a Nonnye that you found recently. I'm sorry if I gave the wrong impression... Maybe this will mean something to you' he said holding out the iPod which Faye had borrowed.

'Where did you get this?'

'From a good friend of yours, she wanted to know what it was.'

'And what in fact is this little box?' Tobias asked warily.

'It's a music player.'

'Do you mean - like a phonomat?'

'Yes, if that's what you call them. Look, here is the play button and the other controls, and here's where you plug in the headphones, and you can read the titles on the screen - except that this one doesn't work of course.'

'So it is the whole phonomat and not just the control box?' Tobias stared at the flat white tablet in wonder. 'Where does one place the music? The cylinder must be minute.'

James explained a digital download and watched with amusement as Tobias's eyes grew wider with each word.

The two men walked as James properly introduced himself, using the story about being a cousin of Faye. Tobias was much more open-minded than James had hoped but his shyness was made obvious by his blushes every time Faye was mentioned.

'The girl you seek is still in the infirmary' Tobias said. 'She has progressed and is now able to speak well. We must be careful however, as I am really supposed to seek permission from Friar Gregory before allowing visitors, but in this case I think it is better that we act on our own as I am sure that too many questions will be asked of you.'

Once at the infirmary, Isla Williams was

brought before James who asked to be allowed to speak with her alone. The duty assistant wasn't sure about leaving the room but Tobias convinced him that James was an expert in matters of the mind and had travelled many miles to see the girl.

Once they were alone, James motioned to Isla to sit down. They faced each other across the table. She sat back with a defiant look.

'Hello' said James.

'Not again!'

'What's the matter?'

'That's all you people ever say... When can I go home?'

'I don't know, but hopefully soon' said James evenly.

'You ca - ca -' she went red with frustration 'can't - keep me here like this! I want to go home, my Mum and Dad will be frantic by now... Why are these freaks keeping me locked up?' She gave Tobias a hostile glare.

James sympathised. 'The monks are trying to protect you and look after you. How did you get here?'

'I don't remember.'

'Well, try and explain what happened before you got here. What was the last thing you did? Even if it sounds crazy to you.'

Isla thought for a moment. 'I was just walking home from school with my mates... We were texting this boy and stuff...'

'Go on, you're doing fine.'

'Well... I grabbed my mate's phone and ran off with it to read what she said about me, and then - I was beside all this water.'

'O.K. This is important. Where did you run to when you grabbed the phone?'

'I just ran round the corner and leaned up against the wall... Well I was going to but' she looked uncomfortably at him 'then there was only grass and I fell over and felt sick.'

'Did you black out?'

'Yeah, I think so.'

'O.K. Thanks. That had better be all for now, I'll let you know as soon as I have any news for you.'

She looked at James quizzically for a moment. 'You're not one of them are you? Only, all they do is say that God's spared me and give me bibles to read... This place is mad! There's no telly', they pretend they've never heard of it, *and* I have to sleep with all these kids in a dormitory. I just want to go home. Why can't you just take me home?'

'Unfortunately I don't know how to yet. But hang in there, the monks really are trying to help you. Just be patient and I'll try to do something. That's a promise' said James.

'Thank you.' She smiled at him for the first time.

'How's the food?' James asked suddenly, thinking that at least he may be able to sort something out for her in the meantime.

'The vegetables taste of dirt, I hate fish and the meat's disgusting. Apart from that, it's lovely' she said with a sarcastic smile.

'I'll see what I can do. They grow all their own vegetables here, that's why they taste different, and the meat could be deer, rabbit, pigeon or anything.'

'What? You mean I'm eating - *bunny rabbits*? URGH!'

James tried in vain to hide his amusement but failed and he quietly had a word with Tobias outside to explain.

'Make the meals sweeter?' exclaimed Tobias 'What a ridiculous idea! The kitchens will not hear of such a thing but I will see if chickens can be prepared for them more often, and as for giving them beef, who do they think they are to demand such expensive fare?'

'Thanks, Tobias. May I ask one more favour of you? I would like to see the man - Mr Oi I think you call him, I'm a bit concerned about him and, frankly, I think he's dangerous.'

Their voices dropped to a near whisper as Tobias tried to talk James out of the idea but after a few minutes of protest, he relented and reluctantly led the way towards the cellars.

'I will wait for you here' said Tobias as they reached the top of the stairs.

James walked past the many shelves of things from his own reality until he found the cell. He stood out of sight and waited, listening carefully.

'Someone's there' said a low grinding voice. 'Come for a look?' he sneered.

James stayed quiet.

'Scared to show yourself, are you?'

The taunting sarcasm echoed round the cellars. James stayed quiet, still hoping to hear more.

'I rec'n I know who you are... And where you live, don't you want to know how?.. These do-gooders don't know nothing!'

James made his way to a pillar a little distance away and peered from behind it. A face was trying to see through the door of the cell, a most vile face.

'C'mon! Show yourself.' He pushed his voice into a high mocking tone 'Is it the little girlie what came down here before?' and then dropped his pitch once more to a low growl 'I know where you live.'

James moved quietly to the next pillar while the ugly head turned and twisted to catch a glimpse of him.

'Oh... No it isn't!.. It's a bloke... Hello mate, what's *your* problem? Scared of being seen are you? Wimp!'

A small, worried group of monks had joined Tobias at the top of the stairs. When he reached them, James refused to say a word until they had moved some distance from the infirmary.

'I don't want him to hear my voice because he could use it to recognise me.'

'But he has already seen you' said one of the group.

'Yes but not very well' said James. 'He only got a glimpse of me from behind.'

'He always knows when I am there even before I reach his cell, I think he can even see in the dark' said another.

'We pray unto the Lord for his soul.'

'Whatever you feel you have to do, Brother' said James 'but don't rely on your prayers. He's as sharp as they come and will always be one step ahead of you.'

He got up to leave, Tobias walked with him towards the main gate.

'Do you know of a woman known as Mad Esther?' James asked.

'I have heard of her, I believe she is one of the town's more eccentric characters but that is all. Why do you ask?'

'I don't know yet, but I think she may not be as mad as people think.'

'People are quick to judge.'

'Aren't they just!'

'Things are changing for the worse are they not, James?'

'Yes they are. I can feel it in the air.'

'I want to help if I may, but I do not know how.'

'You've helped a great deal already.'

James paused and faced him for a moment, something seemed to have gone from the young monk's eyes, they looked suddenly dull as he stared back. James felt a small shiver run up his spine.

'Are you sure you're O.K. Tobias?'

'If by your question you mean "Is all well with me?" Then I must answer No.'

'What's bothering you?'

Tobias sadly looked at the ground and kicked his foot at a stone. Faye's first smile had melted him into a gibbering jelly and he hadn't been able to concentrate fully on his duties since then. He didn't find it easy around girls at the best of times, not that he'd had too much experience of meeting them but Faye was different. She didn't just pose prettily and pretend to have nothing important in her head. She had ideas and opinions about things which she voiced without any of the careful reserve which society usually expected of a young miss.

It was exciting to hear her speak so freely. Part of him was envious. He wished he had been allowed to speak his mind and ask more questions when he was a child. His Father's dearest wish though, was that he should dedicate his life to God and the care of those in need. Tobias had obeyed his wishes and joined the Grey Friars where he studied the legal sciences and explored the wonders of God's creation without having to think about earthly pleasures and sins, at least, not until the day he had seen Faye.

'I wish to know something about Faye' he said eventually, almost squirming under the strain of asking. 'What is it that she really is? I have heard it said that she is a witch, and some call her an outcast and say that she has demons. I do not believe such things but she does radiate a strange and unsettling air.'

James considered for a moment. 'I can assure you that she is not what they claim. It's true though, that she has some abilities which other people don't posses, but that doesn't make her guilty of all the things people blame her for.'

'Do you think she has faith in our Lord God?' He said.

James saw the hope fading in Tobias and felt a sudden sharp pang of the feelings that Faye held for him. He answered carefully.

'She knows that there is so much more to our existence than just the things we can see or the things we believe.'

Tobias looked troubled. They walked on as he wrestled with his thoughts, unease showing clearly on his face.

'You did not answer me though' he said.

'Yes, I know.' James put a supportive arm round the young monk. 'The truthful answer is that she does not believe or disbelieve. She searches for truth whatever that truth is.'

'But the truth is taught to us from the Bible is it not? It is God's own truth.'

'And you accept it just like that?'

Tobias raised his head and met James's gaze. 'It is all I know... She unnerves me with her opinions and her ways. There is something disturbing about her and yet, somehow I know in my heart that she is with us for a good reason.'

'She has a kind of unique understanding of things' said James. 'Look after her well, I know that she cares deeply for you. She may not share your faith but she respects it. It's part of who you are and it makes you strong.'

They parted company and James, still troubled, made his way down the hill towards Maison Dieu Lane, suddenly feeling the full weight of the problems resting on his shoulders. These people were real, their world was real and their problems were now his as well.

He thought about home. Emma would be at work, so would Phil with the summer school. It all seemed so remote though, this was reality for now, this strange place where people saw ghosts and believed in witches, and lived in fear of God because they had seen things that couldn't be explained. Yes, this was definitely reality. It must be because he was here.

Chapter 32 - Madness and menace

The morning rain fell silently past the window of Emma's third floor office turning the scene outside a dull grey, punctuated only by the passing red smudges of London buses.

She stared down at the queue of people waiting to enter the museum. Most of them had bored looking children with them and stood under plastic brollies with their heads down, patiently waiting for the queue to move on a couple of feet.

She turned back to her desk and tried to busy herself with a plan of a site in Somerset where a bracelet and a chalice had been uncovered by a farmer. It had stirred up a lot of unwanted interest from some of the stranger people who hung around the Glastonbury area and the police had been called in to cordon off the site.

Her mind drifted off again. She was overtired from the sleepless nights she'd endured since the weekend and she'd been struggling ever since to concentrate on work. James was supposed to be back at work by now but he wasn't answering his emails or his phone and she had a distinct feeling that something was wrong.

A soft ping sounded from behind her announced an incoming email. She turned to deal with it, half expecting it to be just another memo.

It was, however, from James's boss, inquiring whether she had any idea of his whereabouts. He hadn't shown up for work at all and there was no message to explain it, not that it was a problem of course, and - sorry to bother her - but it was so unlike James.

Of *course* it was a problem. She sent a carefully worded reply, Bcc'd to James, which sounded helpful but actually didn't say much at all, and then left another rather sharply worded message on James's answerphone.

That was it. There was nothing more she could do. She was at work in London and although she had a good idea where of he was, she couldn't do anything about it. She turned back to the window, annoyed that she couldn't get the whole thing out of her head.

◆ ◆ ◆

James meanwhile, had been immersed in some very different problems. He had spent time blending himself into the local life as best he could with new clothes and a hat to help hide his hair. Luckily, the local dialect was not much of a problem because it was class-based, with broad Suffolk being used mostly by the working classes. All he had to do was lose any modern slang, use a more formal tone of voice and people would quite easily accept him as a gentleman.

Rumour had it, that Mad Esther lived somewhere in St James parish out towards Westleton. He came across her on Sandy Lane, shuffling along the road with a heavy basket and moaning to herself and anybody else within earshot about 'lectric stuff' dripping all over the house.

He kept a discreet distance and let her ramble on for a while, hoping to hear something interesting, but it wasn't to be. Most of her coherent words were about disgustingly foul language and blasphemy coming from the voices inside her wall. Eventually he decided to approach her.

'Excuse me, ma'am' he said 'I am from the electric company. I could not help but overhear you saying that you have a problem with your electricity.'

She carried on walking and answered him without looking up 'I ain't got no 'lectric. What d'you think I am? I ain't got no money to pay for your 'spensive services, blasphemin' and laughin' and so on, that's what they do, the demons in my wall.'

James tried once more, using what he hoped would be a more appealing approach. 'The trouble is, madam, we have been losing electricity from leaks in our cables and we have no idea where it is going.'

This time he got the reaction he was looking for, she stopped suddenly and looked him up and down for a moment before straightening herself up and addressing him.

'I'll tell you where it is going, my good man! 'Tis

soakin' into my wall! I don't want it. Devils stuff - and all them bad words and spirits!'

James tried to steer her back onto the subject.

'Would you like me to have a look and see whether anything can be done about it?'

'They do say some awful things, they do - awful - and all that 'lectric dripping down my wall -' she stopped dead once more as if his words had finally filtered through "Yes, Mister 'lectric man. Come you with me and see what I have to put up with, if you please.'

They soon reached her tiny thatched cottage, a dingy hovel down by the road bridge which looked as if one hard push would knock it down. Inside, it smelled of chimney soot and fish, the walls and ceilings were stained with soot and a thin brown film. He soon saw where it came from. The ceiling above a small oil burning stove was covered with a brown oily residue from the flue. Drips of it had set like treacle and were encrusted with dust and soot. The stench made him feel sick.

She had to be reminded at least twice why he was there, the reason being obvious from the gin bottles which covered the table. James politely refused a cracked china cupful of "Medicinal Gin" and watched as she downed it quickly herself, before he could have time to change his mind.

He moved a chair out of the way and pretended to look for leaks while she watched him with a beady eye. Drunk, she may be, but she was still sharp and wanted to see him doing something which looked official.

He held his arms out and frowned as if he was assessing the problem and then pretended to write something down. Much to his relief, she lost interest after a few minutes and shuffled off to her equally grimy little kitchen with her basket.

Once she was safely out of sight, James examined the wall for real. He wasn't sure what he was looking for, but hoped to find some small clue, anything, to confirm his mounting suspicions. He held a hand out towards it and felt a tickle like a small electrical charge in his finger tips as they made contact with the crumbling plaster. A couple of lads walked past on the other side of the wall and in a different reality, swearing with ease as they talked. As their voices trailed off into the distance James heard a mobile phone ringtone, hollow and echoey.

'Now you see!'

James jumped with surprise as the old lady's voice shrilled out from the doorway just behind him where she had silently returned to watch.

'Now you know! All that blaspheming - wicked! - foul and wicked!'

She ranted on again as James collected his wits. He hadn't realised that she'd been standing there and he desperately hoped that she hadn't seen his fingers merge into the wall.

She poured herself another gin and asked what the "Lectric Company" were going to do about it. James took the opportunity to suggest that he might return for a further examination, possibly with a colleague. She agreed to it although it was likely that she would forget as soon as he had gone.

He saw himself out, leaving her alone in the filthy gloom with her gin and started back towards town, piecing everything together as he walked.

He was quite sure now that the wall was actually where a weakening in the fabric of reality itself was forming. It was odd he thought, how the edges of reality were attracted to the edges of a physical space. Isla must have fallen through a weak spot in the wall as she leaned against it with the phone. *I must get word to Tobias* he thought, *there's a chance that we can at least get her back through, and possibly even some more of them.*

Nobody in the streets paid him any attention as he walked and it suited him to be as anonymous as possible. He was becoming a little more familiar with the way of life now and could pick out different types of people by their clothes and the way they acted. Rhiannon's father had been a great help with this, pointing out particular signs which people would use to declare their allegiances. A brooch or pin, a hand shake, even the design on a necktie. Of course, the same thing happened at home. The religious symbol of a dove or fish that people would stick on the back of cars or wear as a lapel badge, a school tie or a company logo and of course, having the right designer label. All of these were signs for others to read, but here it all seemed a bit sinister and secretive.

He pulled his hat down low as he approached a

group of uniformed young men in dark suits. They all had gold lapel badges in the shape of a cross with a large engraved glass eye staring out from the centre. The badge had the nickname the “Eye of the Lord” and was a sign of dedicated True Path membership signifying that God was always watching.

A shiver ran through him at the thought of what it symbolised. Faye had enough problems looming already and the last thing he wanted was for them to find a second gildenhair, himself, in Dunwiche, especially a man. One of the men suddenly noticed him and called him over, holding out a photograph of a young girl.

It took just a moment for James to recognise the subject of the photo. He drew a sharp breath and immediately tried to cover it with a coughing fit as his mind reeled and his whole world suddenly started to spin before his eyes.

He had allowed himself to become too preoccupied with the problems of others and had completely lost sight of the fact that he was a stranger here and only a few days ago had panicked at the thought of venturing too far from Amber Lodge.

Reality flooded back and hit him like a wall. He was sure that they would notice his hands shaking and he struggled to maintain an act of normality and stay casual as he stared at the first picture he had ever seen of Faye.

‘Do you recognise this girl, Sir?’

‘Er - Let me have a closer look’ he said, taking hold of the picture and committing every detail of it to memory while he had the chance. 'Yes, I think I may have done, but not recently.'

'Ah, we have another sighting - good. My colleague here will take your name and details if you please, Sir.'

James, even in his current state, had no intention of giving his details and bought a little more thinking time with a question 'Who is the girl and why do you want her?' he asked as calmly as he could.

'She is just a young soul who needs our help. No concern of yours, Sir.'

James paused for a moment too long. The man narrowed his eyes and parted his jacket to show a cosh in his belt 'Does this help you to remember anything more? Sir?' The undercurrent of menace in his voice was unmistakable.

'No, it doesn't help, but I have seen her. She was walking by the haven, I noticed her very bright hair.'

'And when would this have been, Sir?'

'Oh, about two weeks ago I should think. Yes, at least two weeks.'

Surely the man would know it was a lie. James felt his legs starting to shake but managed to steady them by changing the way he stood. He decided in desperation, on a plan to face them out. It wasn't a good plan though, and if it didn't work, plan B was just to run very fast.

'I see, Sir. And now if my colleague could have your details?'

'Are you the Church Police then?'

'Not *actually*, Sir. But we are working closely with them.'

'Then I would politely request that I withhold my details at the present time.' said James as boldly as he could 'I am sure that you will already know of my association with the Bishop and will understand the rather delicate situation it may cause.'

The group, suddenly unsure of their ground, reluctantly agreed that it would be better that they should be discreet and let James go about his business unhindered. After all, it was for the Bishop. His only task now was to walk away in what he hoped was a normal way.

Not too fast he thought.

Not too slow.

Just confident and with purpose.

Don't look back.

Each step was torture, wondering if they would wait until he thought he'd got away with it before they called him back, but the call never came.

He reached the corner and stepped out of their line of sight. His legs felt as if they would give way any second and his whole body started to shake. He had to get off the street for a while and calm down.

He slipped through a gate into a yard and hid behind a wood pile, hoping that no one had seen him. The men's voices came close by on the other side of the wall and he held his breath, feeling his heart thumping. He could just make out occasional snippets of conversation, they kept saying "The Gildenhair" when they mentioned Faye, as if to dehumanise her. Their voices when they spoke to each other were clipped and hard and all traces of their polite, public persona were gone.

They crudely joked with each other about what they would do to Faye in a way that made James feel sick. She wasn't even human as far as they were concerned, she was a gildenhair. She had demons and they constantly referred to her as "It". There was no love or compassion in anything but their public image as the the "Followers Of The True Path To Salvation".

Their voices and footsteps slowly faded away into the distance. He supposed it wouldn't be too long before they knew a whole lot more about Faye. The feeling of menace was overwhelming and he could see now how easily people could be bullied into complying with them. His initial feelings of homeliness about Dunwiche had completely evaporated and, for the moment, been replaced by paranoia. It wouldn't be too long before his deception was noticed and then he too would be wanted.

He sat, hugging his knees up to his chin and thinking about the photograph of Faye. She had been laughing and her eyes were shining with glee. A vague memory flashed across his mind and he heard Faye saying to Rhiannon "What if I *were* a witch?"

Chapter 33 - A big decision

James made his way via the back streets to Greyfriars. He found Tobias and told him what had happened and of an idea to try to get Isla and some others back to where she should be. Then he went carefully on his way towards Amber Lodge, passing several groups of people on the way.

Most of them were in their late teens or early twenties and all wearing pseudo military uniforms with the "Eye" pinned to their lapels. They must have only just started canvassing the streets because he hadn't seen anything like it happening before.

Tobias had immediately started to form a plan and prepare for action. He'd thought it best to try to get Isla back on her own first, then he would know if he stood a chance of helping more people later on.

Havenside was bustling with activity when James reached it. Comical little three-wheeled motor carts pop-popped to and fro over the cobbles carrying merchandise to a boat which had moored alongside the quay.

Leathery skinned, sweaty labourers were manhandling loads of wood or rolling barrels ashore while foreign looking deckhands stood furtively in small groups. They puffed tobacco through tiny earthenware pipes and occasional hard, guttural laughing cut the air.

A couple of the seamen eyed him up and down as if he was in the way and he stood back to make room. They returned his smile with a glare and it made him feel as if everyone was watching him. He hurried over the bridge, glad not to have been trapped on the quayside earlier while the boat came through.

Amber Lodge was empty, which surprised him. He fully expected Margaret to be in the kitchen, happily busying herself with something as usual but there was no sign of her. It worried him, although he couldn't say why, and added to his ever-increasing feeling of dark foreboding.

He made sure that all was secure in the house before making himself ready for the journey back, and with his original clothes on once more, he walked through the light and into The Grange. It was much easier this time and he managed to do it without blacking out.

◆ ◆ ◆

After changing into some jeans and a T shirt, James went downstairs to check that all was well. Mike had pushed a note through the front door to say that the lawns would be cut on Thursday if it was dry but if not, they wouldn't be cut until the following week because it was his turn with the kids. James didn't actually know what day it was but the lawn outside was still uncut and it was raining. Maybe it was Thursday now. It felt like a Thursday.

Several days worth of post had piled up on the mat and he checked through it quickly, binning all the junk mail unopened. The answerphone light was flashing. He pressed it, half expecting to hear Emma but instead an over-excited American voice wished him “Congratulations!” and told him he’d won a competition he’d never entered. He deleted it and then listened as a work colleague asked if he could phone the office. Emma was next, then work again, he opened a couple of bills and a letter from the solicitor as the messages continued.

The solicitors had sent some forms for him to sign but he wasn’t quite sure what they were for so he tried calling them. There was no answer, maybe it was too late in the day. He tried Emma’s work number and got the answer phone.

Suddenly he remembered that the grandfather clock in the hall would show the day. He had set it when he moved in and had thought it quite quirky and unusual. It was seven minutes past six on Thursday evening. Emma would be traveling on the tube and his work colleagues would not answer the phone after hours even if they were all still working. It was company policy.

He stood back and admired the clock, understanding for the first time just how important it was. It ticked emphatically back at him and he imagined the intricate mechanism behind the face, hundreds, maybe thousands of tiny parts working in such well engineered harmony to produce essential and accurate information for it's reality-travelling owner.

He was now that traveller. He was back home from a journey of immeasurable distance and yet only about fifty footsteps away. The old childhood thoughts came back to him once more about being taunted at school and how he had protected himself from being hurt, not knowing at the time that it was true. He *was* different. He *was* a mystery.

It didn't give him any comfort though, he didn't feel special or super or any of the things that people did in films, if anything he just felt weary.

There was a price to pay for his journey and the payment was in the form of a great weight of responsibility. His actions in Dunwiche had possibly caused changes in the way things would happen. Life there was still continuing even though he had left it on the other side of the light.

Life had been continuing here in his own reality too. He had missed most of a working week, the answer phone messages were proof that he would have to manage his time very carefully indeed from now on, especially as he was starting to feel more detached from everything he once accepted as normal life.

He switched on the computer and checked his emails. He was in trouble. There were several from work and also the copy of the one Emma had sent to his boss, Martin.

He accessed the work server and opened his

folder to review his current tasks. The biggest job was adding a sound track to a new Christmas cartoon, pasting the dialogue clips and effects accurately on to the timeline. It would take a while to download all the files in total so he started the process running and sat down to wait with a coffee.

Faye weighed on his mind most of all, he was scared for her and scared of what he might have done just by being in her reality. The problem was one of knowing what to do now, whether he should continue to act by his instincts or to stay away from the other side of the light completely.

The answer came to him quickly. It was obvious really, he must continue to react on his instincts. Doing nothing was as much an action as doing something. It was like voting, if you didn't vote, your lack of action would still influence the outcome.

He would have to enter the light again quite soon and convey everything to Faye while their minds could touch together in the center of the crossing. In the meantime, he would have to sort out what he intended to do about his own life. He couldn't keep on letting people down at work.

Eventually the file transfer was complete and he opened the film in the timeline, from there on it would be a long and tedious process of pasting and aligning all the sound effects.

A needy, childlike cartoon voice whined out of the speakers.

"Da-ddy-da-ddy--will-San-ta-come-soon?----

Will-he-bring-us-some-pre-sents-and-Can-dy?"

He aligned the sounds with the images on the film timeline and moved on to the next group of files, and then the next. It all seemed pointless with so much happening around him but it still had to be done, he couldn't let himself or the studio down. At least he could think about everything while he worked.

The enormity of the situation weighed down on him as he cut, copied and pasted and trimmed the files to fit the on-screen action. He worked late into the night until his eyes refused to focus on the screen any longer and he found himself absent-mindedly pouring a stiff whisky. He stared through the glass and into the warm inviting chestnut colour of the liquid in the glass. Lights from the room glistened through it and beckoned with the promise of relaxation and an easy way to sleep. He deserved it, he'd been working hard all evening.

Suddenly he snapped out of his weary stupor and realised what he was about to do. This wasn't the time for a drink. He raised the glass to his nose and sniffed, imagining how stale it would smell on his breath the next morning along with the hangover it would give him. He put it back down and instead, opened some long-life milk from the fridge and took it up to bed. Tomorrow, he would do a final check on the sound track and then upload it, along with an apology.

At about the same time, Emma was sitting in a bar in south London with a guy she'd met through a dating agency. He was nice enough and he made her laugh with his easy charm and witty conversation over dinner but her mind just wasn't on it. Crunch time had arrived. He phrased his questions very carefully, asking if everything was O.K. and if she would like to meet again. She could see the doubts etched across his face, he'd been so nice all evening and she knew that under normal circumstances she would have been far more fun.

'Look, I really have enjoyed tonight' she said with as much conviction as she could muster. 'It's just that -'

A frown passed over his face, obviously she had "Issues". 'It's all right' he said, 'you don't have to explain'.

'No, I really have enjoyed myself, but there are some things happening to a friend of mine at the moment and it's weighing on my mind - Sorry.'

'Look - you don't have to answer me now, here's my number, give me a call if you still want to.'

Emma took it. She'd been through this kind of thing several times before, sitting through evenings listening to people with emotional baggage, the desperately lonely, the one-night standers and the "Listen to me boasting all night" types. It was always the same if you didn't want to meet again, you'd say you'd phone but both parties knew that you wouldn't. The trouble was that she actually liked this guy.

'I'd like to meet you again' she said 'if you want to. I'm sure I'd be a lot better company another time.

This problem is not really mine, it's a friend - not an ex or anything - just a guy I've known since uni' who's in a difficult situation and he told me all about it the other day.'

'Well, if you're sure.'

'Yes' she said, 'I am sure.'

Next morning James completed the soundtrack and uploaded it to the work server. He felt relieved at having finished the job, but this time there was no satisfaction in it. Everything paled into insignificance when compared to the events of the last few days. He knew he would have to make some life-changing decisions about his future and he would have to make them now.

It wasn't actually that difficult. Faye was his first priority, it was as simple as that. She was part of him and he was part of her. He had visited her world and had been drawn into the lives of the people, her friends, their problems and their fears.

He would have to give up work. It was better than trying to keep struggling on, only to let them down repeatedly. They would find it tough for a week or so but no one was ever indispensable. The money he'd been left, along with the house was enough to last him his whole life and more but he'd never considered using it before. It was too much money to imagine as his own.

He sat at the desk and typed a formal letter of resignation, explaining the reason as an ongoing family problem. Next he sent an email to Emma, asking her to forgive him for dragging her into it and for causing friction between her and Phil. He explained where he had been and also something of his decision to quit work, then he sent a similar email to Phil.

Finally he left a note for Mike, saying that he may be away on business for a while and, could he please carry out the things on a list he would leave for him.

With the note taped to the shed door for Mike to find, James walked into the village and posted the letter before he could change his mind. He knew it was the right thing to do but doubts still nagged at him. He had a strong work ethic and it felt uncomfortable to throw away a good job and face an uncertain and dangerous future.

As soon as the letter left his hand and dropped into the box, a weight lifted from his mind. The tie which bound him to a normal earthly routine was broken.

He was free.

Chapter 34 - Loneliness and fear

The walk back from the postbox felt surreal and James found himself looking at the village with new eyes. The hub of his life had, in a month, shifted from the bustle and noise of London to quiet little Ashwell Green in deepest Suffolk where the crows and the occasional tractor were usually the only signs of activity.

Emma was right. He had changed and he could see it for himself now. Something in the deepest recess of his mind had unlocked and allowed him to see a little more of who he really was.

As he pushed open the side gate, James paused for a moment to look at The Grange. It had an atmosphere about it which reminded him of Amber Lodge in that it seemed to exist entirely by itself, still part of the village but separated by an invisible and indefinable boundary.

He felt detachment and loneliness sweep over him once more as he made his way over the lawn to the back door. Maybe it was something he was going to have to get used to. He'd never really recovered from the time when he'd lingered in the void for a few minutes and had returned slightly out of his own time. He felt a sudden need for comfort and reassurance and there was only one place he could get that.

He picked up the receiver of the old phone in the hall and dialed. 'Hello Mum. I just thought I'd call and see how the old fogeys were bearing up. How are you both?'

'We're fine, love. Your father's washing the car. I think he's in love with it. We're both looking forward to seeing this new place of yours. When can we come? The pictures were fab!'

'Unfortunately not for a few weeks. I'm going to be away for a while so I'll phone you when I'm back and you can come and visit me then. Sorry it's so far to come.'

'We'll look forward to it. It's so nice to hear your voice, James. You're always so busy that we never get time to talk.'

'It's nice to hear *your* voice too. Give my love to Dad... You know I love you both very much don't you?'

'Yes, of course we do... Is anything wrong, James?'

'No, honestly. Nothing's wrong... I s'pose I haven't seen you for some time and, as you say, I'm so busy. But it doesn't mean that I don't miss you.'

Her voice sounded doubtful 'O.K., as long as you're sure.'

'Yeah. I'll speak to you soon, 'bye, Mum.'

' 'Bye James, look after yourself - and eat properly!'

James placed the receiver back down on it's cradle and stood for a moment while the empty quietness of the house settled around him once more.

It was time to prepare himself for the trip back through the light. This time he suspected that it would be a long absence so he recorded a new answer-phone message and wound the clock. Then he checked that the taps were all off and that the windows and doors were all secure and that all other loose ends were tied up as far as possible. Finally, he went upstairs and undressed, an uneasy feeling creeping into every bone in his body.

The day so far had been warm but dull and drizzly, the grayness of it seeming to become more overbearing as time went on. He sat cross legged on the bed for several minutes, listening to the muted sounds from outside and wondering what Faye would find on the other side of the light when she appeared. He feared for her safety, and for Margaret, Rhiannon, and Tobias, and for himself.

A low rumble of thunder echoed round the clouds which hung low over the village. He went over to the window and looked out, delaying the moment when he would have to make the decision to go by looking for another flash. The wind picked up and rattled the window gently, blowing fresh air through the cracks between the panes. It smelt vaguely metallic. The hairs on the back of his neck stood up as he realised what it implied. This was it, he could put it off no longer, it was time to go.

He walked over to the wall and held out his hands, allowing himself to be taken forward. He felt himself floating away from the the floor and turned to watch his now soul-less body standing in the room as everything faded away into the distance.

As the sense of self became more distant, the feeling of oneness became much stronger. The memories and feelings of both James and Faye intertwined and drifted with each other in the void until a small pinpoint of light appeared and a new sense of self-awareness started to form from them.

◆ ◆ ◆

Slowly, the shape of the light changed as it grew and it started to take on a hazy form which eventually came into focus and stabilised as the bedchamber of Amber Lodge.

Faye started to feel the effects of gravity and as her feet lightly touched down onto the floor, she steadied herself and looked around at her room. It felt a little different after her absence and odd things had been moved. She adjusted the scent bottle to just where she liked it and straightened up her line of shoes, realising immediately that she, like James, was procrastinating.

Irritated with herself for not wanting to face the truth of her situation and the thoughts and images which she now shared with James, she went to the wardrobe, selected some clothes and got dressed, noticing with grim humour that they matched the darkness of her mood.

Amber Lodge was deathly quiet. Dusty sunbeams bathed the walls of the room in a pinky-orange afternoon glow which on any other occasion would have made her heart sing but now, she only saw it as serving to strengthen the shadows.

She crossed the room, keeping out of the sunlight, and peeped out of the turret window, making sure that she could not be easily seen from outside. Several people were on the quayside opposite but none of them looked suspicious, she recognised most of them as local traders.

The chandler was talking to the landlord of the Lion and Lamb. Two women with baskets were walking towards the cottages where a fisherman was sitting outside on a bench mending his nets. Two men, one carrying a clipboard, came out from a warehouse and stared over the water towards Amber Lodge. She pulled back a little and waited to see what they would do, feeling her heart quicken until they turned slightly and gestured towards the lighthouse. With much relief she realised that they were probably officials of some sort and must be discussing some quayside matter.

Faye risked moving closer to the window so that she could see further. A boat was approaching the channel, an old rusty tub with a broad beam and a shallow draft. Dockhands started to appear and make ready to receive it and the bridge started to rise and swing aside.

She leaned closer to see the lane below, aware that all eyes would be on the boat. It was all clear apart from the customs men who were waiting to log the boat. One of them walked towards the front gates and disappeared from view only to appear a few moments later with a lit pipe. Suddenly he turned back towards the gatepost and laughed, waving his pipe at another person who was standing out of sight behind it.

Faye pulled away from the window, suddenly frightened. Had they already discovered where she lived? Was someone watching the house that closely? Images flashed vividly, along with the memories of the cruel words which James had overheard. They flooded her mind. She brushed away a tear and tried to think what to do.

The bedroom door creaked loudly through the stillness as she gently pulled it open. She stopped dead as she heard a slight movement from downstairs.

Faye's blood ran cold as she realised that someone may already be in the house with her.

Chapter 35 - Paranoia

A soft low humming noise came from somewhere below. Faye couldn't think what it could be, it was constant and could only be noticed because the house was otherwise completely quiet. A door moved slightly downstairs and she froze with fear until Starlight appeared at the foot of the stairs. The humming noise was now slightly more noticeable and she suddenly realised what it was. The prediction engine was still running.

She took a step out onto the landing and waited for a moment. Starlight began to purr and sharpen her claws by picking on the carpet at the bottom step, her way of asking for food. Faye relaxed and went down to her, knowing at last by her behavior, that at least the house was still secure.

The morning room had a warm electrical smell and Faye quickly switched off the prediction engine, tore the chart paper off the roll and studied it with interest. The ink lines were at first glance just a jumbled group of curves and jagged peaks but with a little careful thought and some help from James's knowledge of how the machine worked, she made sense of it.

There were five days of activity plotted and she

could see how the curve of the temperature plot rose through the mid afternoons and showed the effect of the residual heat which would cause warm evenings. The jagged lines were a prediction of electromagnetic activity and on the third day's reading they went absolutely wild along with most of the other lines. On the fourth day, all the lines suddenly jumped to new positions at the same time and began to trace out a new and different pattern of behavior until the end of the chart.

It looked as if an extremely violent event was predicted and that could mean only one thing!

Fully aware of the implications of the chart, she placed it inside the prediction engine cabinet along with the book and and closed everything up. Once Starlight had her head down in a bowl of food, Faye checked the downstairs rooms, making sure that the curtains were all half closed so that she could move around without being easily noticed from outside and that she had something in every room to use as a weapon. Then she wound the clocks, realising for the first time that they were different to the ones in James's world.

It lifted her mood having something to do and she found herself sifting through his thoughts to find out what else he found strange about her life. It seemed that he found everything strange. Eventually the silence started to close in on her and she found herself beginning to go "Stir crazy", a phrase from James's mind which she found most odd although she understood very well what it meant.

She watched the boat once more from the shadows by the window as it came alongside the quay, deckhands throwing ropes to the men onshore who secured them firmly to the mooring rings. The covers over the hold were then untied and raised up on metal frames until they formed a canvas awning the same dull reddish colour as the sails of a wherry.

Being too scared to leave the house in daylight and not knowing what else to do, Faye went up to the turret room and read until the daylight faded too much to continue.

It was time to venture out and she left the turret room in search of her hooded cloak and long, black boots. They would be perfect for moving quietly around the town. She made sure her hair was tucked well under the hood and left by the back door just in case the man at the front gates was still lurking around.

He wasn't. The lane was deserted when she finally got there so she made her way to the bridge and crossed quickly. The sea was calm and gave no clue to its secrets as it had done to James. Yellow light spilled from the open portholes on the boat and snatches of conversation in a guttural, foreign tongue drifted out over the water. She kept to the shadows, avoiding anywhere which had too many lamps or people. Several times she shrank into a doorway to wait until people had passed by, but no one challenged her.

There was tension in the air. The atmosphere was heavy and tingled with a kind of charge. It seemed to Faye, that even nature itself knew that something was soon to happen and, like her, could only watch and wait.

An ivy covered wall nearby shimmered and fragmented for a moment and Faye saw the swell of the open sea through a gaping hole where the wall had been. A fierce gust of cold wind blew spray from the waves into the street before losing its power as the hole closed up once more and everything returned to normal.

That was it. She'd had enough of being brave, or was it foolhardy? She turned and ran back towards home in panic. Her hood fell back on to her shoulders as she ran but she ignored it and kept on going until she reached the quayside.

An old woman was standing on the deck of the market boat, leaning over the rail and having a quiet puff on a pipe. Faye froze in panic as the woman looked up. They stared at each other for a few tense seconds before Faye suddenly bolted for the bridge, not caring if the woman raised the alarm or not, just wanting to reach the safety of home.

Heaving the gate open, she rushed up the path and pushed the key into the door, cursing with some of James's choicest words as she fumbled at it in haste. Finally it turned and she swung the heavy door open and rushed inside and slammed it shut behind her. The sound of the bolts being pushed across echoed loudly through the stillness and Faye, still panting for breath after the long run, felt her legs turning wobbly so she sat down on the hall chair for a moment to recover.

As the minutes ticked by and her heart rate settled down, she realised that maybe the woman either didn't know or didn't care about the situation.

Or had she quietly informed one of the Young Masters?

Three loud knocks rudely crashed through the silence and reverberated through the house, jolting Faye straight back into fear. She stayed rooted to the chair, frightened to make even the slightest noise. The knocks came again and she froze, hardly daring to breathe for fear of being discovered but then a voice made everything change for the better.

'Faye!.. Faye!.. It's me, Rhiannon... Are you there?'

Faye was just about to answer when a new fear gripped her. *What if she is not alone? What if she is being forced to call out?* She quietly stood up and tiptoed through the hall to the morning room, hoping to peep through the windows to make sure but the door creaked as she pushed it.

'It's me!.. Rhiannon!.. I know you're in there 'cos I just heard you! Come on, let me in!'

Faye crept quickly over to the window and peered out. Rhiannon was on her own, just as she had said. The panic subsided.

'O.K. I'm coming' Faye shouted at the door, 'just give me a moment.'

The bolts were slid back and the key turned once more, then finally the door opened to reveal her visitor. Rhiannon immediately gave Faye a big hug.

'Oh my God! I'm so glad to see you... Why didn' you tell me you had a cousin? Where have you been? It's an age since I've seen you.'

Once they were safely locked in, Rhiannon took off her cloak and followed Faye through the house to the library. She asked if Faye had seen the Young Masters out on the streets earlier in the week. Faye replied that she had not, but that she knew of them through James.

'What is happening currently in the town?' asked Faye while they made themselves comfortable on the rug in front of the fireplace 'I admit to being quite scared of what I have learned and I am eager to know.'

'The True Path know your name now' said Rhiannon 'and probably where you live as well. The Young Masters suddenly stopped asking people about you today so all in probability, they have what they want... Damn that Joshua Leadpenny! Dad thinks they may even be watching your house by now. Have you seen anyone lurking around?'

'Yes. There was a man at the gate today' replied Faye, 'I cannot be sure that he was watching the house but I must assume it.'

'Well, you'd better be careful. People are getting very jumpy now 'cos there's more and more tension in the town. There were two fights at the Kings Arms the other night and another at the Baron. Some folk are saying that the Nonnyes are part of the problem and want to round 'em up and - well I don' know if they would actually do anything but-'

'Do you notice anything about the air?' cut in Faye.

'Well it feels like the thunder is coming, and people say how heavy it feels but whether 'tis actually in the air or in people,s minds I don' know.'

'A smell?' Promted Faye.

'No - not really. There's always smells in the air.'

'But this one is different. It is underneath all the usual ones. Take a very gentle sniff, so gentle that it is hardly a sniff at all.'

Rhiannon closed her eyes and gently breathed in through her nose. 'Only the coal in the scuttle and the fire grate' she said.

'No, not the smell of the room, try to concentrate harder. Pretend you are trying to recognise the ingredients of a scent.'

Rhiannon looked puzzled 'Now I think of it, 'tis more like the smell of the electric generating sheds rather than coal.'

'The smell is not from the generating sheds, it is everywhere, it is on the wind. I can smell it even from the direction of the sea.'

Rhiannon looked at her darkly 'Is it something to do with the Judgement coming?'

Faye said nothing, but leaned over to Rhiannon and hugged her tightly. The two girls held on to each other in silence for a moment.

'Do not call it "The Judgement" said Faye, 'It is not a punishment and you must not listen to those who say that it is. Remember what James told you.'

'I do remember' said Rhiannon releasing Faye

from the hug. ‘Have you noticed that I don’ say I’m going to Hell any more? ‘Tis a bit strange to do and I still feel guilty for not saying it.’

‘I have, and I am proud of you’ said Faye in a mock-patronising voice which made Rhiannon smile once more. ‘We have to protect ourselves as best we can. There is nothing we can do to stop the Rift happening but we can at least try to face it and ride it out.’

‘Can we at least have a lamp on in here?’ asked Rhiannon ‘It’s so ghostly dark and quiet, every time the house creaks I jump out of my skin.’

‘I dare not, it is too risky. I was so scared when you knocked I even took time to check that you were on your own before I let you in. What brought you here at this time of the evening?’

‘I don’ know really. I hadn’t seen you and I was worried that you’d been found or even taken like they did your housekeeper.’

Faye was stunned.

‘They took - the Larkins?’

‘Well, ‘tis only what I heard’ continued Rhiannon ‘but people are saying that the parish constables came and took them from their beds at night. Anyway, I just wanted to make sure that you were safe.’

Tears started to prickle at Faye’s eyes but she brushed them away and pulled herself together.

‘Does anyone know that you are here?’

‘Dad thinks I’ve gone to bed early, but I saw your monk friend on the way here so he knows. He said he’d been keeping watch here for you and that no one was home, I nearly turned back then, but something made me continue and when I got here the gate was open so I knew that someone was in.'

Well, I am glad you came' said Faye, 'I just wish I knew what to do.'

They sat together on the rug in the dark silence for a while, each girl lost in her own private world of thought. Each girl wondering how they were to face the Rift, and also their own fears.

The pitch black of the night had now completely closed in and they could no longer see anything but the occasional star through the window. Faye whispered to Rhiannon that they should go to bed and get some sleep as they could achieve nothing more that night.

They felt their way to the door and then to the stairs, creeping up the sides of the staircase trying not to make the steps creak although some still did, making them both jump.

Finally they reached the bedchamber and collapsed fully clothed on the bed. Rhiannon fell asleep almost immediately but Faye lay for a few minutes listening to the sounds of the night and wondering what scurrilous deeds were being done while the town slept, before she too, drifted off to a deep and much needed sleep.

Chapter 36 - Plans and poison

While the girls were sleeping in Amber Lodge, a small door to the meeting room in Scotts Lane stood slightly open. It was dark inside but that didn't bother Luke Bavent as he slipped through it. He felt for the handle of the inner door and opened it, spilling light from the gas lamps into the tiny entrance porch.

'You can shut and lock the outer door now, Luke. We are all here' said a voice from inside.

Luke did as he was bid and then took his place at the table, looking round to see who else had been summoned to the meeting. He nodded a respectful greeting to High Elder FitzJohn and also to Elder Leadpenny, Elder Valenes and his son, Robert who sat with him on the Young Masters committee.

'Pour yourself an ale, Bavent' said the High Elder. 'I apologise for the lateness of the hour but I have called this meeting in order to finally unveil the details of my great plan to you. Others are to know nothing of what we discuss. Please keep in mind that you are all bound by the secrets you already hold.'

There was a general murmuring of agreement from around the table along with some apprehensive looks. FitzJohn continued. 'Then, Gentlemen, as this is to be our final meeting for now, a "Last Supper" if you will. Now let us get down to the *real* business.

As you all know, the gildenhair has been the main preoccupation of our people in recent weeks. She is generally feared by them now and they will be more than willing to see her "demonic" tendencies exposed. I see no wrong in using her for our own ends with a demonstration of her possession.'

Heads nodded in agreement. FitzJohn studied the faces in the room and continued.

'You have arrangements in place as we discussed at our last meeting, Arthur?'

'Yes, High Elder.'

'Good. Then I will leave it all to you. You can use Mr. Bullman if you wish and afterwards, you can do whatever you want with the gildenhair.'

'Yes, High Elder' said Leadpenny hiding his pained and embarrassed expression from the others. FitzJohn watched him with disgust for a moment and then snapped back to business.

'Now, gentlemen, I can now reveal to you the final details of the plan.

Think of it! The day after the Lord shows himself unto the earth once more, a new and great church rises from the chaos to impose order and discipline among the people. We will lead them towards true enlightenment with a kindly but firm hand.'

'But how will we know when The Lord will come?' said Valenes. 'Surely we will receive a sign.'

'The signs are already there for all to see if they only take the trouble to look' said FitzJohn with a serene smile. 'It is my belief that there will soon be another occurrence of what the common people call "The Judgement" and if we survive it, we will be able to calm their fears, bringing them flocking through *our* doors while the orthodox churches wrestle with their consciences and try to do what is "right".

'People will look to a strong leader, and they will indeed be given one. They will follow the example *we* will set for them. The gildenhair will be shown to them as the puppet of the very Devil himself and we will use her as proof to them that the predictions in the Elucidatum Divinicus were indeed correct. She will be displayed in public for what she is and she will sway them.'

'Will they not be uneasy about such a thing?' asked Robert Valenes 'Surely we must still show care and compassion for her, at least in public.'

FitzJohn raised one eyebrow but it had the desired effect.

'My dear boy' he said with a chillingly measured tone. 'After such a day of mass destruction do you really think they will be in a mood for forgiveness? Do you really think they will have a care for anything except their own self preservation? Of course they won't! If I know anything about human nature they will beg to see her hanged!'

He looked around and watched as the faces in the room gave away little clues as to what their owners were really thinking.

'Gentlemen, I did not ask you to attend a tea party. Each of you has demonstrated a ruthless desire to gain power and you have all lived well on it so far. You must be careful not to fall for the very stories we tell the common herd. Remember that they are weak, easily led and gullible. They believe in witches and magic and demons and also the idea that the Lord is to bring unto them a great punishment.'

Bavent saw a chance to address his leader directly about something he had long been fascinated by.

'High Elder. As we are together, bonded in a state of final understanding with you, may I please ask a rather bold question?

'You may ask. I may answer, but there again, I may not, as it will entirely depend on your motives. Do not however, ask me the wrong question.'

Bavent swallowed and thought for a moment while the burning eyes of his master observed his dilemma without prejudice.

'How is it' he said steadily 'that we actually know that this Judgement Day actually will come?'

'Do you doubt me?' Asked FitzJohn with more than a hint of menace.

'Absolutely not, Sir' said Bavent with a steady return. 'I ask only in this room where we know so much more than those outside. I ask it because I firmly believe you know that it will be soon. Not because I have doubts.'

FitzJohn let the menace hang in the air for a moment more and then suddenly beamed at Luke.

'My boy' he said. 'I can tell you have spirit in plenty for this. Not many would dare to ask that particular question of me. I will answer you in part for now but one day I am sure you will learn more.

'There are times when one must dance with the devil in order to learn his secrets, and many years ago I did that very thing in my youth when I had the same fire in me that I see in you this night.

There was a man, you are not old enough to remember him, but some gathered here will know of whom I speak. To my shame I befriended him, naively thinking that people were cruel to judge him as they did. At first we had many long and fascinating discussions about the illegal sciences and his observations on them. It was exciting to my young mind for a while until one day he went too far.

I realised then, that he was just as people said, a dangerous heretic and a lover of the lower races. Needless to say I did not visit him again but I remembered much of what he told me and since then I have used it in God's name.'

FitzJohn then produced a plan and spread it out over the table.

'This, gentlemen, is to be our new and great seat of office. As you can see, I have provided for a grand public entrance leading directly into the open area of worship. Columns will hold gilded statues aloft which will serve to deliver phonomatic sound through the trumpets they hold so that all may hear.

They pored over it, amazed at its scale and

grandeur, each feeling proud and honoured to be one of the chosen few.

Luke Bavent was on fire. Youthful lust for power shone from him as he gazed at the plans. The ale had gone to his head a little but he felt that he was privy to the start of something wonderful. He was above the ordinary people. He was one of the elite. One of those who knew how it really worked. He was closer to God and could look down on the little people of the church as if they were ants, scurrying about their business in the belief that they knew what was going on. They knew nothing!

Robert Valenes felt the same. What an honour it was to be a part of the secret inner circle at the start of a new great power. He looked at his father, who held up his tankard and gave him a conspiratorial wink. They would be part of it together.

Leadpenny was smiling. The High Elder smiled back.

'Arthur, my good fellow, it is time for you to take your leave of us. May good luck follow you. You will need your sleep.'

'He has the gildenhair to deal with' said FitzJohn as soon as Leadpenny had gone. 'However it is time now to don our red sashes and salute our Father in Heaven.'

Each member took out their red sash and held it out in turn to the High Elder who kissed it and uttered a silent prayer over it. He then produced a silver chalice and decanter from a small alcove, holding them high for all to see before placing them at the head of the table. Then he offered a prayer over the decanter while the others stared in wonder, having never before seen the ritual unfolding before them. The High Elder spoke softly.

'Oh Lord our God.
We offer ourselves to you this night
as your humble servants.
Grant us, we beseech thee, the
power of your holy spirit.
That we may stand before the
people of this great land,
and lead them into glorious salvation.

The emerald green liquid was poured carefully into the chalice before another prayer was uttered by the High Elder.

'I take this cup in Your name
O Lord, and drink -
that I may receive the blessing of
the truth of Your Great Majesty.'

The liquid almost touched his lips. He pretended to swallow, making sure that it appeared to the others that he had taken a good gulp. The atmosphere in the room was now highly charged. Each was offered the chalice in turn, and drank from it gladly as the High Elder repeated the prayer.

The High Elder waited and watched for their eyes to start glazing over. Robert Valenes suddenly felt the room spin and stared at him in horror. Fitz-John assured him that he would be fine and that he should relax and accept the truth into his heart.

The others followed quickly, each one feeling

the sweaty heat of the room engulf them while they watched the lights which sparkled so prettily before their eyes until they passed out one by one, in a white ecstasy.

FitzJohn checked each one and made sure that they were comfortable before he locked up and left the building. As he walked round the corner to his private motor carriage he looked at his pocket watch and was glad to see that there was still half an hour left before they would be moved. He would be safely at home during the night's events.

The ugly figure of Mr Bullman watched from the shadows as the motor carriage slid quietly past and wondered how long his freedom would last.

The monks would discover his apparent escape in a few hours and would be frantically searching for their scary "Mr Oi", never thinking that anyone would actually be hiding him.

He allowed himself a small grin at the thought before turning his attention back to the question of his continued freedom. His use to the High Elder was limited and he had to find an escape route before someone else did to him what he had done to others.

Ever since he had arrived in this strange place he had survived on his wits. You didn't run an armed gang in London without being sharp. The day he'd tripped and fallen right through a wall was one of the luckiest he could remember, the bullet would have got him but for that. He chuckled as he remembered it. He'd thought at the time that he must be dead and even had the "Am I in heaven?" moment until common sense had kicked in and he realised that he wouldn't be seeing anything if he really were dead.

This place was his new life, his second chance. He'd been patient with the monks for long enough and now he had a job to do with the promise of some money. He could easily set himself up here without the complications of a competent police force or people trying to bump him off. It would be easy, they were all so naive and trusting here.

He looked up at the church clock, it was time to go. He made his way to the little door and felt for the key he'd been given, and slipped it into the lock. Inside, the room was smelly and hot, whatever they'd taken had made their breath reek and he wasted no time in getting to work. He took the heaviest first, pulling the limp body through the door and out into the empty street, thankful that they hadn't yet invented CCTV and good street lighting. After a quick check up and down, he lifted Walter Valenes over his shoulder and carried him round to the front of the building and through the main entrance.

Once inside, he carried him downstairs to the cellar and laid him out on a plinth on the floor. Then he removed all the unconscious man's clothes, dressed him in a robe. He placed his head on a small pillow and made sure that the limp body was resting in a comfortable position, as per his instructions.

Next was Robert Valenes, he was placed on a plinth next to his father and dressed in a similar style. Finally Luke Bavent was brought down to join them.

When he had finished, Mr Bullman stood back and admired his handiwork. Three motionless bodies lay before him, each one with hands together as if in prayer and looking as if they were stone effigies ready to be place on top of a tomb. The first part of his job was done and now all he had to do was sit with them and make sure they didn't come round too soon.

Chapter 37 - Closing in

Next morning Tobias left his bed earlier than usual. It was time to put his plan to help Isla Williams into action.

Before first light he had made his way down to the infirmary and released her. He told her only that he was going to try to get her back to her family and that it may be her only chance. The two of them now walked together along the edge of a field towards Mad Esther's little house as the sun crept above the horizon.

The air was stuffy and humid as it had been for days and it was getting worse. The sun looked dirty and washed out through a thin layer of ashen haze which had been drifting in on the wind. Wild heathers on the heath were attempting to turn to their autumnal purple and the ferns were turning brown but the days were not mellowing out to their usual warm late summer glow.

As they neared the edge of town Tobias explained a little more of his plan.

'When we get to our destination there will not be much time so you will have to follow my instructions without question. Do you understand?'

'Yes' she said uncertainly.

'We are to visit a small cottage beyond the bridge at the end of this field and when we get there we must act quickly no matter what happens. It is just over the road there, do you see?'

They crossed the bridge and made their way down the sloping path to the cottage. Tobias gently tried the door but it was locked so he turned his attention to the window and after a moment of fiddling, pulled it open.

'As I said before' he whispered, 'when we are inside you must follow my instructions without question. Things may happen very quickly or not at all, I am not sure which.'

'Yeah, but you've done this before, right?'

'No, never.'

'You're joking!'

He levered himself through the window and then helped Isla to climb through. They both looked around at the filthy room and the bottles in disgust.

Tobias put his hand near to the wall and felt a tingle from it just as James had told him. He plucked up the courage to touch it with a finger tip, it passed right through the plaster and he pulled back suddenly.

'What's wrong?' whispered Isla.

'Nothing. All is as it should be. Now, you must take a risk. If it does not work you may hurt yourself. Are you ready?'

'What do you mean? "Hurt" myself.'

'You must run at the wall.'

'You're joking, right?'

'No, just do it... Now!'

Emily ran towards the wall but not with any conviction. Tobias thought she was scared of hurting herself and would pull up short so he gave her a hard push. She fell forward and faded right through the wall and disappeared.

Tobias was completely aghast at what he'd just witnessed even though he had been expecting something strange to happen. The shock of seeing Isla disappear right before his eyes was too much to take in and he stepped backwards into the table sending all the bottles crashing to the floor. Angry cries came from upstairs as the old woman woke. He fled.

In Amber Lodge, Faye and Rhiannon had risen and were eating breakfast alone in a gloomy silence, Rhiannon only breaking it to voice an occasional thought.

'It will be a stifling hot day - yet again!'

'Yes.'

'I can still smell that electric smell.'

'Hmm.'

'It won' go away - just stays at the back of my nostrils, I wish I didn' know about it.'

'I saw something quite worrying last night' said Faye.

Rhiannon stopped her. 'Please don' tell me, 'tis frightening enough without hearing yet more.'

Faye made a cat's cradle of her fingers and rested

her chin on them, deep in thought. She had woken with a strong feeling that the Rift was at the heart of all the problems and that all the smaller issues were just symptoms of it.

She felt guilty for including the arrest of Mr and Mrs Larkin amongst the smaller issues but when viewed dispassionately, it was true. It would do no good to try to help them because all she would succeed in doing would be to get caught herself.

The morning so far had been just as the chart predicted. Faye could remember the rising temperature curve and the start of the violent swings of the electromagnetic activity plot line. She knew she couldn't stop the Rift but if there was a way to understand more about it then maybe she could help in some way.

There was something she was missing, a small detail which would give her a direction, maybe it was right under her nose and she couldn't see it.

Movement?.. Direction?.. Why did the small weak points between realities mostly occur in or near walls? She wasn't sure what she was searching for, it was as if the key to finding out was always just beyond her reach.

'Why just in certain places?' she said out loud.

'What?'

'Why do things only happen in certain places. There is something missing, something I cannot see. I should know it but I cannot quite work it out.'

'There's no point' said Rhiannon shaking her head in resignation. 'There is nothing we can do.

We may as well sit here and wait to die, maybe we should pray that God will take pity on us.'

Faye suddenly snapped and before she knew what was happening, she had rounded on Rhiannon, anger and frustration boiling to the surface. She tried to keep herself from shouting and instead, heard herself speaking with a cold steely edge to her voice.

'If you so much wish to pray, then you should go and do it. I will *not* join you, there are more important things to do.'

Rhiannon's eyes welled up with tears and she stared back at Faye as if she had been slapped in the face, and Faye, now upset and just as quickly full of remorse, reached out and took hold of her hand.

'I am *so* sorry' she said, tearfully. ' 'Tis just that a huge dread resides in both of us and I cannot bear to see you give in to it. Please forgive me.'

Rhiannon wiped her eyes. 'You scared me' she said with feeling 'I never knew you could be like that.'

'Nor did I' said Faye wiping away her own tears. 'I scared myself.'

'You know something? said Rhiannon still a little hurt. 'You're in a foul mood 'cos you're thinking too much and you need a break from it. Come on, let's go and look round the market boat, the traders are up at the crack of dawn.'

Faye stared at her incredulously.

Rhiannon stared back at her in frustration 'Don' you realise what I'm trying to say? If you do something else the problem will work itself out. Many times I've found something as soon as I've stopped looking for it. Come on, get your coat and let's go.'

All was quiet as Tobias reached Havenside and he stood for a while to watch the gulls circling and swooping nearby.

Amber Lodge stood opposite, it looked stern and imposing in the thick morning light, casting a long formless shadow over the calm waters of the haven. Two young men appeared from an alleyway and walked towards him. He stepped out to meet them in the open.

'Morning, Brother.'

'Good morning.'

'And what are you looking for, Brother?'

'I am just taking the morning air.'

'Aah, so you are, Brother. And is the air to your liking?'

'It is.'

'And have you come to pay a visit to the gildenhair, Brother? Are you a friend of the gildenhair, Brother?'

Tobias was appalled at the growing arrogance of the Young Masters and he ignored them, walking on. Knowing that they would dare go no further with their comments, at least for now, he crossed Havenside and entered another alleyway to get away from them.

Suddenly he was grabbed from the shadows and flung against a doorway with a hand pressed over his mouth.

'Easy does it, Brother. I won' hurt you unless you force me to.'

Tobias waited as the hand was slowly withdrawn so that he could speak. He vaguely recognised his would-be attacker who was now glancing nervously left and right is if in fear of being discovered himself.

'What did they say to you, Brother? Those two young bastards.'

'Nothing, just a taunt... Who are you?'

'Believe it or not, a friend... If you're who I think you are.'

'My name is Tobias... And yours?'

'Thank the Heavens for that! Tom. Tom Owen.' He released his grip. 'I found my Rhiannon missing from her bed this morning and I can only hope and pray that she came to visit her friend else I don' know what to think.'

They stood together for a while in the shadow of the doorway and watched as the two girls appeared from the side of the house.

'See?' said Rhiannon to Faye as they reached the bridge. 'I told you there would be no one about at this time of the morning.'

From the cover of the lighthouse nearby, a lone figure gave a signal across the water, and on Havenside the two smartly dressed men started to move unhurriedly out of the shadows and into the open as if to casually cross paths with the girls. Tobias and Mr. Owen moved quickly to make sure they reached them first.

The girls meanwhile, kept their heads down and crossed quickly before heading directly towards the market boat. It was already a hive of activity in preparation for a long day of business and the men could do nothing but watch as Tobias and Mr Owen walked up to them.

‘They are here for you’ Tobias said softly ‘don’t look round, just keep walking with us. We should stay in the open among people as much as we can, and hope that they will not dare to make a move in public.’

Chapter 38 - Sanctuary

As they walked towards the town centre, the streets of Dunwiche seemed on the surface to be building up to their usual Saturday morning bustle. But an underlying tension hung in the air. Traders shouted their wares without any humour and their customers were unusually sullen and quiet.

Tobias wanted desperately to tell Faye about what he had seen at Mad Esther's house but there was no opportunity to speak to her alone. He was still shaken up by the experience and needed her to reassure him or at least explain what had happened, but it was no good, he'd have to wait.

He had no idea what they should do next, only that they should try to find out if they were being followed. They all stopped at a fish stall and used the opportunity to check the street for any suspicious looking individuals but could see no one.

'This miserable sense of gloom is affecting everyone and I think we should try to guard against falling prey to it ourselves' Tobias said to Tom. He nodded and hung back so that they could both keep a better watch over the girls.

'May I ask you a question, Sir?' said Tobias, 'What is it about Faye, which draws you and your daughter so close to her?'

'She is an outsider just like us I suppose' said Tom. 'We are foreigners here.'

'Have you not noticed though' Tobias continued, 'how she looks right into you sometimes? Right inside to your deepest thoughts? There is something about her which scares me a little. Look at her, she is feared by the True Path. People sometimes curse at her openly in the street just because she is different and yet she still stands firm in the face of it all.'

Tom nodded thoughtfully 'Yes, there is something of the darkness about her. She lives in the shadows between and people are scared of that.'

'Between what?'

'Just between. You find a name for it. Heaven and Hell, life and death, light and dark. I don' know. You're quite sweet on her though, aren't you young man? I can tell.'

Tobias blushed. 'Truthfully, I must admit that I am. I think that I have strayed from my chosen path' he said under his breath.

Tom pulled a disapproving face. 'That's your guilt talking' he said 'If you like her you should say so and be done with it.'

Tobias thought for a little longer. 'I think that I have grown to have strong feelings for her, against my better judgement, as she unnerves me with her words and her ways.'

'Are you sure that your feelings are against your own better judgement or are they against the judgement of others?'

Tom suddenly moved forward and spoke to Faye. 'Stop for a moment, there are men at the end of the street.'

They turned round and started to walk the other way but the men from the quayside were now following just a few yards behind them.

Tobias led the way quickly to the door of Great St John's Church and opened it, ushering them inside. The interior was quite cool and smelt musty and old.

'We will be safe in here, they will not dare to follow and we can claim sanctuary' he said looking back at the door.

Once her eyes had adjusted to the light inside, Faye surveyed the scene before her. The neat rows of wooden pews. The stone arches. The paintings on the walls. The altar and the cross at the far end.

'It is very finely decorated' she said out loud.

'Shhhhh. you must keep your voice down' whispered Tobias.

From the organ pipes somewhere far above, a small chord floated out on the air. A simple and pure melody joined in with it and meandered gently down through the sunbeams which shone through the stained glass windows. A soft deep bass note vibrated the cool air, descending as the tune moved on and causing a momentary beating sensation as the bass notes overlapped.

Faye was almost immediately overcome by the beauty of it. She sat down and listened as the music started to evolve gently. She looked at the images on the walls and at the stained glass colours of the sunlight as it shone on the stone pillars and the lilies in the side chapel.

Something inside her stirred, something from the most deeply buried recesses of her subconscious.

For the second time in her short existence she saw in her mind's eye, the swaying of branches and the pattern they made, each one affecting the others around it. Ripples on a pond running evenly out to the edge and then being reflected back to the centre. The moving oceans. The seasons. The planets and even time itself, flexing and adjusting to maintain equilibrium, everything moving in harmony and perfectly balanced.

As the music swelled she could imagine herself once more in the void, bathed with the light that shone so brightly with every conceivable colour and hue at once. It was so beautiful. Images were now flooding into her mind at such a pace that she could barely grasp them.

She stood up and walked slowly towards the chancel, muttering softly to herself as she placed her hands on a stone pillar and then the walls and the altar rail, seeming to find answers to silent questions in them. As the last chords played the music moved softly towards a conclusion. Tobias took her hand.

She turned to look into his eyes. 'Please do not ask' she said 'as I would only disappoint you yet again.'

'Ask what?'

She pursed her lips. ‘Tobias, I can read your thoughts as clearly as if you were to write them down.’ She led him up towards the altar ‘There is such beauty in this place, ‘tis a pity that it is used to follow the teachings of men instead of listening to the voice of nature.’

‘Yet again you defy all my attempts to understand you’ said Tobias withdrawing his hand.

She took it back in both of hers and gripped it tightly, staring up at him as she spoke.

‘Dear Tobias. I know that my words have offended you on several occasions. ‘Tis something I never wanted to do and yet I cannot hide behind a lie. Despite your hopes, I cannot share your faith. What I saw then was not your God. I did not have a holy vision. ‘Twas a vision of the nature of all things which I saw in my mind’s eye. I understand now, I see how it all works and I am no longer afraid.’

‘I think I am afraid of *you*’ said Tobias.

She smiled up at him and squeezed his hand.

‘No. Seriously, I am afraid of you. You say things which are against everything I was taught to hold true. You bewitch me with your smiles and you shatter my hopes, and yet I am still here.’

An uneasy silence fell. Tobias now felt as if he were swimming against a strong current of all the ideas and teachings he’d ever had. Faye waited as he wrestled with his thoughts, guilt and unease showing clearly on his face.

‘I have to know something’ he said eventually, almost squirming with discomfort. ‘What is it that you really are?'

Some of the strain on his face eased as he heard himself speak and now it was Faye's turn to feel uneasy. She knew very well what he was really asking and she suddenly felt exposed and vulnerable.

'I do not really know' she said quietly.

Faye felt her cheeks start to burn. She spoke slowly, choosing her words carefully.

She could feel him watching her intently but for once she could not look him in the eye. It felt humbling to have to voice her innermost secrets and to trust another with them.

She plucked up the courage to look up at him. He stared back at her in silence. He was a troubled bundle of conflicting emotions. There would be more difficult questions to come but she hoped above all that Tobias would be strong enough to keep himself on the course he had chosen on the day he first spoke to her.

Chapter 39 - No sanctuary

The latch of the church door clanked loudly and a young smartly dressed man walked slowly into the open space of the nave. He studied a painting for a few moments and then spoke in a confident voice without turning round.

'This is a beautiful building. I have never been inside it before.'

The four of them said nothing but waited for him to continue.

'A church of course, is an interesting choice for you to seek sanctuary, Gildenhair. How are your demons? Are they writhing within you? Are they wishing you would leave?'

Still they said nothing but Faye could feel Tobias tense up as the man spoke.

'We mean you no harm of course, only to help you. To council you. There is no need to be afraid.'

Tobias broke their silence in frustration. 'Then why is it that you hunt her down like a common criminal?'

'We care about our town and its people. We only want to Help her' replied the man in an annoyingly calm but slightly mocking voice.

He turned and faced them, openly staring at

Faye. ‘Ahh, a fascinating sight. I understand you can see into the minds of all those who stand before you. Tell me. What do you see in me?’

‘You mock her even in a church!’ Tobias spat the words out.

‘It is her demons that mock her, Brother. Look at her, she is a walking blasphemy. The Lord wiped her kind from the face of the earth. She is here as the guest of Satan.’

Tobias was fuming with rage. ‘It was disease and the bad air which wiped out so many people! People of all kinds, not just those with gold or red hair. Not just those with blue eyes. Why is it that people always pick on those who are unusual and find ways to punish them?’

‘Have you forgotten your faith so easily, Brother? Are you now tainted by the same demons?’

Faye spoke. 'You asked me what I see in you. I see a frightened child in the body of a man.'

The young man forced a grin back at them as if their words meant nothing to him. He looked Faye up and down once more. She stared back at him for a moment before speaking again, holding her hands out to stop the others from intervening.

‘I suspect that there are others waiting outside.’

‘Of course.’

‘And I assume that you have no intention of leaving us to go about our business.’

‘That is correct, Gildenhair.’

‘Are you sure that you wish to continue with this and accept the consequences?’

Faye waited for a response, staring directly into his eyes and reading his thoughts. He was noticeably unsettled by her words and tried in vain to cover it up with another forced smile. After a few painfully long moments she broke the silence.

'Very well, I will leave with you.'

'You can't!' cried Rhiannon in dismay.

'I must' replied Faye. 'There is no choice in the matter.'

'A wise decision, if I may say so' said the man.

'You may not' said Faye staring him down.

Both Tom and Tobias understood her reasoning and each gave a resigned nod of agreement. Faye slowly and gracefully walked towards the man who suddenly seemed a little keen to keep a yard or so between them. He held the church door open wide for her and then followed, giving them all a final appraisal as he left. Tobias reminded him of just one word as the door swung slowly shut.

'Consequences.'

'Why did you say that? asked Rhiannon.

'To keep him scared.' said Tobias. 'There is nothing else we can do. We cannot stop them from taking Faye.'

'God, you're so practical, I just wanted to hit him, the horrible, grinning little insect!' She hit her hands together in anger. 'What do we do now?'

Faye walked out into the street where several True Path members were waiting for her along with a small crowd of onlookers. Someone in the crowd spat at her but was sent away by one of the uniformed Young Masters. Others just watched as Faye walked slowly past them to meet her captors.

She was politely requested to take a seat in the back of a motor carriage and was then driven off towards Scotts Lane with a guard sitting on each side of her.

Not a word was spoken during the journey. The motor carriage glided gently to a halt outside the front doors of the meeting hall. She was ushered out past a similar gathering of curious townsfolk. Then she was led in through the front door, past the curtain where she had once hidden, and through the main hall to an office where Elder Leadpenny was waiting.

'Ahh. Young Miss, we meet again' he said with a smile while making a flourishing gesture towards a chair. 'Would that it were in better circumstances' he beamed.

Faye said nothing.

'We have been looking for you for quite a time... You are hard to find' he said to fill in the silence.

'I have been openly walking in Dunwiche and, had one of you merely asked me in an honest way, I would have come of my own accord' said Faye staring into him. 'Instead, you set out to catch me as if I was a thief.'

'Ahh, but *would* you have come? You must have known we were looking for you... To help you.'

'To help, I presume, in the same way a fisherman sets a net to "Help" a fish to the table... I do not consider myself to be in need of your help.'

'And that, unfortunately, is a symptom of your condition.'

He gave her a leering smile and continued. 'We wish you no harm, my dear. It is not your fault that you have demons, we only wish to see them banished. It is for your *own* good that we have "Caught you" as you put it.'

'Then may I please leave? We have now discussed the matter and I still have no need of your help.'

Leadpenny leaned forward over the desk towards her. 'I am afraid the answer is no. You cannot help yourself. You are a blasphemous creature and must be cleansed of your sins before the Lord your God.'

He signaled for the office door to be opened. A small group of church women were waiting outside and they led Faye away, back through the main hall to a side room.

Faye looked around at the cell like room with its vaulted ceiling and tiny window set high in the wall. Then she looked at the bare wooden table, and with suspicion at the bucket of black tar like liquid which stood on the floor in the corner. Then she looked with rising fear at some leather restraints which were lying on a stool nearby and at the faces of the women who surrounded her. One of them was Ann.

They crowded in on Faye, shushing her desperate cries with promises that she would not be hurt and that it was for her own good. One woman forced her hand over Faye's forehead and prayed over her.

Faye felt violated and tried to escape.

Pushing past them, she made a bid for the door but someone grabbed her hair and yanked it hard. She was jerked backwards roughly into the arms of some of the women who were still making soothing noises at her while they grabbed for a hold on her. She kicked as hard as she could and made contact with somebody. The woman let go and howled in pain as a wooden sole hit her in the mouth.

The others retaliated by getting much tougher with Faye. They squeezed her arms and legs tightly to hurt her and stop her movements while one of them roughly pulled off her shoes and hurled them into a corner. Her bracelets were ripped from her arms and thrown after them. Faye managed to pull an arm free and tried to scratch at a face which got too close but she was grabbed again and pinned down until they could secure their hold on her. One of them held her tightly from behind while the others struggled against her thrashing limbs, to get her clothes off.

When they had mostly managed to undress her, Faye was made to wear a crude sackcloth garment. She struggled far less while it was pulled over her head because it was so rough that it scratched her skin. When she finally ran out of fight, they stood back and stared at her in pity, making whispered comments to each other and shaking their heads.

Faye made full use of the short break as an opportunity to get her breath back. She had moved beyond fear. Tears of anger were now silently running down her face and she looked at them one by one, assessing them and making plans for her next move.

Two of the women were prejudiced against her and two more were extremely scared of her but one of them was worried about their treatment of her and seemed full of self doubt. Faye spoke to her.

'Why do you treat me worse than a dog?' Is *this* your love and your compassion?'

'We mean you no harm' stuttered Ann, her eyes wide with fear in case Faye revealed that they had spoken before. 'You should not have tried to fight with us, we only do this in love.'

'Some love!' spat Faye. 'What would *you* have done in the same situation? I have been tricked, I came here of my own free will and you have done this to me. Am I not entitled to put up a fight?'

'You are with demons' said another woman. 'It is *they* who fight with us and we know that you cannot help yourself.' She smiled at Faye as if to reassure her.

'A fine excuse for yourselves, I am sure' spat Faye. 'I am sure it will be a worthy assuagement of your guilt.'

She said nothing more and after a moment of indecision, one of them stepped forward and tried to take her arm. Faye slapped her hand away and prepared herself for another battle but they were ready for her and she was grabbed quickly.

The sackcloth scratched and cut, hurting her breasts and rubbing raw patches on her skin where the women were holding her tightly. She soon gave in. They lifted her onto the table and held her down, her long hair hanging over the end of it like a waterfall and her eyes stained and smudged from still silent tears.

'She does not cry' said one of the women in surprise, 'the tears run but still she does not cry.'

' 'Tis a sign of her possession' said another, coldly.

'Poor thing, it must torment her so' volunteered another.

Ann said nothing.

Faye looked at her for a moment, and then at the other faces around the table. 'This is all for nothing' she said. 'You waste your time with this nonsense. Soon you will understand and you will see what evil is harboured in the minds of others in this "Church" of yours.'

'She speaks foul' said one the women,' 'tis time we got on with this.'

Ann fetched the bucket and placed it under where Faye's hair fell, stirring the liquid with a stick until all the lumps were dissolved. Then she carefully worked the mixture into Faye's hair with her fingers, making sure that all of it was caked in black. She leaned in close as she worked and whispered.'

' 'Tis only a mixture with soot and ashes.'

'What are you saying to her?' said one of the older women.

'I was reassuring her that we mean her no harm, Mary.'

She leaned forward to Faye once more and whispered "I am truly sorry for this and for my part in it.'

'I think we should all say a prayer for the poor thing' said Mary. 'She seems to be more at peace now.'

Faye stared blankly up at them all as they recited prayers over her, wondering how on earth they could believe that she was at peace. She started to shiver as the cold sooty mixture ran down her neck and congealed in pools around her shoulder blades. She wanted to cry *so much* but refused to let herself succumb.

After the prayers. Ann came forward with a cloth and dabbed gently at the black streaks on her face, saying that it was time for her to be allowed to rest and reflect on her actions. The others agreed and in a short time Faye, with her hair now stained and dull, was cuffed at the wrists and ankles and allowed to sit on the stool.

The door opened and a figure stood in silhouette against the light. It was Leadpenny. He walked into the room and surveyed Faye for a moment before addressing the others.

'Thank you, ladies. The Lord's work has been done well. How are you feeling, Young miss?'

'How do you think I feel?' Faye replied without looking up.

'I confess that, were I in your position I would feel frightened and helpless and alone.'

'Oh! An attempt to be sympathetic to your prisoner' said Faye sarcastically. 'To let them know that you understand their plight and that it pains you to see them like this'

'But it does, my dear. It does.'

She looked up and gave him a hostile glare. 'Do not try to be friendly towards me, I am your prisoner and you are my jailer.'

'Of course you are not my prisoner, we only-'

'Yes. You only want to help me... So let me go free!'

'If only we could. But you are not yet in your right mind and..'

' 'Tis *rubbish* that you speak!'

Leadpenny paused and then changed tack 'I think it best that we leave you to calm down. I am sure the dear ladies' he beamed round at them 'will provide you with some food and make you comfortable.'

He opened the door and held it back while the ladies filed out carrying Faye's belongings. Then he came back inside the room and perched himself on the edge of the table, taking time to look her up and down.

'What now?' said Faye after at least a minute had passed in silence.

He said nothing but just just sat and continued to look her up and down in an unsettling way.

'Well?' she said, fearing what was in his his mind.

'We will be completely alone later, my dear.' He smiled one of his most sickly smiles. 'Just you and I, alone together.' His face flushed with nervous excitement as he spoke and Faye's blood ran cold as her worst fears were confirmed.

Chapter 40 - An accidental fall

Emma didn't know what to expect as she drove into Ashwell Green. The gates of The Grange were closed and bolted so she left the car on the verge and let herself into the grounds via the side gate, shouting for James as she stomped towards the house. No one answered and the emptiness started to weave its lonely cloak around her.

'JAMES! Where are you? Come on, I know you're there...'

Nothing stirred. Her voice seemed to be swallowed up by the silence. She tried to shake off the feeling of isolation by marching noisily over to the tree to get the keys.

'He's gone away, Miss' said a voice from the other side of the lawn. 'He didn't say for how long.'

'Oh... Thank you.' Emma grabbed the key from its hiding place and walked over to meet the owner of the voice.

'I'm his maintenance man. Mike's the name, only I'm not s'posed to be here today, I just called in to see that all was O.K. while he's gone.'

'Did he say where he was going?'

'No, only that he's away on business again, he comes and he goes. Do you know him then?'

'Yes, I'm an old friend of his. He said he would be back soon. I think I'm a bit early so I'll stay and wait for him to return, I have my own key.' She held up the key and smiled winningly. 'Could you open the gates for me before you go? I need to get my car in.'

'Of course, Miss.'

Once she had parked and taken her overnight bag inside, Emma relaxed a little. She had been worried about staying there on her own because she felt like an intruder but now that Mike knew she was there, she felt a little more justified. She made a cup of tea, noting that James had virtually nothing in his fridge apart from T.V. dinners, a pint of milk, butter and some eggs.

◆ ◆ ◆

Faye had been alone on the stool for hours, occasionally trying to ease her stiffening limbs by standing and shuffling around. It was difficult to keep her balance because of the ankle restraints. She had stumbled several times but managed so far to save herself from falling.

Occasional sounds would filter through to her and she tried to keep her mind alert by trying to interpret them. Leadpenny was still in the building, she could hear his walk. The ladies had gone though, she'd heard snippets of their conversation and also the squeak of the door as they were leaving. She had also worked out that there was another large room somewhere because of the hollow sound of an unfamiliar door. There were also some echoey stone steps somewhere, and another person who only came out when all was quiet.

Ann appeared later with some food and a cushion for the stool. She was distressed by Faye's sorry state but dare not do anything about it. She dried Faye's eyes for her and talked of her own doubts as she tried to make her more comfortable.

'This has become too much for me' she said in a low voice. 'I dare not go against the Elders or anyone, even my own husband. Times were, when we all had our place and followed the path, but now the Elders control everything and no one dare say anything against them.'

'You could leave' said Faye.

'I could not. If a Path member harbours doubts, the worship leaders visit their house and council them. They say that their family will break up and they will face ruin and shame.'

She looked sadly down at Faye. 'I wish I could set you free. I would indeed but I do not have the courage. Besides, Elder Leadpenny has the only key.'

'He is a horrid man' whispered Faye. 'He makes my flesh crawl.'

Ann knelt and whispered into Faye's ear. 'I agree with you but he has so much power in our church, and such sway! His word is always taken without question and I would not ever dare to cross him, or indeed, any of them.'

Faye felt a dreadful sinking feeling as the words hit home. Until that moment she had been plucking up courage to tell Ann about his threats but her strength had finally been defeated and she sunk into a state of numb blankness.

The light from the high window in her room was starting to fade and she miserably wondered how long it would be before she heard the inevitable footsteps of Leadpenny coming in her direction. Everything kept playing over and over again in her mind. Leadpenny's threats to her were the thing she feared the most though. He would be back soon and she could do nothing to stop him.

She tried to make herself block him out by thinking of other things but it didn't work for long. She tried thinking of friends and the good times she'd had during her short life. Tobias, Rhiannon, James and Mr and Mrs Larkin, rose petal picking. Her mind kept switching back to Leadpenny. She *had* to escape.

With desperate effort she managed to stand and take some shuffling steps towards the door. Maybe it was unlocked, she couldn't remember hearing the key being turned. Anyway, she'd be stupid not to try.

She tripped and fell over on the floor. A sickly warm feeling swam round in her head and she felt as if she were still falling. She could hear Leadpenny's footsteps running towards the door and the fading sound of the key being turned.

She tried to cling to a firm conscious thought to try and save herself from blacking out.

James! Think of James... Imagine his world.'

Leadpenny stared around the empty room in disbelief. The girl had gone and he was now left with the job of explaining to the other Elders how a shackled girl could escape from a locked room and get out of the building without being seen.

He was sure he'd just heard her cry out. The thought struck him that she could be hiding behind the door hoping to escape so he pulled it swiftly away from the wall to reveal nothing.

He went back into the meeting hall and walked round the rows of seats to see if she had managed to slip past him somehow and hide, but the meeting hall was empty. *Damnation to her!* he thought. How she had done it he couldn't imagine and his mind started to whirl with possibilities.

Maybe she was possessed with such powerful demons that she could control the dark magic by herself. Now he thought about it, Catherine had said the girl had the look of the Devil.

He shuddered at the thought of his wife and her temper but he had to agree that she may have been right, he'd seen the signs for himself in the Elucidatum. Whatever the girl was, she must have tremendous power, and it started to dawn on him just how lucky he might be that she had gone.

Chapter 41 - Dr Who

Emma had been reading for most of the afternoon while she waited to see if James would appear. The Grange had its own kind of quietness. It wasn't silent at all, occasionally a creak or a sharp crack from another room made Emma jump. Even the soft, whirring sound of the fridge echoed its way all the way through to the living room.

She shut the door and closed the curtains on the early evening light before switching on the TV and flicking through the channels for something to engross herself in. She found an episode of "Dr Who" and settled down with a cup of tea and a cushion to cuddle, wiggling herself deeper into the sofa to enjoy it on James's big screen.

A loud creak came from the ceiling above her head and she muted the sound to listen. Maybe it was James. She hoped it was, it would be such a relief to see him.

'JAMES... JAMES, IT'S ONLY ME. I HOPE YOU DON'T MIND BUT I LET MYSELF IN TO WAIT FOR YOU.'

There was no reply. A few moments passed without any sign of him. She un-muted the TV and carried on watching, presuming that the noise was probably just a floor board settling or something.

'Help me' said a girls voice off screen.

The Doctor shouted 'Hold on tight, I'm coming!'

The off-screen voice came again 'Help me, please.'

Emma was just wondering why the voice came from the left of the screen when The Doctor was shouting to the right when a movement caught her eye. The door of the room was slowly swinging open and in the light from the hall she could see a silhouette of a figure.

Her blood ran cold.

The filthy and wretched figure of a girl flickered eerily in the light from the TV. She held her hands up to show that they were cuffed together. Her lips moved but no more sound came out. She shuffled towards Emma.

'What the - !' exclaimed Emma who's first thought was that she was seeing a ghost but then another thought suddenly struck her.

'Are you - Faye?' she asked. Tingles like tiny shards of glass were running up her spine as she tried to come to terms with the scene before her.

The girl nodded slowly. Emma jumped up and ran to her aid.

'My God! I can't believe this... What happened to you? Sit down and I'll get some stuff to clean you up.'

Faye looked back at her gratefully and waited while various items were collected to make her more comfortable.

Emma rushed up to the bathroom and found

the first aid kit, filled a bowl with warm water. She grabbed a couple of flannels, some soap and a towel, then balancing it all carefully she made her way back down to the living room.

She cut the sackcloth away and disposed of it, muttering to herself in disgust at the dirty state that the poor girl had been left in. Then she fetched her dressing gown and laid it gently over Faye to keep her warm.

Phil would be amazed. Emma thought how she'd just love to see his face when he was confronted with the truth. It would serve him right for giving her such a hard time over everything. She reached into her bag for her phone and started to text realising that he could probably help *if* he would believe her.

'I am sorry' said Faye as she watched Emma with the phone. 'I have caused trouble for you.'

'No. Not at all' replied Emma. I was just texting a friend because he can probably find a way of getting those cuffs off.'

Emma showed Faye the phone. 'It's just a phone' she laughed. 'I suppose you don't have them where you come from.'

'We do not' said Faye. 'But I have seen such devices before although they did not work.'

'Look' said Emma holding the phone so that Faye could see. 'You tap the buttons and the text appears on the screen, and when you've finished you just press "Send" and the person at the other end gets it on their mobile.'

' 'Tis a very clever thing.'

Just then the phone rang. It was Phil. Emma stood up and paced the room as she spoke, failing completely to notice the expression on Faye's face.

'Yes, Phil. She's actually here!'

'Yes. With me, here in James's house.'

'I know. I drove here to wait for him.'

'No. James isn't here, just Faye... You should come.'

'Because she's in need of help. She's handcuffed.'

'No, it's not a joke. Please!.. Get in your right car now, and come.'

'See you in a couple of hours then. Bye.'

'You can *speak* into it?' asked Faye incredulously. 'Why do you fiddle with the buttons when you can speak into it?'

'I don't know' Emma laughed.

'And it plays a tune!'

'Yes. And it takes pictures and does lots more besides... Our world must be really weird to you.'

Starlight wandered in from nowhere in particular and jumped up onto Faye's lap, purring loudly and rubbing herself against Faye's welcoming arms.

'Oh, that's James's cat' said Emma giving Starlight a stroke.

'I know' said Faye. 'She is my cat too. She come and goes between us at her will.'

'You mean - the cat goes between both sides?'

'Yes. She is very fickle and she goes where she likes.'

'Wow!'

The metal cuffs were quite heavy and rough. Emma had managed to push some lint under them to stop them rubbing but she could see that they would have to be removed before too long.

'I've got an idea' She said, 'I won't be a minute.'

A short while later she returned with a hair grip. 'I'm going to have a go at those cuffs myself. They look as if they're quite crude and I just may be able to undo them.'

She straightened out the hair grip and started poking about in the key hole of one of the cuffs. It soon fell apart and she started work on the other one. It too, parted with relative ease and after a few minutes Faye was completely free.

Emma grinned triumphantly at her. 'Do you fancy a nice hot bath now? We could try to get rid of that awful black stuff from your hair, it would make you feel a whole lot better.

Chapter 42 - Inquests and answers

High Elder Ian FitzJohn stared out over his office desk with a look which could only be described as dangerous.

No one had ever seen him in such an ugly mood which made those present in his office very nervous indeed. Pipe smoke hung in the still air except for immediately above him where it rose rapidly, giving the effect that he was burning with silent rage.

Leadpenny looked up at him from the small chair he been given, trying to make out the features of his earthly lord and master against the harsh lamplight. He was actually frightened. The two uniformed Young Masters who had shown him in, had taken up position on either side of the door so he was trapped. He did his best to face the High Elder over the huge black and gilt desk.

'Well?' Asked FitzJohn, his thin, reedy voice cut the air like a knife.

Silence hung heavily for a few more moments as Leadpenny plucked up the courage to speak. 'I have no excuse, High Elder.'

'I gave you a simple job and you failed.'

'With respect, High Elder...'

'You failed to prevent a girl who is no older than your own son, from escaping. A girl indeed!'

'But, Sir. You must understand the circumstances of her escape, she must have used some kind of magic.'

FitzJohn raised an eyebrow and considered for a moment. 'Leave us!' he commanded the two Young Masters. They filed out and closed the door. He waited until he heard the chairs scraping at the end of the corridor before continuing.

'How stupid you are! Magic?.. Really? There is no such thing as Magic!'

'But she has demons. She is a witch according to some... Even you have said -'

'You are such a fool!' FitzJohn sneered.

'High Elder. Listen to me. Please! Just give me the chance to explain and then tell me how I could have acted differently.'

FitzJohn leaned forward and clasped his hands together in anticipation, expecting to hear a desperate excuse from a frightened man who was out of his depth.

'Go on' he said. Watching with sadistic interest as a glimmer of hope flickered across Leadpenny's face.

'I spoke with her upon her arrival' said Leadpenny 'and then I had her shown down into the side room where the ladies of the Inner Circle carried out your instructions. All the while, she was secured with cuffs on her wrists and also her ankles. They were never removed.

I locked her alone in the room afterwards. She was there for several hours and it was only when I heard her make a loud noise that I unlocked the door. I could swear she was still there as I arrived, but as soon as the door opened she had disappeared.'

'And what sort of noise was it that she made?' asked FitzJohn.

'As if she had fallen over.'

'And you went immediately to the room?'

'I thought she had fallen. She had moved around the room on several occasions during the afternoon, I could hear the chains scrape along the floor. I only wished to make sure that she was unharmed.'

FitzJohn sat back and considered once more. Leadpenny was many things but he was not known to be a liar, in fact he often accepted blame too readily.

'Is there any chance that she was helped?' He asked, the cutting edge in his voice receding a little.

'I cannot see how. I had the main doors locked as well as the meeting room door. After the ladies had gone I busied myself preparing the manifest until I heard the noise from the side room.'

'The problem is of what to do from here.' said the High Elder. 'What would you do if you were in my position?' He leaned forward with interest.

◆ ◆ ◆

Phil pulled up behind Emma's car and stared up at The Grange with an unexpected feeling of apprehension. Until now he had been totally sure that there must be a logical explanation for everything and that it would sort itself out in the end. But to actually meet someone else who claimed to have shared the experience was either part of a huge con or... He didn't know what to think.

Emma answered the door, quietly explaining that Faye was fast asleep on the sofa. Phil followed her into the living room and stared down at her with a puzzled look on his face, for once he didn't know what to say.

Faye stirred and blinked her eyes open, meeting his gaze with a young, sleepy yawn and a stretch.

'How are you feeling now?' asked Emma.

'I am more rested now, thank you.' replied Faye, pushing herself up to a sitting position. 'I must consider what to do now that I am recovered. There is not much time left.'

'This is Phil' said Emma gesturing towards him.

'Yes, I know.' said Faye holding her hand out and looking him directly in the eye.

Phil shook it politely, still unsure of what he was witnessing. The girl was certainly real enough and very pretty in an ethereal way but she had a presence about her which suggested hidden depths and a seriousness beneath.

He was surprised at himself for these observations because in any other circumstances he wouldn't have had such thoughts. This girl however, seemed to generate a powerful presence, the like of which he'd never encountered from someone so young.

'I see you've removed the cuffs already' he said awkwardly to Emma.

'Yeah, I had to try, they were hurting her. I hope you don't think I've wasted your time.'

'No. Not at all. I'm finding it all very interesting.'

Faye looked up at him pointedly. 'Do you still not believe what you have heard about James and myself?' she asked.

Just for a moment he was caught by the directness of her question.

'I must admit it's a bit hard to swallow' he said. 'But you are here and, well, I don't really know what to think for the moment.'

'What will you do now?' asked Emma.

'I am not sure yet' said Faye seriously, 'I know I must go back.'

As Faye continued to speak, Phil sat quietly and listened carefully to everything she said, slightly subdued but still ready to find fault.

Faye spoke with passion about time, space, reality and rifts, and the reasons James and herself were convinced that another rift was due. As she continued, Phil found himself concentrating less on catching her out and more on what she was saying.

'You're quiet, Phil' said Emma.

'Yeah. I've just been taking it all in. It isn't quite what I was expecting to hear I must admit.'

'Are you willing to believe James now?'

'Aah' said Phil defensively. 'That's a difficult one to answer. At the moment I'm just reserving judgement.'

'Well, at least it's a start' said Emma. 'So, back to my original question. What will you do now?'

'I must go back' said Faye. 'There are several reasons for it. I must confront the True Path and also protect my friends as there is much injustice to bring to account before it happens. There is nothing we can do to stop the rift but we may be able to influence the change which is to come into all our futures. Firstly though, I will return and face my persecutors with a clear head.'

'How can you even think of doing that?' asked Emma. 'I would just stay here and hide from them until it's all over.'

'I cannot. If I stay here I will change the lives and the futures of many people and if I go back, 'twill be the same. The difference is that if I go back I may be able to change them for the better.'

'What if you can't, though?'

'Then at least I will be in the correct place. I do not belong here and that in itself may cause a problem.'

Phil was quiet. He had to admit to himself, although grudgingly, that she seemed to be all she appeared and if she was putting on an act she hadn't slipped once.

Emma suggested that Faye should get a good night's sleep.

'I will sleep in James's room' said Faye.

When they reached the landing, Faye stopped and stared out of the window at the evening sky. 'Do the fires burn every night?' she asked.

'What fires?'

'Over there' said Faye, pointing into the distance.

'Oh that! It must be the glow from a town. All the street lights make the clouds glow.'

'Oh' said Faye. 'The lanterns must be extremely bright.'

'Yes, I suppose they are but there are probably thousands of them.'

Faye stared out at the distant sodium glow and thought to herself *So many people!*

They continued across the landing to James's room. Emma made sure that Faye was comfortable in the bed and then perched herself on the edge.

'I don't know how you can do this' she said. 'You know, go back there and do whatever it is that you have to do.'

'I must. There is no other way.'

Emma gave her a haunted look and Faye saw into her soul.

'Do not worry about us' she said. 'All will be made right in the end.'

'How can you *say* that? How can you be so sure?'

'Because it will. It always will. Nature will always find its balance, 'Tis the way it must be.'

Faye gave Emma a tiny wave with her fingers before the light went out and the door swung slowly shut. She wished she had more time to spend exploring the strange new world she found herself in, but it would have to wait for now, maybe for ever.

The ripples comforted her as they danced on the ceiling. She watched them in wonder for a while until her eyes felt heavy and she eventually fell sleep.

Chapter 43 - The final hours

Next morning Emma rose early and took a drink up to Faye but her room was already deserted and the bed neatly made. She wandered back out to the landing and stood for a moment, blinking in the bright morning sunlight.

Footsteps sounded behind her. She spun round just in time to see Faye emerge from the same room. Her long tumbling hair was dressed with Celtic braids and held by a jeweled clasp which matched her stunningly embroidered black dress.

'Good morning' she said. 'I arose early to prepare for the day.'

'Wow!' exclaimed Emma. 'Look at you!.. You look - amazing!'

'So, where did you just come from?' asked Phil, staring at her from the door of his room.

'I returned to my home to see what is happening there. I came here only to say goodbye to you both, and to thank you for all that you have done for me.'

'That sounds a bit final' said Emma.

Faye looked solemnly at her. 'I had a dream last night' she said. I dreamt that all the churches in Dunwiche were placed on a chess board and that when a piece was taken it was erased from the game as if it had never been there to take.

I then dreamt of being inside one of the churches. Two or three motionless figures sat in almost every pew. They were grey with only the slightest hint of colour as if they had been frozen or turned to stone. I then felt the building being picked up and moved with us all inside it and when it was placed down onto a new square all the people vanished and I did not know my name.'

'Wow!' said Emma. 'Scary dream!'

'I thought I would tell you in case it is useful. I am not used to dreams yet.'

'Well, thanks' said Emma, a little unsure of how to respond. 'I'll keep it in mind just in case, but it sounds more like it could be useful to you.'

'And now it is time for me to go' said Faye quietly.

Emma gave Faye hug. Phil was surprised to find that he also felt a little choked by the sudden finality of her words and he moved forwards awkwardly to join in.

'I hope it all goes well' he said. 'Give 'em Hell.'

'Come back and see us, won't you?' whispered a tearful Emma. 'I want to know that you're O.K.'

Faye said nothing more. She slowly released herself from the hug and gripped their hands in silent thanks for a moment before turning back towards the bedroom door. They both stood and watched as it closed behind her and they listened to the sound of her footsteps crossing the room.

Just for a moment the world seemed to tip backwards and the dust in the air seemed to shimmer and sparkle before silence enveloped them like an ominous cloud.

'Do you feel a bit giddy?' asked Phil.

'Yeah... Weird!' answered Emma, wonderingly.

◆ ◆ ◆

High Elder Iain FitzJohn had gone back to the church in the early morning to see Mr Bullman.

'How are they? Well I trust?'

'I kept 'em just as you told me to. They should come round soon if your doses were correct.'

'Good. Did you have any problems with them?'

'No, not really. One of 'em gave me a hell of a fright though, he sat up and stared at me while I was eating but I talked him back to sleep, gently-like.'

'Do you think he was actually awake?' said FitzJohn, suddenly concerned.

'Nah. He was right out of it, just stared straight through me. I've seen it before when people are out of it like that. You just talk calmly to 'em and reassure 'em, it's just common sense really.'

'Well I hope he doesn't remember anything' said FitzJohn sharply. 'We will take them back up to the meeting room. There is a way through via the minister's office which we can use.'

'When do I get paid?'

'When the whole business is over.'

'I wouldn't mind something now. Goodwill you might say.'

'Very well Mr Bullman, take this for now.' FitzJohn took a box containing a new watch from his pocket. 'You will have to wind it every day, it is not like the ones you described to me.'

One by one, they carefully carried each of the bodies back to the meeting room, placing them exactly where they had been the night before. FitzJohn rinsed out the chalice and decanter, replacing the contents this time with unlaced alcohol. He took a large swig to put the smell of it on his breath and offered some to Mr Bullman who declined.

FitzJohn saw him out and then sat in the chair he'd occupied the previous evening and opened a book. After an hour of reading, someone stirred. FitzJohn calmly slid the book into the desk drawer and positioned himself so that he looked as if he was asleep, and waited.

Luke Bavent opened his eyes and looked around in an unfocused daze just as Walter Valenes grunted and moved. FitzJohn took the opportunity to stretch and open his eyes. Bavent was now vacantly staring at him so he feigned surprise and sat up to look around at the other still sleeping churchmen.

'What happened?' said Bavent ''Tis daylight outside, we must have been here for the whole night.'

'I have no idea' said a yawning FitzJohn. 'I feel so fresh though, 'It is as if I have received perfect sleep.'

He chose his words carefully. To suggest to the still drowsy Bavent that he had "Received" perfect sleep was, he thought, a touch of genius.

'What time is it?' asked Valenes as he came

round.

' 'Tis morning.'

'What has happened to us?'

'I know not, but I have a feeling -'

Valense cut in 'I remember we were having a meeting - and the plans - then we... '

'I say!' said Bavent. 'Did any of you see the lights? They were so wonderful, and when they became one and - The Lord spoke unto me!'

Chapter 44 - The morning of the Rift

The atmosphere that same morning in Amber Lodge was dark and oppressive. Faye ascended the stairs to the turret room and stared up at the sky.

High up was an ominously thick, dark blue haze under which flat strands of stark white cloud drifted like pieces of torn paper. Lightning flickered constantly on high but there was no thunder, and the ash which had been floating on the breeze for days had settled over everything giving it an eerie appearance as if the ghost of winter had shrouded it in a dusting of snow.

Oddly, the vanes of the radiometer were racing. They usually did it in sunlight but never in the half-dark like this. Faye surveyed the scene with morbid apprehension, knowing that later on this day the chart showed a massive disruption before all the lines reset to zero.

She went down to fetch her long black velvet cloak. One thing she had learned from Rhiannon was how people were swayed by appearance above all and it was just the right time for some theatre. It was Sunday and if she had learned anything about human nature it was that frightened people would turn to God in a crisis.

She ran across the bridge and through Havenside to the nearest church, flinging the doors open and finding the place packed with people. She shouted as loudly as she could.

'THE DAY IS HERE!.. YOU MUST LEAVE THE BUILDING AND STAY AWAY FROM WALLS IF YOU WANT A CHANCE TO SURVIVE! GO!.. SPREAD THE WORD TO OTHERS, THERE IS STILL TIME!'

Everyone was stunned into silence for a moment and she fled while she had the chance, hearing sudden noise and mayhem behind her. In the next church she did the same, and the next, until she found herself on Scotts Lane. Without hesitation she flung the doors open and ran inside ready to do the same but was stopped in her tracks by the scene before her.

A hole had opened in the floor in front of the inner door and through it she saw nothing but blackness. It slowly closed as she watched in horror. Once it had closed completely she reached carefully forward and tested the door handle to make sure it was solid. It was, so she pulled the door slightly open and peeped inside. Someone was speaking.

'The Lord is with us today' the voice of the High Elder said reverently. 'He has spoken and we have listened.' The congregation craned forward to hear. 'We have listened, and we are to be rewarded.'

Silence followed while three robed men entered and stood before them. The Minister went down to them and uttered a blessing over each.

'My friends' he announced. 'We stand on this day, at the beginning of a new era. You see before you three of our number who have been chosen by our Lord to receive a vision. A vision to help us negotiate the Path of Truth in this troubled time. Let us listen with open hearts, to their words as they bear witness unto us.'

While murmurs and amens swept round the packed hall once more, Faye carefully eased herself through the door. No one paid her the slightest attention, they were all staring eagerly ahead trying to get a clear view of the action. So while the three men each spoke of their "visions", she slipped unnoticed to the rear of the centre aisle and waited nervously.

The last sentence was now being spoken by Luke Bavent and The High Elder was standing to make another announcement. It would not be long before she was seen. Her heart raced and every fibre of her being was on alert as the inevitable moment drew ever closer. She let her cloak slide to the floor.

'Please sit' said High Elder FitzJohn. 'Many of you may have heard a rumour that we have the gildenhair with us this morning and that we intend to show her off before you but I can assure you that we do not have any such intention. It would be wrong to condemn her - to' He faltered as he saw Faye at the end of the isle facing him. 'However, Err - I am-'

All eyes turned to follow his stare. A member of the Young Masters tried to grab her by the arm but she shook him off and carried herself slowly and deliberately up the isle, all the time trying to stop her legs from shaking.

They watched her in apprehensive silence, hurriedly averting their eyes if she looked over in their direction. FitzJohn was thinking hard, everything he had so carefully re-written for his speech was now useless. Leadpenny was looking scared and the others looked confused.

FitzJohn watched her as she slowly and deliberately turned and faced the people. He tried to think how to handle the situation; Her impressive surprise appearance had given her the upper hand for now but he must try to take back control and keep it.

'So... You have returned to us' he said carefully.

'I found your hospitality a little overwhelming' Faye replied clearly with icy coldness.

'Then may I welcome you on behalf of us all. Would somebody please fetch the young miss a chair?'

'I will stand if I may' said Faye, still coldly.

'As you please, my dear' replied FitzJohn. He faced the congregation. 'I had not expected to see our guest today. As some of you already know, she came here yesterday with some of our Young Masters and we offered help to her.'

'I did not regard it as an offer of help' said Faye loudly so that all could hear.

'I am sure of that' he replied patronisingly. 'Our young guest is troubled, and one of the signs of a troubled soul is denial.' Several heads nodded in agreement. 'Tell us, child. Why *did* you come back to us today? What mysterious power brought you to the Lord's house?'

'No mysterious power brought me here. I came of my own free will. I ask only that you listen to my words and judge me as you feel within your own hearts.'

A murmur rumbled round the hall and a man stood, pointing to the window. 'See? The sky is black now. 'Twas lighter before she came here. I don't care what she says. She is with demons!'

Faye lost her patience and retorted loudly so that all could hear.

'There are more important things than to listen to this claptrap! There is to be a catastrophe upon the Earth and whatever measures you take, it *will* happen. It starts even as we speak! You may call it a day of judgement and you may pray about it but you will not make a difference to its course. Nature will always do what it needs. I came here to warn you all to stay away from walls and buildings. Stay outside and you will have a better chance.'

Voices shouted out from the main floor adding to the tension and rising fear among the more vulnerable members of the congregation.

Robert Valenes was starting to behave strangely, pointing to the air and exclaiming in wonder at things unseen. Luke Bavent started to laugh in an odd way at Elder Valenes who was staggering towards a chair, apparently drunk.'

'See?' shouted someone. 'See how she has bewitched them?'

FitzJohn tried to shout over the noise but no

one took any notice so in desperation he grabbed his Elucidatum and thew it down hard on the floor. The noise made everyone pause for a moment and he bellowed at them to sit down while he had the chance.

'Never before have I seen such behavior in the house of God! You should hang your heads in shame. All of you!' The gloves were off now, he thought. 'SIT DOWN, VALENES!'

'He's bewitched!' someone shouted again.

'HE IS NOT!' shouted FitzJohn, temper overtaking him.

'Then, what is he then?'

'He's poisoned, that's what' shouted another. 'Look at his sweating brow.'

A voice rang out from near the front ' 'Tis whimsey weed with which they are poisoned. I know it!'

Faye was staggered to see Rhiannon. She was disguised in a demure dress and Sunday bonnet, and as such was almost unrecognizable.

She came forward and stood next to Faye. 'I know the signs well' she continued 'because I use it in some of my cures. They've been drugged with it. I can tell.'

FitzJohn stayed quiet, things were going very wrong. The Minister took over and asked everyone to stay calm and quiet while they tried to make sense of what remained of their service.

'Now... Calmly, Girl' he said. 'Tell us who you are and how you can account for yourself.'

'Some of you already know me' said Rhiannon,

defiantly staring round the gallery above. 'I am the one who treats your wives and daughters for ailments when you won' help them yourselves. I am the one who's been told she is going to Hell.'

The minister held a hand up to silence any comments from the hall. 'And you can explain your accusations, child?'

'Yes' continued Rhiannon. 'Whimsey weed is a good treatment for worries and fears when it is taken in tiny doses. When I first found out about it I took some, but I took too much and it made me see sparkling lights and wonderful things which were not really there, just like it does now to them, and I can prove it.'

She took Faye's arm in hers and continued. 'I made some scent for my friend. This friend. The one you all love to call a witch. And I put a couple of leaves of whimsey weed into it. She wears it now, I can smell it on her and that is what caused them to go doolally, not some demon... You people will believe anything! You should listen to her and do what she says. She knows things and I believe her!'

'That is enough, girl' said the minister, firmly. 'I will not have rudeness and such a lack of respect in this holy place.'

Rhiannon led Faye over to Bavent and the two Valenes men. Nothing happened for a moment or two but then, all three started to look unwell as the effects started to grow.

'See?' shouted Rhiannon. 'They're all dosed with far too much of it. Even the smell of it makes them see the visions.'

'I still maintain the gildenhair is the cause' shouted the man again. 'All the heathen girl has done is prove it!'

'I agree!' shouted another.

'And me!'

The crowd started to leave their seats and rush forward. Rhiannon grabbed Faye by the arm and begged her to run but Faye refused.

'Go! Save yourself! I will be fine!' She pushed Rhiannon towards the vestry door and shouted a final warning to the throng as she turned on her heel and vanished through the stonework.

Chapter 45 - The Rift

Faye, still dressed in her dark finery, stood at the turret window of her bedchamber and looked out over the waters of the Haven. They were flat and still. Lightning continued to flicker high up in the murk and her head started to ache from the heavy atmosphere. Nature seemed to be imposing a frighteningly rigid order where it usually allowed freedom and change.

The sea, dark and almost completely calm stretched away like a mirror to the distant horizon. Several intensely dark shapes swept around in the distance and spread out seemingly at random. Where they touched, the fabric of reality dissolved leaving only an intense blackness.

She shuddered and turned back into the room, suddenly aware that she had no idea what else she could do. She felt helpless.

A distant rumble of thunder broke her train of thought but this time she felt no joy in it, only a feeling that the inevitable was coming. She opened the panel and went up to the turret room and stared out over the town, wondering if the people she'd left in the meeting hall were still arguing.

Grabbing hold of the telescope, she pointed it

towards Scotts Lane but the meeting house was partially hidden by the surrounding buildings. In other places though, she could make out figures running and knocking on doors to warn others. Panic was everywhere and families tried to keep together while others ran wildly about. Children wandered lost and groups of men fought in the streets.

She aimed the telescope towards the outskirts of town and saw a row of distant figures standing in an orderly line on the bridge near Mad Esther's cottage. Relieved, she realised that Tobias had started the evacuation of the Nonnyes and was himself in a safer position out there in the open.

A disturbance to the south caught her attention and she swung the telescope over towards it. A glow of fire from one of the streets was sending bright orange sparks flying up into the sky and a fight had broken out among some people who were trying to get to a boat.

She shivered and spun round, suddenly feeling that someone was behind her as a tingle ran up her spine, but no one was there. Her hair started to stand up on her scalp and a sensation of extreme panic swept over her as the radiometer suddenly stopped spinning madly and came to an abrupt standstill.

The clock stopped ticking.

A crackly finger of light started to descend from the sky directly above. Faye watched transfixed as it travelled a jagged path slowly downwards. The feelings of panic started to recede only to be replaced by a dizzy remoteness and detachment.

Fingers of electrical charge started to rise from high points nearby. A charge reached up from the weathervane above her head. It jerked and twisted as it grew in strength and climbed upwards, straining to be the first to make contact with the descending bolt. Her feet felt lighter and her hair floated weightlessly around her face.

Time outside had slowed considerably and the rain had ceased to fall at a noticeable speed. The individual droplets now floated downwards so slowly that they almost hung in the air like shimmering jewels. Above her the two fingers of charge had almost reached each other and the light from them was growing brighter as they sought to link together.

A blindingly bright light appeared as they finally touched. It spread back back upwards towards the clouds and the suspended raindrops nearest to it started to boil and slowly explode. Just for a moment the town was lit up as bright as a summers day before the dark shapes swept through and erased it from reality.

Faye looked around. The room was still starkly lit by the time-frozen flash but everything else had gone.

A voice, eerie and distant spoke in her head.

Faye?

She turned her head and saw James standing in the air watching her.

Every time you think something, your voice ap-

pears in my head his voice said. *It's really quite strange standing here looking at you and your voice doesn't come from your mouth.*

Your voice speaks in my head too she thought back. *Where do you think we are?*

I don't know, but I guess that we are somehow suspended in the Rift, or stuck outside it.

The dark shapes continued to sweep around outside, not actually visible themselves but visible by what they revealed or erased. The rest of Amber Lodge suddenly reappeared with sunshine reflecting brightly from the roof tiles but there was no sun, just the blackness of the void all around it. Stars shone and then disappeared as did parts of the sea, the town and the sky only to be wiped out again out as more dark shapes swept over them.

Why are we here? thought James.

I do not know, replied Faye. *We are protected by the room though, 'tis the one thing we can know for certain.*

A hole opened in the blackness and a bright, sunlit sky shone through it and spread out in front of them. Dark storm clouds from somewhere else rained heavily through into the sunshine.

Nature is finding its level thought Faye. *'Tis fighting with itself to find a balance from this chaos.*

Yes, thought James. *Nature is tring to heal.*

The sky and the sunlight were erased leaving only blackness, although sunlight still reflected from the roof tiles of Amber Lodge. Somewhere outside in the black void, it rained. The dark shapes swept in once more and wiped the sea into view.

A cafe sat near the edge of a sunny beach with a car park behind it. A few people sat on the beach and a young kitchen hand opened the back door of the cafe and threw some rubbish into a bin.

That looks like the Dunwich I know, thought James. *I can tell the make of the cars.*

' 'Tis also partly my Dunwiche thought Faye, looking at a familiar road which was slowly washing into view over the beach. *I know those houses, they are on the corner of Maison Dieu Lane and St James' Street.*

Why are we here, though? thought James once more. *We must be here for a reason!*

Maybe we must do something to bring this to an end and it appears we are only ones who are on the outside thought Faye. *When I wanted to escape from the True Path, I yearned to be in your world, and then I was there. Is it possible that we can bring about an end by the same method?*

Dunwich was wiped out by the dark shapes once again and they both stared out at total blackness.

O.K... What do you want to think of? thought back James.

I love my Dunwiche, thought Faye *'tis the only place I have known. My only memories are there but it is a place with a troubled heart.*

I can understand that! thought James to her. *I found your Dunwiche pretty scary. I want to go back to my friends and the things I know but I think we have to aim for much more than that... I think we have to face our deepest buried feelings, the ones we ignore because they are too painful. The ones which are too frightening to face in life.*

Rain suddenly lashed the turret from where a hole had opened in the blackness to reveal clouds. Faye looked up and saw that the rain and mist near the lightning were still completely frozen. The hole widened and the clouds spread out until they met with the open sea. Moments later the dark shapes swept over and erased it again.

Whatever we think of, thought Faye, *we must yearn for it together.*

I don't think I'm good at yearning... No previous experience you see.

You have yearned! thought back Faye. *You have yearned to belong to someone. You have yearned to know who who you are and where you came from. You have yearned to meet me as I have yearned to meet you because we are the same... We both have a void in our hearts.*

They turned to face each other and moved forward to a gentle embrace and as they touched, a huge flood of raw emotion overwhelmed them and they clung to each other tightly.

Images and stories of their pasts flooded through them and with those cryptic images came glimpses of who they were, who they had been and the realities they had seen. And as they clung to each other their thoughts gradually fused together and became the same.

A low shaking started in the air and climbed in pitch until it became audible. The lightning bolt expanded to a blinding intensity and the sound climbed higher in pitch until it exploded into an ear-shattering crack of thunder.

Then

nothing.

Chapter 46 - James

From silence, a slight sensation of sound came. A kind of distant knock which echoed into a blur. Then from the blackness came a pinpoint of distant light.

Indistinct humming noises mingled with sharp sounds before they took shape as speech. The sharp sounds became words floating from somewhere above and a slow awareness that "above" was a direction, and if there was a direction there must be an existence.

Voices started to sound familiar as the words from a TV high on the wall of the room sounded out, thin and echoey.

'The missing girl, Isla Williams is found safe and well' announced a news reader. 'Isla Williams, the girl who has been missing for two months was spotted wandering alone in Ipswich town centre on Sunday morning. We have an interview with the woman who found her'

'Well, she was just walking past the window of the cafe where I work and I recognised her from her picture' said the woman on the screen.

'How did she seem when you found her?' Asked the reporter.

'She was a bit confused and she kept asking what day it was, and saying about being in a car park and not knowing how she got there. I took her inside and gave her a drink while I phoned 999 and then we just sat and I waited with her. She didn't say much more really, just sat there staring. Poor girl.'

The newsreader then announced 'Suffolk Police gave the following statement at a press conference earlier today.'

The sound changed to that of a packed room with a rather uncomfortable sounding voice reading from a prepared statement.

'Isla seems to be well and is relieved to have been found. She is confused about where she has been over the last few weeks but signs indicate that she may have been with a group of people, possibly in some form of commune during this period of time. She has been well cared for and is unharmed. She has already been reunited with her parents but will remain in the care of the authorities to continue her recovery for the time being while we continue with our investigations.'

Questions were shouted as reporters, radio and TV stations each tried to get their questions answered. The noise was deafening for a few moments until the same voice spoke once more.

'I cannot give any specific details about the case at the moment but I can reveal some general information to you in the hope that someone may come forward to help us with our enquiries.

As yet we have no idea of the motives the group

she was with, but it seems that one of the members gained her trust and eventually helped her to escape. He is described as tall with shaved hair and wearing only a simple robe and what were described as "Jesus" sandals.

If anyone recognises this description or knows of the whereabouts of a group of people who may dress in this way we would urge them to get in touch with us.'

A sudden increase in volume of the voices and an alarm sound came into focus along with more awareness of light and moving shadows.

'James... James... Mr Hadleigh... Can you hear me?'

A light shone brightly and a reaction came as facial muscles tightened to try to shield the eyes from the light.

'He's coming round.'

'Oh thank God for that' said a familiar voice... 'At last!'

James blinked and squinted while his eyes got used to the light. Emma was beside him and so were a doctor and two nurses who were fussing about with some machinery by his bed.

'You are safe in hospital' said the doctor, smiling down, 'your friend is here to see you. Take it easy.'

James stared up at Emma who smiled back at him warmly.

'There's nothing to worry about... You had a car crash but you're O.K. now. The car was a mess though' she grinned. 'You're tougher than old boots.'

James tried to speak but was told to lie back and relax by a nurse so he rested for a minute or so and thought about how to form the words, then he tried again.

'Where - Where's Faye?' he managed at last.

'Who?' asked Emma. She stroked his head. 'You were alone in the car. You were going to your new house. There was no one with you. Nobody else is hurt, not even the other driver. Relax. Just take your time. Everything's fine.'

'You know... Faye!'

'No, sorry' said Emma. 'But whoever she is I can promise you she wasn't with you... You're safe, so relax and save your questions for when you have the strength.'

A tear rolled down his cheek and Emma mopped it up, giving him a sympathetic smile which he found frustrating. He started to wonder if anything of Faye and Dunwiche were real. But it seemed so real! The trouble was, that a car accident was such a completely feasible reason for his current surroundings and state of mind.

Again he was told to take his time and try to rest, and as he had so little energy, his eyes soon drifted shut.

When he opened them next, Phil was sitting beside Emma and it was dark outside. They sat with him quietly while he ate a piece of toast and drank some milk before venturing into a conversation of any sort.

'You look better' said Emma. 'I think the sleep

did you the world of good.'

'Thanks. I feel a bit better' he said, feebly. 'What day is it?'

'Tuesday' said Phil.

'Oh Thank God for that' said James. 'I've only been here for a few days then.'

He pushed himself up and had a good look at his surroundings. The glare of the fluorescent tubes made everything look harsh and the institutional cream walls and glass screen reminded him of how much he hated hospitals.

James looked at the sympathetic faces of his friends. They looked so familiar and yet there was something different about them. Nothing much, maybe was just that they were tired.

He thought back to the final moments in the rift and the way the raindrops around the lightning bolt had hung in the air because time had stopped.

Reality must have changed but there was no easy way to see how while he was in hospital. Faye and himself must now be even more out of step with the timeline of everything and everyone around them. At least two months had passed since the near miss that *he* remembered on his first visit to The Grange but everyone else thought the accident had only been a few days ago.

He wondered what the recent past had been for them. Maybe he could piece things together by pretending to not remember due to the accident. Then he could move on seamlessly with all the changes.

The ripples of change would be spreading out

like those on a pond, making ever smaller changes until eventually, there would be a point when all the seams and joins in reality and time were invisible once more. But he still felt he needed some proof.

'Was the TV on at all while I was in here?' he asked Emma.

'No. There was no point was there? You were out of it' she replied.

'So why was it on today then?'

'Because I put it on while I waited for you to come round. They told us they were going to wake you up so I came here to be with you when they did.'

'So I couldn't have heard the news or known what was going on outside this room the whole time?'

'You were under sedation the whole time. Honestly, James! What is this about?'

'I don't know. Maybe I'm just a bit confused.'

Over the next few days, James continued to recover well but decided to keep all further thoughts of Faye, time and reality to himself. He was desperate to escape from hospital and find out what had changed in the world outside. No one knew Faye anymore and he seemed to have lost a couple of months somewhere.

Finally the day of discharge came. He packed his belongings into a bag and met Emma in the ward visitors room. They were to drive to his family home in the village of Ashwell Green in Suffolk which had been left to him months ago.

Emma was excited because she had never seen

the inside of the house before and was fascinated by the idea of James living alone in a house with the ghost of a young girl walking the floors at night.

'I would be really frightened to live there' she said to James. 'How can you possibly think of sleeping there all on your own with a ghost appearing and staring at you in bed or something?'

I don't think she does that' said James forcing a laugh and trying to steer clear of any specific comments about a ghost he had no idea existed until that point. 'I'm not even sure I will ever see her.'

They turned into the one and only lane which led into, and out of the village.

'I think that must be where it happened' she pointed to a gouge in the verge as they rounded a bend near the village. 'Do you remember? The little hoon in the red hatchback that hit you wasn't even hurt. Typical! Dangerous little idiots like that never seem to get hurt themselves!'

They drove past the the pub, the old school, the post office, the rusty village hall and the farm. Emma drove carefully through the open gates of The Grange, down the gravel drive and parked in front of the fountain which was dry and covered with ivy.

'Ooh' she said with a shiver, 'I just had a strong feeling of deja vu. How strange!'

James smiled but said nothing. It was more proof at least to him, that he hadn't imagined the whole thing while in hospital.

'What a lovely garden!' said Emma as she took stock of the place. 'You'll need to get it under control before it takes over though.'

'Yes, I suppose so' said James, weakly. 'I suppose I'll have to do a lot of things - again.'

Emma didn't notice his comment, she was keen to see inside so James unlocked and showed her through the front door.

A motorbike stood at the back of the hall with a drip tray underneath it. He assumed that Mike would call by shortly to introduce himself and hurry away with it.

On one side of the hall the oak paneled library was as he'd first found it with wheeled steps, piano and synthesiser under dust covers. The room on the other side was comfortably furnished as he remembered it from the first time he'd seen it.

When they reached the kitchen James quickly talked Emma out of trying the oven, suggesting it would need a thorough cleaning before they used it. She took his advice and offered to go out and find a shop or a takeaway so they could eat.

James said he would stay and make a start with getting the place habitable but as soon as she had started the car he went upstairs to the light and passed through it.

Chapter 47 - Faye

'Mrs. Larkin!.. Mrs. Larkin... 'Tis Miss Jane. She's comin' round!' An unknown girl's voice shouted across the landing of Amber Lodge in a strong Suffolk accent.

Faye opened her eyes and stared blankly round the room as distant clanks and knocks from downstairs disguised the reply but she could make out the occasional words. 'Oh my Lore - - as soon - - You stay there, girl!'

Her room looked much the same, large and rectangular except for the open circular area which extended out from one corner into part of the turret. The walls were still plain and bare except for the huge carved stone fireplace on one side and the ancient and faded wall tapestry on the other. She stared at it, noticing the area where there had once been just a faint discolouration. It now had a coat of arms, faded but definitely where it hadn't been before.

Someone had put all her clothes away and her shoes had been filed neatly in pairs on the floor instead of the higgledy-piggledy line she usually left them in.

Footsteps echoed across the stone floor in the

hall below, changing to a softer clump as they came up the stairs. Moments later Mrs. Larkin came in, followed by a rather droopy looking girl in a slightly stained black and white uniform.

'Oh, Thank goodness' exclaimed Margaret. 'You're back with us! How do you feel? Would you like some tea or something? How about a nice, big slice of cake to set you up? Go on, girl, fetch some tea and a slice of cake for Miss Jane.'

The girl scuttled off and Faye noticed that Margaret had an impassive expression on her face.

'You've been hurt' she said firmly. 'It was quite a bang you took to your head and you woz knocked out.'

Faye wanted to ask why she was being called Jane but Margaret held a finger up to silence her. 'You must rest' she said. 'And you must keep up appearances, 'specially in front of the staff. Beatrice is a good girl but she's a bit slow and easily frightened by things she don't understand.'

They heard the kettle clank on the stove in the kitchen. Margaret relaxed her expression a little and sat on the edge of the bed, holding Faye's hand.

'Now, you take your time and see how you go. I'm sure you will get used to being back on your feet before long' she said.

'Why is there a coat of arms now on the tapestry?' asked Faye.

'That? 'Tis the Dunwiche coat of arms of course! 'Tis also your family coat of arms. Your family dates back at least eight hundred years and shares its name with the town. She smiled down at Faye. 'I think that bump on the head shook up your senses, Miss Jane of Dunwiche.'

I have a family?' asked Faye incredulously.

Margaret put a hand on her forehead. 'You're still quite hot on your forehead round the bump, Miss Jane' she said with concern. 'I think, a little more rest before you try to get back to your feet. The doctor says you may have shaken yourself up more than you know, 'specially after what happened... Do you remember, Dear? About what happened?'

Faye had no idea, of course, and had to think really quickly how to react so she was careful not to reply too specifically.

'I do not remember entirely. 'Tis a little blurred in my mind' she said, hoping for an explanation, or at least a hint of what the recent past had been. Margaret said nothing more and once again recommended rest until she was a bit stronger.

Beatrice entered with a tray and placed it beside the bed with a little bobbing curtsey.

'Thank you, Beatrice' said Faye.

'Ma-am' replied Beatrice as she made for the door.

'That's it' said Margaret, gently to her. 'You just take it easy and do what you know you must do. We all want you to be well in time for tonight. Now I must get along after Beatrice and make sure she don't burn anything with the iron again.'

Faye shuffled herself up to a sitting position and reached for her tea. She felt quite clearheaded even though she had a small swelling on her head from an apparent collision with something hard. She realised she would quickly have to become Jane for the sake of everyone around her even though she still thought of herself as Faye. So Jane it would be. Jane of Dunwiche.

Obviously quite a lot must have changed, and she was keen and also slightly scared to find out what the changes were. The moments she spent in the rift with James were precious to her beyond anything and she, like James had done, sifted through their combined memories while she was alone.

At least the rift was over and she was alive. She would have to get used to living a new life as Jane for the time being, coping with the changes to her recent past as she was confronted with them.

Beatrice was a bit of a surprise but not nearly so much as the discovery that she now had a family history. A history also implied that she now had a past which stretched back further than her own existence, a strange idea for her to grasp. The fact that everyone else had such a past was no help to understanding how she would feel about it over time.

Her next thought was of Rhiannon and Tobias. Did they still exist? Were they still her friends? Did they even know her? Maybe she had other friends that she didn't yet know. The idea shocked her for a moment and brought into sharp focus once more, the enormous effect of the rift. Everyone so far seemed completely unaware of it and obviously had no memory of any other reality. Maybe even Margaret didn't know... Maybe.

So many questions would have to be answered and she would have to learn so many new names, places and stories but that would be for another time.

It was raining outside and she felt something she'd never before experienced. Cold. The temperature had dropped by several degrees and her arms had tiny bumps all over them. The season had finally given way and the atmosphere was changing along with it.

As the planet continued its journey around the sun and Autumn set in properly, people started to wear jackets and coats and the leaves changed colour. There was something settling about it all as if nature was relieved to have a break from all her summer growing.

Many times, Jane would walk in the fallen leaves, kicking them up and scattering them in childish excitement. Everything was changing in a natural way for once and it was all new to her and many more wonders were to come in time.

Chapter 48 - New beginnings

December finally came to Dunwiche and also of course to Ashwell Green.

Both Jane and James would have claimed it was only a turn of phrase because to them, the orbit of the earth had finally reached the place where December happened.

Quite a lot had changed for them both, and over the last few months they had each learned to cope with a past which was entirely new to them.

James decorated his tree on the first weekend of the month and made plans for a party for his friends and some of the people in the village he'd since met.

In a snow laden Dunwiche, Jane helped as much as she could with the Christmas preparations for Amber Lodge. Margaret had insisted that as lady of the house she must let the staff have their fun. There was no tree as the custom had never been started but on Christmas Eve there was an enormous Yule log burning in the fireplace in the morning room.

Her sixteenth birthday had apparently been on the day of the rift, although only she was the only one who seemed not to know.

James now takes his duty to time and place very

seriously and is much more detached from the normal everyday hustle and bustle of the life he used to lead.

The people in Ashwell Green know him as their landlord and also as a fairly regular visitor to the pub. They think he is a musician who has made a lot of money for himself before giving it all up to take on the responsibility of The Grange.

He sometimes leaves a note for Mike saying that he will be away for a while. They assume in the village that it means he'll be in a recording studio or on a stage somewhere but nobody ever asks him. After all, he's a really nice guy even if he's a bit strange but, well, you know how these musician types are.

To his friends he is still a bit of a lovable nerd who sees everything from a slightly sideways point of view but they always knew that. It was just James.

Jane is now learning to be the lady of the house although Margaret often has to remind her to walk down the stairs like a lady rather than to run down them like a child. In general though, she takes her responsibilities very seriously, after all, Amber Lodge has standards to uphold.

She is generally regarded by the people of Dunwiche as quite a reserved and mysterious Miss. There are rumours circulating around the town that she has something of a secretive nature about her. After all, she is the great granddaughter of Daniel of Dunwiche and he was rumoured to have carried out some dark and sinister experiments in his time, as were others in that family. Her few close friends however, know of her kind nature and unyielding inner strength and they love her for it.

Her parents are never mentioned, and every time she tries to find out about them the subject is changed with quiet comments made about it being "so sad". Jane has the impression that they died while travelling abroad a few years earlier and she is credited with great strength of mind for the practical way she has coped with their loss.

Both James and Jane (although she still sees herself as Faye) are able to cross the boundaries their realities quite easily and they both walk through the light on a regular basis. Emma once found the computer switched on when she was absolutely sure it had been shut down. Soon after, she caught a glimpse of Jane as she was entering James's room. She swore later to James that she had seen the ghost.

And what of the others who touched their lives for better or for worse?

Rhiannon is still Jane's friend but she now has her own business in part of her father's shop selling perfumes, cures and linaments. She still treats "Discrete ailments" in a private room at the back of the shop and because of it, there are people who whisper that she is a witch. But some of them still pay her for a quiet consultation when they need a cure for something unusual or to help heal a bruise which they cannot explain away to friends.

Rhiannon is a good listener and a good healer

for all her tender years. She is aware that she is privy to many of the town's secrets and also that she is constantly being watched by those who seek to keep knowledge as something to fear.

Tobias, Rhiannon's gentleman friend is currently studying medicine with the monks at the priory and is allowed to work at Greyfriars Hospital as a student.

He is still shy at heart but also has a strong presence of mind which is useful for dealing with Rhiannon who can be quite a handful when she wants to be. He is learning to cope with the guilt of not entering as a novice at Greyfriars as his father had wished but he has a fascination with science which cannot be dampened. Sometimes he even privately reviews the forbidden sciences with a little help from Jane who, of course, has a library full of books and notes on those very subjects. The three of them share a bond of close friendship but only Jane really knows why it runs so deep.

The Nonnyes are unknown. They had never existed in Dunwiche after the rift. Those who had queued to go through the wall at Mad Esther's house fitted seamlessly into their previously normal lives without any memory of what had happened to them.

Emily went back to life with her family. The "Commune-style group" she had been with during her absence had never been traced.

The True Path are a borderline cult. Many ordinary folk considered them to be far too zealous and also to hold some odd beliefs. Some even considered them harmful to the vulnerable and weak minded.

Mr Bullman is still at large somewhere in space and time but nobody knows where. It is likely that wherever he is, his presence will eventually be noticed by the trail of destruction he will undoubtedly leave behind.

Mr. and Mrs. Leadpenny are still unhappily married and Mrs. Leadpenny is continuing her discrete affair with Ian FitzJohn, a local wealthy businessman and fellow member of The True Path. Arthur Leadpenny is still regarded as a creepy and lecherous man by the women of the town - but he *does* sell such delightful shoes!

And finally, Starlight. She continues to walk quite freely between Jane and James whenever she feels the inclination to do so.

She asks for herring when at Amber Lodge and then curls up on the chair by the window in Jane's bedchamber. Whereas at The Grange she asks for tuna and then sits under the wisteria on the porch to daydream for hours in the sunshine, so in fact, she has the best of both worlds.

As cats usually do.

THE REAL DUNWICH

Dunwich as it actually exists, superimposed over "Dunwiche".

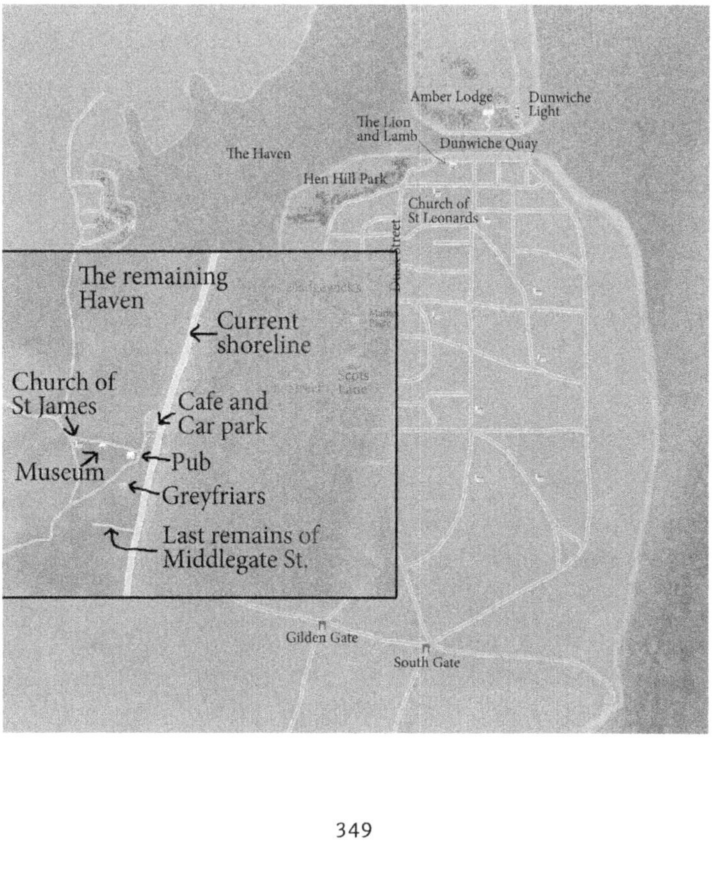

Suffolk is one of Englands most beautiful counties. It has a rich history which is well worth some investigation as there are so many fascinating events and places to choose from. One of those places is Dunwich which sits on the Suffolk coastline just to the south of Walberswick and Southwold.

Dunwich was an influential city 800 years ago but most of it is now under the North Sea (see map). All that remains currently on land is the western end of the original city but a visit to the small museum on St James Street will show just how much influence it had in its past.

You can walk along St James Street and visit the museum which has a superb model of Dunwich as it probably was in the twelfth century as well as many artifacts from its history. Turn right towards Greyfriars and the beach or left to visit St James's Leper Chapel although both are now just ruins.

If you follow the road to the beach you will arrive at the area where Maison Dieu used to be. The nearest point to where it was situated is the cafe by the beach. The last remaining part of the Palesdyke was just behind the cafe.

The car park for the cafe was once part of The Haven and if you look out from there you can see the whole of The remaining Haven although it's mostly dry now.

TRUTH AND FICTION

They say that truth is stranger than fiction.

The idea that a whole English city was washed away by the sea seems far fetched, but actually, it's true.

I once met someone who was convinced that electricity was invisibly dripping down the walls of their house. A horrible thought to live with when you think about it!

On one occasion during my teens I remember having to call on a customer who lived in a tiny attic room in a once grand Victorian house. The room had oozes of brown oily crud hanging like stalactites all over the ceiling. It was caused by dirty fumes from two paraffin heaters which apparently were kept on all year round... and my visit was on a hot July day!

There are still some religious organisations that heavily control their members and perform rituals over them in the belief that they are helping a troubled soul.

For this book I found old maps to find street names of Dunwich as it was before it was washed away by the actions of the sea. All the street names in "Dunwiche" are real and some are still locatable under the North Sea.

Some of the characters in this book are loosely based on the historical residents of the real City of Dunwich as it was about 800 years ago. They all once actually lived, worked, stole or were imprisoned there.

"Starlight" is one of our cats. Our other cat is named "Moog" after Dr Robert Moog, the father of electronic music synthesis.

The idea of an analogue computer of sorts (the prediction engine) is entirely possible. I own two huge analogue music synthesisers and I used one of them to see if I could actually make it do the things I wrote about in this book -

It could!

There may be other realities out there somewhere in time and space but I have no idea where. I imagine though that Starlight does.

You cannot walk through walls so don't try it unless -

A. You found a way to reach another reality or

B. You have bandages at the ready.

Printed in Great Britain
by Amazon

79089437R00212